FOR MY FR11

1..... 7 I MET YOU.

There's Always A Light

The Journey of a Warrior

KEEP STEPPIN'

Dervin Walker

signature

R 6/23

A Deviah Book

Dedication

I would like to dedicate this book to two special sunflowers, my wonderful children, Derishe' and Daniel, who have brought pure love and happiness into my life. They have been an inspiration and motivation on my life's journey.

There's Always A Light
The Journey of a Warrior

<u>Introduction</u>

This book documents my life challenges, one of which led me to jail for almost a year. My sudden battle with cancer was also a major inspiration for writing this book. My life story will inspire you to never give up. This book is to appeal to the disheartened to know that there is always a light even in the darkest moments. With all the challenges, I have always found a way to keep moving forward.

Regardless of the challenges, you are faced with in life, love will always win. Life is an adventure; enjoy its challenges. Stay close to family, friends, and the community. With all these people around, you will never have to fight alone.

My main message is spread love, do good, and take responsibility for your actions. Treat people well, with respect, and be understanding. Taking care of humanity is as important as taking care of oneself. We are one unit, one people, and we cannot survive without each other. Until mankind understands this, we are destined for doom.

Life is a gift. Enjoy, love, and cherish it. There will be obstacles on the journey. Some we can avoid and others we cannot. It's good and bad. In the darkest of times when you can't see your way out of a situation or feel alone because it's so dark that you can't see around you, your faith in God will be your only light. Only then will you see a way out. Miracles happen every day. My story will show you many along my journey. With that light, you will see all the possibilities. He is the light.

There's Always A Light.

Table of Contents

Chapter 1

Childhood Days in Jamaica

The Foundation

It all started in the community of Rio Bueno, Trelawny, Jamaica, W.I. Rio Bueno is located on the north coast of the island. One of the many unique things about this community is that the Rio Bueno river runs into the Caribbean Sea. It has one of Jamaica's deepest natural harbors. The main road between Kingston and Montego Bay ran along the coast through the community which made it a very busy town. It was a prominent fishing village because of its proximity to the Caribbean Sea. Ships would dock in the harbor frequently which would attract prostitutes, pimps, drug dealers, and all kinds of hustlers. There are two air strips on the outskirts of the community that were regularly used to export marijuana. There are two political parties in Jamaica, the Jamaica Labour Party (JLP) and the People's National Party (PNP). Rio Bueno was a Jamaica Labour Party stronghold. The JLP was represented by the color green which I'll talk more about later.

Three major farms were surrounding the community which provided work for a lot of its residents. All this land was owned by three or four families with small lots in the inner section as if they designed it like that for the workers on the farm. Because of the river, sea, Baptist and Anglican churches built in the 18th century, and historical Fort Dundas, Rio Bueno was an attraction for tourists and locals looking for something different to do. All these activities provide opportunities for the locals to make a living. It was like everybody was selling something: alcohol, food, fruit, vegetables, carvings, seashells, fish, juices, herbs, and spices just to name a few. Everyone knows everyone in my community. It was as if we were all family.

I am the youngest of five in my immediate family. I had a big brother and three older sisters taking care of me. My mom stayed home to take care of us while my dad was living and working in Kingston. My dad would come on the weekends, or we would go visit. We usually spent most of our summer break with him in Kingston. There were four houses in my yard: ours, my grandparents, and my two uncles. I had ten cousins in the yard, six of whom were boys who were like brothers to me growing up. Other kids in the village would come to our yard to play with us. We even had our little soccer team with my brother as the coach.

My grandfather was a fisherman, a farmer, and the calmest man in the village. He would ride his bicycle over two miles one way to the neighboring village, Braco, where he had his fishing boat. He would do this every morning around five o'clock and come back home around eight o'clock with the catch of the day. My grandmother would then sell it to the people in the village. My grandfather was a chain smoker. He would have his breakfast with a few cigarettes in between before heading back out to the same village he fished at. He would stay there all day working the farm until the sun went down. He would then take the journey back home, along with a few other farmers from my village. He would do this every day like clockwork. I remember we used to look out for him in the evenings; then we would race to meet him. Whoever got to him first got to ride the bicycle to the house. He would take off from working on the farm on Sundays.

My grandmother was the total opposite of my grandfather. My grandmother was hardly ever sober, and when she was drunk somebody was getting cursed out, even the dogs. The whole village knew her to be like that. People would even mess with her to get her started and she wouldn't stop until she fell asleep. If anyone messed with us she would take them on, although we weren't spared from her fiery tongue. My grandparents lived together but they slept in separate rooms. For the most part, they got along; it was the drinking that caused the problem between them.

My Aunt Cindy is my mom's younger sister, the youngest of my mom's siblings. She was the disciplinarian; she didn't play. She was ready to spank you for any and everything wrong or right. Sometimes it was just a misunderstanding. She was the best though. She didn't want us to end up like most of the kids in the village. Manners and respect were a must. What I love most about her is that she never left my mom's side. She was always there for us. When you get to know my mom, then you'll see how important my Aunt Cindy was in my family.

If you ask me to describe my mom with one word it would be ANGEL! My mom is a devoted Christian. She has been a Christian since before I was born. She is one of the humblest people I know. I've never heard my mom curse, argue, call anyone names, and hardly ever saw her mad. I have never seen my mom wear pants, get her hair done or wear nail polish. She is always wearing a hat outside and the only time I have seen her dance is in the church. There are five of us, with me being the youngest. My dad was in Kingston working and my mom was carrying all the weight without a complaint. Keeping clothes clean for five kids was hard especially when there was no water in the pipes, but what was much harder was feeding us. My mom would get up early to prepare breakfast for us before we left for school which was no easy task. Before we got a gas stove, it was a wood fire. My mom would have to light the fire first which was a pain especially if it rained the night before or it was still raining. Sometimes her eyes would get watery from the smoking firewood. Even after we got a gas stove, she would use wood or coal because the gas was very expensive. She saved the gas for the days she was not feeling well or when it was raining. Some days she used both. My mom would make breakfast, get us ready and send us off to school. I didn't even mention waking up five kids. I remember being half asleep with breakfast in front of me.

After my mom would send us off, she was cleaning up, washing, and getting lunch ready before we returned for our short lunch break. While doing that she would be thinking about dinner. It was 24/7 taking care of us. My mom was also very active in the church. We would go to church every night except Friday and Saturday. On some

Sundays, we would go three times for a 5:00 a.m. prayer meeting, 11:00 a.m. midday service, and then 7:00 p.m. night service. I was always sleeping on or under a bench if not on my mom's lap. Everyone in the village showed much respect to my mom. Most called her Mommy.

My dad is a different breed. I always admired him. As a kid, my dad was just different from everyone I knew. He was super strict but fun to be around. He lived in Kingston where he worked and later took over a company. He would come on the weekends, sometimes for an extended stay. When my dad would come, I got excited because I knew we were going to do a few things for the weekend. I would throw a tantrum if I was not in the car with him. I loved helping to wash the car even though I would make a bigger mess. My dad would take as many kids as possible that could fit in the car to the river or the beach. We would play soccer or cricket. Most Saturday evenings, we would drive to get ice cream, stop at the Columbus Park in Discovery Bay, or just drive around while my dad showed us places or just talked about something.

My grandmother lived in Runaway Bay and sometimes we would go visit her. My dad would give us the best of everything. We had bicycles, real soccer balls, and all the gear for cricket. The grown-ups would borrow our gear sometimes. My dad loves music, and he had a stereo system in the house. He was always adding something to it, fixing something, or just playing music. My dad regularly bought new records and had a nice country music collection. We had a microphone that we would get to use sometimes. My maternal grandfather had a sound system and a dancehall in our yard. My step-grandfather, the man my paternal grandmother married, also had a sound system that my dad used to operate and perform on. My dad was a dancehall artist. That was kind of how he connected with my mom. People in my village had mixed feelings about my dad. He had his boys that he would check on when he was around; other than them he did not mix with many other people. We were not allowed to go to anyone's house other than my cousins' three houses down the street at my mom's Aunt Vera's house.

My dad was hard-working, ambitious, and very smart. Some of the people in the village thought he was a show-off. My dad drove an asphalt truck and paved roads all over Jamaica. Sometimes when he was working close by or passing through he would stop by and, as he did with the car, he would pack the cab with kids. He would drive up the hill, turn around, and come back down the hill. The best part about that was he would play with the horn while showing us his skills with the clutch and gear shift. Even the grown-ups loved it. My dad was a very good truck driver. As a kid, he was like a superhero driving that big truck on those small Jamaican streets, especially in the country areas. Anywhere my dad pulled up to, people would gather around the truck in awe. It was the cleanest asphalt truck ever. It looked like a milk truck. My dad also loved fishing so he would take us out in the ocean with him. He would go night fishing with one of his few boys sometimes. My dad was also into horse racing. He had a major connection in the business with owners, trainers, jockeys, groomers, and the whole works. When my dad came to my village, men would be checking him for a winner. My dad would go to bet at numerous shops on Saturday morning. Then he would sit in the living room, and when it was race time, he would listen to the races. Sometimes my dad would be riding a broomstick in the living room all excited.

My dad knew someone everywhere we went. Some people just knew him as the man that drove the clean asphalt truck. I remember my dad took us on long road trips. He would do this on Sundays when the road was not that busy. Most of the gas stations were closed on Sundays so he would travel with a big container of gas in the trunk. When we were in Kingston with my dad, it was much of the same, just more action. We would go for ice cream on Sunday afternoons, then my dad would drive us around and show us everywhere. One of my favorite places was Beverly Hills. The view was awesome, and the big houses were inspiring. He would even take us through the ghettos. My dad knew a lot of gangsters. He was good everywhere we went. He is very kind, so he treated them very well. Even the police used to come to check on my dad. He would always tell us that he never had a problem all his years in Kingston because he treated people well and minded his business. My dad never used to go to church, but he would take us anywhere on the island to go to church. He would pay for us to go on

13

the church bus. The only time I would see my dad in the church was at a funeral. To sum it up, daddy was an interesting boss-like figure that I wanted to be like. You will hear much more about him throughout my story.

My paternal grandmother was a woman who I admired a lot because she was doing the things that I saw only men doing. My grandmother lived in Runaway Bay. In the yard, she had a bar and she would show movies on a billboard-sized screen with a projector. She was a boss lady. My dad must have gotten it from her. She would always have people around; some doing odd jobs as she always had something going on, some stopping by just to visit or ask for a favor. There were a few regular drinkers that were always there. Like my dad, my grandmother was kind to everyone. The one thing I remember most about her is that I was getting something every time I visited. Sometimes she would sneak a couple of dollars in my hand, or she would just put it in my pocket so my dad wouldn't see. Daddy would always be telling her that we are good, "keep your money." Granny Stella, as we called her, was heavy set so she moved around slowly. Most of the time she would be sitting down. I remember times when she would be telling my dad about the pain she was feeling, mostly in her legs. She was very calm and quiet; you could hardly hear her speak.

My paternal grandfather lived in Hope Bay, Portland. He had a small house literally on the sand. He was a fisherman. I remember visiting him a couple of times, but I don't have much memory of him. There was a hurricane, so he pulled up his boat and tied it on the side of the house. He then went further inland to ride out the storm with the family. During the hurricane, the house fell crushing the boat. My grandfather was devastated. He went to the hospital and died. I think he had a heart attack. This was the first time I heard my dad cry. He cried for hours. We drove to Hope Bay to look at the devastation and make the funeral arrangements. There was nothing left of the house but the sand-covered floor. Growing up, my dad always said I'm like my grandfather because I didn't like wearing a shirt.

As early as I can remember, my life was centered around church and school. I went to basic school (pre-school) in the basement of the Baptist church. I remember learning our ABCs and counting 1,2,3. We would sing everything while rocking on the bench. After lunch, we got to take a nap with our heads on the desk. Sometimes, they would walk us down to the beach where we would pick up seashells. Whenever there was a ship in the harbor, I would get scared. The ships were so much bigger when you saw them up close than when we would see them passing out in the ocean.

When I was six years old, I started all-age school. I had to walk to school. At first, it was scary walking there. We had to walk on the main road which was a two-lane winding road without any sidewalk, the main thoroughfare between Montego Bay and Ocho Rios. At first, mommy walked with me. Like with every other time in my life, I had older siblings that would hold my hand and take care of me. There was a certain part of the road where we would wait until there was no traffic coming; then we would run because it was so narrow. In the front of the school was the main road and at the rear was the Caribbean Sea. Danger everywhere!

During break and lunch, some kids would sneak and go swimming. I would never do that. I was scared of drowning, and I was the kind of kid that knew my boundaries. My older siblings set a standard for me, and I followed. The principal and the teachers always talked about how well-behaved my siblings and I were. That made me want to remain on my best behavior. Some parents came to the school to argue with the teachers about disciplining their kids even though they would never show up for a parent-teacher meeting. My mom and my Aunt Cindy would not miss a PTA meeting and there better not be any complaining about us. We were never allowed to fight. If you got into a fight, you were wrong and in trouble. My mom would promise a spanking that she hardly delivered but there was no escape from my aunt. If we got in trouble at school, we would try our best to let it stay there to save ourselves from a second spanking. The method of teaching at my school was kind of crazy. It was more about punishing you to learn rather than teaching you.

I remember my first-grade teacher for being the most caring. She taught us about personal hygiene, and from six years old until this day I never forgot the day she taught us to bathe with warm water then rinse with cold water to close our pores. At that time, we only had cold water but now I have access to both and that's exactly how I have been showering because it makes sense. The principal on the other hand was all about discipline. She whipped us like slaves. I even think she was cautious with me and my siblings because of my dad. My dad did not ever want anyone putting their hands on us. I will never forget being in a class studying for the common entrance exam. This was the test you had to pass to go to high school. The principal would pop up anytime she felt like it and take over from the teacher. She came in with a whip in her hand which was a half-inch thick electrical wire. She would start in the front and work her way down asking each kid questions. The simplest question would make you struggle and before you knew it, you got lashed at lightning speed. For example, she would say 6 x 7 and if you answered right she would flip it quickly and say 7 x 6. It was not working because very few kids went to high school. It was still a lot of fun going to that school. We played before school started and on our break, lunchtime, as well as after school.

The most special thing to me until this day was that we prayed before starting, and then we got together after lunch and prayed again. I'll talk more about that later. My parents hardly ever let us go on school trips. There was one trip that they allowed us to go on that I'll never forget. It was my first time riding on a train. We took the bus to Montpelier which was a few miles from Montego Bay. We rode the train from there to Montego Bay where the bus was waiting at that station. We also went to Freeport in Montego Bay to see the ship that was docked in the harbor. We went to tour the factory that made the D&G sodas. It was a very exciting trip; even the bus ride was fun. It was a bus that only carried tourists. We had to wear a uniform to school. The boys wore khakis, and the girls wore a dark blue dress with a white blouse. We all wore black or brown shoes. My mom would dress me in the mornings. My shirt would be tucked in my pants and my pants waist was up to my belly button. My mom expected me to keep it that way all day. It was a hard thing to do, but you were expected to keep it clean. The worst thing that could happen would be to fall in the grass and get that green stain on your khakis. We would usually wear that same uniform for at least two days. When we got home from school, the first thing we did was take our uniforms off and hang them up.

Some kids would be out playing in their uniforms after school. I was not allowed to do that. I was expected to go straight home after school. Some kids only had one pair of khakis so when it got really dirty their mother would wash it after school and hang it on the clothesline to dry for the next day. Sometimes, kids would miss school because their uniform was dirty, especially when it was raining. Sometimes it rains in Jamaica for days even weeks.

After school I would get to play but only in my yard. I was not allowed outside the gate. That was a problem because the other kids would come to my yard to join me, my siblings, and my cousins. If you didn't behave, you were not allowed to play in my yard. After playing it was dinner or homework and then shower. Some nights I would have to go to church with my mom. Our church was almost a mile up the hill from my house and we walked back and forth. Rarely did we ever get a ride. At night, the street was very dark. There were some nights when the moon would be shining so bright it was like daytime.

On Sundays, my dad would drop us off when he was home. They would come to have Sunday school in my yard every Sunday evening, and on Monday nights there was a meeting called young people's meeting. We would study the Bible verses and recite them. We even had to do that in school. There was one morning out of the week that we would have devotion in our classes and each student would have to say a Bible verse. Some students would try to get away with John 11:35 "Jesus wept" but the teacher would tell them to say another one. It was easy for my siblings and me since we had to study it in Sunday school, church, and at home. It was always like I was from two different worlds. I had my blood family and my church family. My mom was closer to her church sisters and brothers than most of her own family. I was born and raised in the church. We did not miss any church events. We were on almost every church trip. We even cleaned the church. You will hear a lot more throughout this book about that world.

My grandfather had a woodwork shop in our yard. Back then when people in our community died, especially older people, they would not go to a morgue or funeral home. They would put ice on the body in the house and they would make the casket in the workshop in my yard. The workmen in the village would go to their regular job in the day and then they would come together in the shop at night to build the casket. There would be drinking, singing, shouting, and sometimes arguing about which way to make the casket. At first, it used to be scary but over time it became normal. I remember sneaking in there one day when there was a casket that was finished and waiting for the day of the funeral. I opened it and laid down in it just to see how it felt. If the person that died was a family or close friend of my family, we would go to the digging of the grave. That also was mostly done at night with lots of people gathering around the spot drinking and singing while the men took turns to dig and shovel the dirt. They would also have what they called a nine-night before the funeral where mostly older people would sing all night, drink tea, and eat bread. There were certain people in the community and neighboring villages that were known to be good at this type of event.

The people in my community were very close for the most part. There were a lot of petty arguments, but everyone would help and protect each other especially if someone was sick or there was a death. People in the community always thought we had money so there was always someone coming to my mom for help. The older I got, I realized my parents were not rich; they were just kind. We were not allowed to beg for anything or accept anything from anyone. There were vendors in the schoolyard who would sell candies, fruit, snacks, and even little toys like blow horns and balloons. They would try to force us to take stuff from them because they knew my mom would pay. We were not allowed to eat from anyone. We were not even allowed to be talking when we went out. My dad had some different kinds of rules.

As I mentioned before, my community was aligned with the Jamaica Labour Party, the green party. My first exposure to politics was at a very young age from my grandfather. He would talk about Sir Alexander Bustamante all the time. He was the leader of the Jamaica Labour Party and Jamaica's First Prime Minister. My grandfather had a picture of him in his living room. The People's National Party, PNP, was aligned with Cuba. They were known as the Socialist Party and my grandfather hated that. I would hear him saying he would never share his land or his house with anyone. I remember hearing him say that he would set his house on fire with any occupant. My grandfather had a special love for Bustamante and the JLP because he gave acres of land to the local farmers for them to work, and then paid a reasonable price for said land. Until this day, the land my grandfather got to work and paid for is still in my family. Leading up to the 1980 general election, it was a very violent time in Jamaica. It was more about the bigger fight between America and the Soviet Union. The JLP was aligned with America and the PNP was aligned with the Soviet Union and Cuba. There were lots of Cubans and Russians in Jamaica since the PNP was the ruling party at that time. The American government put its support behind the JLP to get rid of the Soviet Union's influence over Jamaica. It was bloody. The main road that connected Montego Bay and Ocho Rios ran through my community on the north coast of the island. All the campaign motorcades would have to pass through my community.

When it was the JLP passing through, it was a party and when it was the PNP, it was a war. As a kid, I would be in great fear when the PNP was passing through. My dad would make sure he was home with us when this type of event was happening. It would make me feel safe when he was there with us. I remember nights when my dad would say no lights, and we would be there in silence in the dark. The worst of these kinds of events I can remember was when Prime Minister Michael Manley had a conference at Sam Sharpe Square in Montego Bay to announce the date of the general election. There was a steady flow of buses, trucks, and motorbikes going through the community. There was also a heavy presence of soldiers and police. My dad was not into politics even though the contracts for making and fixing the roads were handed out by the politicians. My dad was very diplomatic with what he did. Since those days, I have felt something inside of my soul that I must grow up to defend my community. I also realized that when the PNP is in power, they wouldn't do anything for my community. In Jamaica at that time, everything was controlled by politics. Everything changed after the election and the Jamaica Labor Party won. That was a historical event in Jamaica and more so for my community. It was like a jubilee. Everyone, from the smallest of kids to the elders even if they had to be picked up and carried to the streets, was present. Anything that could make noise was used to make noise. My dad and some of his friends and family cooked in the backyard. It was the biggest celebration I have ever seen in my community.

As I got older, my siblings started taking more responsibility for me, especially my big brother. I started hanging out with him more and more. He was responsible for me in many ways. When it was time to take a bath, he would make sure I got mine. I remember playing around with the rag and water until he was ready for me. Sometimes I would rebel telling him I can bathe myself. He would help me to get dressed. I was very close to my mom. It was hard to separate me from my mom. In church, I had to sit next to my mom. I might drift away to play but I would come right back, especially when it was time to sleep. The church had two conventions every year and my family never missed any of them. There would be one in Kingston in March and the other in Norwich which was a little community next to Port Antonio, Portland. My dad would take us and then pick us up at the end of the week. It was Sunday to Sunday. Sometimes we would go on the church bus.

We stayed in boarding houses all over the community. In Portland, there was a school across from the church where most of the people would stay. Since it was summer, the kids were off from school. The men stayed in different quarters from the women. It was a problem separating me from my mom until I was much older, and the women started complaining. Then my brother had total responsibility for me when we were not at church. The older brethren would look out for us as my brother was also a kid. For the whole week, we would go to church three times per day with prayer meetings at 5:00 a.m. Then we would have breakfast, shower, and get dressed for midday service at 11:00 a.m. After midday service, we had dinner. Then we would have some time before the night service.

My brother always took great care of me. My siblings and I got along very well. Sometimes there would be no water in the pipes so we would go to the river to bathe. Sometimes the whole village would be at the river washing clothes or bathing and it was an everyday hangout for some. I went to the river with my brother and his friends one evening to bathe, and I had almost drowned. Unlike the sea, some parts of the river have an edge. I was at the riverside next to my brother waiting on him to bathe me. I stepped out and the next thing, I was under the water jumping up and down with my hands up, but my head could not make it above the water. I felt someone grab my hand and pull me up. It was my brother. I was so shaken up; I just wanted to go home. From the veranda of my house on the hill, you were looking in the river running in the sea. There was my mom sitting on the porch not knowing what had just happened. My brother told me not to say anything because my mom would not let us go back to the river. From that moment, my brother became special to me. He saved my life.

My brother loved birds. He had lots of pigeons and a few different kinds of doves. I would go with my brother and his friends in the woods where they would search for bird nests with eggs. They would mark the spot and keep checking until the eggs had hatched. They would take the baby birds home before they grew feathers, and they would feed them until they could eat on their own. I learned from them and started doing the same with my friends. Saturday mornings, my brother used to sweep the yard. I had to join him when I got older. We did not use a traditional broom. We used a stalk from the coconut tree. The coconut broom was the stem that the coconut would be hanging from on the tree. We would sometimes go into the woods to get a special bush and tie them together to sweep the yard.

My oldest sister left to go to a boarding school located outside of Ocho Rios. It was an all-girls Christian school. I loved visiting her. She always had something for me, and her friends would be all over me. I loved the attention. I never forgot the first time she took me to Woolworth in Ocho Rios. She is the firstborn in my immediate family, and I am the last, and our birthdays are a day apart.

To go to high school in those days, you had to take the common entrance exam. Hardly anyone from my all-age school passed this exam which means only a few kids from my community went to high school. I am not sure if it was the wrong curriculum, or if it was their method of teaching. You got two chances at taking this exam. First at 11 years old and then the following year at 12 years old. This school starts with grade 1 and goes through grade 9. If you fail the common entrance exam on both tries, you keep going until you get a chance to take the technical exam. If you passed it, you got to go to technical school or take the grade 9 achievement test. If you pass that test, you would get another chance to go to high school. In this case, you would start at grade 9. High school started at grade 7 and went to grade 11. If you fail all these exams in all-age school, you continue until you graduate in grade 9. Then you could go to private school, learn a trade, or get a job. My oldest sister graduated and went to a private school. My big brother and my other two sisters passed their common entrance exams and went on to the William Knibb Memorial High School. This school was located in Martha Brae, a community outside of Falmouth, Trelawny.

To prepare for the common entrance exam, we did school lessons. When it was time for me to do my exam, we were in Kingston. I would have to go to Trelawny and then go back to Kingston where we were spending time with my dad. This journey was three hours in one direction. My dad said it did not make any sense to do all that because I was not going to pass. I was happy to hear that because I did not want to go. My mom was not going for that. She said I was going. My mom came up with a plan which was she and I were going to take a passenger bus to the country the day before the exam and stay at our house. I would go do the exam at the Duncans all-age school which was in the town next to Rio Bueno.

After the exam, I would get on a special bus that runs from Montego Bay to Kingston. The driver knew us very well as we rode with him all the time. My mom would then get on the bus when it got to my community. I did not like the plan but I had no say in it so that is what we did. The test was hard for me. I answered the questions I knew then guessed on the rest of them. Everything went as planned, and we made it back to Kingston safely. A few months later on a Friday mid-morning, I was dressed and ready to go to the annual high school fair with my older siblings when the news came that I passed the exam and could go to said high school. All I remember is that my mom said to take off my clothes; I wasn't going anymore. I was devastated. Going to the high school fair was like going to Great Adventure for an 11-year-old kid. I guess it was some form of superstition that something bad would happen to me. I cried so hard, and my siblings begged my mom to let me go, but my mom would not give in, so I did not go. You would think that it was the perfect gift for me to go celebrate but that is how it was in my family.

Starting high school was life-changing for me. I had to start getting up much earlier to get to school on time. My new high school was almost 20 miles away from my community. There was no school bus, so I had to find my way to and from school. The passenger buses would refuse to take students sometimes because our bus fare was half the price of regular passengers. We would hitchhike sometimes on pick-up trucks, dump trucks, flatbeds, or tractor-trailers, and sometimes random drivers would stop and give us a ride. There were many days we had to go back home because we did not get a ride. One of my scariest rides was riding on a tractor-trailer. I had to ride on the platform between the cab and the trailer. When we got to Falmouth which was 16 miles, then we would have to travel another mile and a half to Martha Brae where our high school was. Some days we did not get home until night. The journey to and from school was very exhausting, especially for an 11-year-old kid.

My first year in high school was a struggle. Most of the schoolwork was unfamiliar to me. I had one sister in 8th grade, another in 9th, and my big brother in 11th grade so they would help me with my homework. They were busy with their schoolwork, but they always

23

found time to help me. My mom would help me sometimes. They kept me back in 7th grade. Now the friends I made moved on, and I was in a class with a new set of kids. It did not take me long to make some new friends that turned out to be lifelong friends. My two best friends and I are still close to this day. By the time I got to 8th grade, things started getting better. I started understanding the schoolwork more and I was getting a hang of the transportation situation.

One of the best things for me the first year in high school was having my big brother that was a senior. It didn't hurt to have two big sisters either. The seniors would do what we called "grub" to the new students. They would do stuff like tell them to blow out a light bulb, polish their shoes, carry their bag, and just about anything else that came to mind. I remember having one encounter where an older male student told me to laugh in Spanish. I said something to him, and he kicked me. I went and got my brother and pointed him out. My brother was well respected by both teachers and students. He apologized to my brother and that was it. The word went around as to whose brother I was, so I did not have any more problems with grubbing. My brother finished school and went to Kingston to live with my dad and further his studies. My sister shortly followed and transferred to a school in Kingston. Now it was me and my youngest sister on the road.

My community was known as a JLP stronghold in the northern Trelawny constituency. The men from my community were known for being violent. After the JLP victory in the 1980 election, men from my community and other men aligned to the JLP took over what was called a Cuban site in the PNP stronghold of Falmouth. These men were now living there so I would run into them on the streets all the time. Sometimes it was these men that would give us a ride home from school, even forcing bus drivers to take us. They would come to soccer games and high school dances sometimes. These men were known as gangsters. Kids from my school would see me hanging out with them so I started getting treated differently by my friends. My friends started calling me "bad youth" or "Ryo" which is the name of my community. My community is spelled Rio but pronounced Ryo.

I played soccer but I was not good enough to make the school team, but both of my friends were good players, especially Keven (Keegan) Simpson. Everyone knew me in school. The JLP member of Parliament came to my school to speak at our devotion in the auditorium one morning. He recognized me in front of everyone and it was the best feeling. He also lived in Martha Brae, a short walk from my school. My friends walked with me to his house one day to check him for some money. They were amazed at the way he treated us. While going to school I started hustling. I was buying candies from the wholesale store and selling them back to the students. At home, I started a little chicken business, something I learned from my big brother. I would buy the chicklets, raise them to a certain size and then sell them to the people in the community. Sometimes I would pluck them, bag them, and sell them to the shop keepers in the community for resale. I also raised pigs and goats. I had a group of friends in my community; some were actual family. I would hustle with them sometimes but could not let my parents know.

I remember one time when we walked a few miles along the main road and searched the bushes on both sides for empty soda bottles that people would throw out the windows of vehicles. We cleaned the dirty ones and then put them in crates and sold them. Once we got a load of conch shells from divers after they harvested the conch. We did a lot of work cleaning and polishing them to sell them to tourists or wholesale to the people that sold fruits and carvings on the side of the road. That did not go well and we did not make any money. My grandmother had property in my community. Since she lived elsewhere, she asked the lady next door to watch over her property. There was a lot of fruit from the fruit trees on the property that I would wholesale to people that sell on the side of the road.

My dad got saved in the church and became a Christian. As I mentioned earlier, my dad was not a churchgoer. He said he had a dream and from there everything changed. He did not just become a Christian and that's it. No! He was extra serious about it. Everything was about the church, religion, and spirituality. It was all mixed up, and it started getting overwhelming for me. There was no father-son or much of any regular talk. It seemed like it was all about religion. My dad would sometimes talk about the Bishops and Pastors as if they were some type of spiritual beings. I remember he used to call the Bishop "The Man of God". He would sometimes say: The Man of God can hear us talking even when he was nowhere around. My dad would act as if he thought this man was watching from somewhere. I never understood it, nor did I like it. It was too much pressure. My mom has been a true devoted Christian all my life. Now my dad was acting as if he was schooling my mom about the Bible and religion. My dad would give a lot of money to the church, and he would also buy instruments or anything that was needed for the church. My dad decided the business he was in would affect his newly found spirituality, so he sold the truck and closed the business down. He gave a portion of the money to the church. By now, my dad was well respected in the church circles. He even started moving up in the ranks.

With all these changes going on with my dad, my mom, big brother, and my sisters already fully in church, I started to feel like I had to figure my way. I was mad that my dad sold the business and did not consider that my brother and I were becoming of age where we could have learned the business. I was not against church or Christianity, but it was not the way I knew it should be, and I was not going to be pressured to act otherwise. I was a good kid that became rebellious. Some people started describing me as the black sheep of the family. It got harder and harder for me to keep up with my schoolwork after missing day after day because I had trouble getting a ride to school. They did not expect much from me in the first place, so it was like whatever for me by this point.

By the time I was a senior, I started hanging out more and more with the thugs from my community. One of my cousins was driving a car for the member of Parliament and doing anything and everything. Some days I would link up with him after school and ride around with him until he was ready to head home to our community. I always loved music; so with my dad not into that lifestyle anymore, I was hanging out where the music was any chance I got. I remember being at a house party one night and I heard my mom was outside looking for me. I got mad that she came there to get me because I usually knew my time to go home. She would be waiting on me, mad! When I went outside to her, she said my grandmother did not come home so I should come to help the rest of the family look for her. I was happy that she was not there to embarrass me in front of everyone. We searched and found my grandma over a wall in the gully. We went to get the police and they took her to the hospital. She never made it back home. She died in the hospital.

After I finished school, they wanted me to live in Kingston with my dad and I refused. I was happy to be done with school and did not want to go back to any school. Living in Kingston with my dad meant I would be subjected to his extreme religious practices and all his other strict rules. I stayed in the country with my mom where I stepped up my hustling game. I had more time to attend to the chicken business. I was already doing this business so I raised the number of chickens I would buy. I set up a pen that my brother had started before he left to live in Kingston with my dad. He intended to extend his chicken cage, but I turned it into a pigpen so now I had chickens and pigs. I started hanging out more with the politicians in the community. There was an election coming up so there was a lot of action going on. Lots of money was being spent and contracts were being handed out. I started getting more and more involved as I was bonding more with these guys while feeling like I was standing up for my community and the member of Parliament that I got to love and respect greatly. There were only a few that I would hang with even though there were always a lot of guys around. There were even a few women that became like one of the guys. It got to a point where I started going on campaigning trips, what we called motorcades.

One night I came back, and my mom was sitting up waiting for me. I felt so bad putting her through all that stress with her not knowing if something had happened to me. The real thugs would look out for me making sure I was good. One of the most memorable acts of kindness I can remember anyone showing me was when my friend (cousin) Round Bread left his girlfriend at a party to walk me home. It was a mile away and in the dark just to make sure I got home safely and then he went back to the party. That's the kind of loyalty I was taught and still practice to this day. The late leader of my community who had a direct link to the MP gave me a contract to demolish an old building in the town center. I was 14 at the time so I was not eligible to vote, so the older men were mad that I got it and not them. They couldn't do anything about it. I loved the member of Parliament because he was spending a lot of money in the community fixing the roads, the basic school, drains, and walls. He was always around, hardly missed a funeral; he knew everyone by their name. He was like one of us.

I was making money so I started buying the kind of shoes and clothes I liked which would make my dad mad. I remember my dad came from Kingston and saw me wearing a pair of Travel Fox sneakers and he got mad. He asked me what the police would think when they saw a young boy like me in shoes like that. He said they were going to think I was a gangster and wonder where I got the money to buy shoes like that. One of the guys I hung out with was a tailor so we would buy the material, and he would make all kinds of different style suits for us. To my parents, my dressing was not Christian and to me, I was just wearing what I liked.

The closer the election got, the deeper I was getting into politics. At this point, the people in my community started calling me Councilor. We were campaigning everywhere in the constituency and beyond. The island got more violent, and I even received some threats to my life. The construction of a new villa started in the area and some of my friends got jobs there. Everything seemed to connect to politics, so I decided to get a job there as well. It was fun being around the guys and I was getting paid. After my first day working, someone called my dad in Kingston and told him. My dad was mad, so I did not go back. As I mentioned earlier, ships would dock in the harbor and sometimes deliver corn to the factory that made grains for the animals.

My grand uncle was one of the supervisors that hired the men to work on the ships while it was being unloaded. He gave me a few night shifts since I was always bothering him about it. All this was fun for me while making my own money. There was a fisherman that sailed his boat from Ocho Rios to my community. There was a little fisherman house on the beach, and he stayed in there. Sometimes I would sit on the beach with him talking while he mended his net, fixed a damaged fish trap, or just got his gear ready to fish. We became close friends. I would sit with him and other fishermen from my community listening to them talk about their different experiences at sea. Sometimes there would be a pot on the fire while they talked.

I got along with mostly everyone, especially the grown-ups. I was taught from a very early age to have manners and respect for others. I have always had a soft heart for the people in my community because most were very poor and did not ever get to live as my family and I did. When my dad sold his business, he remodeled an old workshop my grandfather had in the front yard by the side of the road. He named it Seaview Goods and Supplies. He sold mainly supplies for the fishermen. Some days when I was serving in there, I would give them the stuff for free or they would promise to pay another time. They never did. The people in my community thought I was cool and different from my family. While all this was going on, my dad was quickly moving up the ranks in the church. He had been driving all over the island for years, so it was nothing for him to drive his car to these rural places to preach in different churches. The churches were mainly in Portland and St. Mary.

I was a God-fearing, spiritual kid becoming a young man, but I was attracted to the streets, and everyone knew that. When my dad changed, it was like he expected everyone to follow, especially me. My sisters and brother were already following in my mom's footsteps, even though my dad made it seem like they weren't doing good enough. After a while, I felt like I needed to stand up and be myself so I chose to be myself. Between fearing for what would happen and the embarrassment in the church, I started causing my parents some pain even though I had never gotten into any trouble, not even a fight. I would have a few beers here and there, never smoked and even though I got home late a few times, I never stayed out.

When I was 17 years old, my dad decided to take me to the American Embassy to apply for a visitor visa before I turned 18. Before 18, he would be my sponsor but after 18, I would have to apply independently. My dad was a businessman with his visa and traveled for years. He took my oldest sister to Miami with him once or twice.

All my siblings had their visas before me. My sister Gillian would go to stay with her Godmother in Canada during the summertime. My dad took me to the Embassy, and I got a ten-year visa.

The general election was getting closer and closer. It was the first week of February. There was a hurricane on September 12, 1988, called Gilbert. It was the worst to ever hit the island. There were a lot of monetary and other kinds of donations from foreign governments and private groups to Jamaica. Most of these donations were channeled through the government in power which was the Jamaica Labour Party (JLP). This was the party my community was aligned to. There were a lot of rebuilding contract grants for housing, free-housing materials, and even cash handouts. All this was happening in the heat of the election campaign, and I was all up in it. My sister Gillian was pregnant with her first son. On Sunday, January 15, 1989, we were all dressed and ready for church when she started having contractions. My mom sent me to get this guy with a minibus to take her to the hospital. I drove back to the house with the guy, and they left. I took my church clothes back off and went to meet up with my boys at the regular spot.

When my mom came back home and found out I did not bother to go to church, she was really upset. A few days later on Wednesday, I was at our usual hang-out spot and my mom sent someone with a message for me to come home. When I got to the house, my mom told me I should pack my stuff because my dad was coming to get me. I immediately said I was not going to live with him. We were going back and forth until she said they were sending me to live with my Uncle Leslie in America, and I was leaving Saturday. I was shocked. My uncle and his family came to Jamaica that past October to bury his father and I traveled around with them the whole time they were there, so we had formed a bond. That was something that would just happen when I met people. Before my uncle migrated, he lived in Kingston and would just come through sometimes to visit for a few hours or a day at the most. I had never even had a sleepover. I was determined I was not going anywhere, especially with just a day's notice.

My mom went to ask my area leader to talk to me. He was someone I looked up to. He was the boss. Everything flowed through him, and he always made sure I was good. He treated me differently than most of the other guys. He sat me down and talked to me. He said I should not let an opportunity like this pass me by, and he did not think our party would win the election which was two weeks away. He and my uncle were good friends so he knew I would be in good hands. After talking to him I decided to go even though I was still mad that I had no time to process the whole thing or say goodbye to my friends. I packed my stuff, and my dad came to get me on that Thursday night; we left for Kingston early Friday morning.

My big brother Rohan was living in Kingston with my dad at the time, so we talked Friday night and he made me feel better. Before I left, two of my dad's friends stopped by the house. One of them was my mom's first cousin. They both worked on cruise ships at the time. I remember one of them told me not to bother with the big gold chains. Saturday morning, January 21, 1989, my dad gave me a book of Proverbs. He told me to keep it and study the words of wisdom. He prayed for me; then he and my brother drove me to the airport and sent me off on a plane to a place I had never been before—the United States of America.

Chapter 2

The Migration to the US

New World

Dressed in what we called a three-piece suit and dress shoes, I landed at the JFK airport in Queens, New York. I walked through the airport with my suitcase in my hand looking around to find my way to my uncle, a real-life scene of the movie *Coming to America*.

It was in the middle of winter and almost everyone was wearing jackets and boots, and some even had on gloves. I found my uncle, and he had two of his friends with him. He gave me a jacket to put on while he took my suitcase. It was pretty lightweight because I did not bring much of my clothes. In Jamaica, we had the impression that clothes were cheap in America so why carry your old clothes there. Now we were heading to the car. My uncle was in front, and his two friends were behind me. One of them I recognized. He was from my community so I would see him around when he visited. When I stepped through the sliding glass doors to the outside, a different kind of cold hit me and I stopped. One of the guys behind me tapped my shoulder and said "gwaan mon" as in "keep going". They laughed and started telling me all about winter. Driving home in the car, they were talking about everything. But all I can remember was me just looking around. We stopped in the Bronx where the guy from my community lived. Now I was in semi-shock, not what I expected America to look like.

He lived in a building, so we took the elevator up a couple of floors. When we got inside, he had food and drinks ready. The music came on and the talking continued. It was like a welcome party, but the problem was the guest was not feeling up to it. I felt tired as I wanted to sleep and was wondering what it was going to be like and where I was going to live. I was also thinking about Jamaica. We chilled there for a while and then got on our way. I was in deep thoughts and looking all around as my uncle drove. While driving, he was asking me about people in Jamaica and reminiscing about three months ago when we were together in Jamaica. Finally, I got to my new home in Morristown, New Jersey. My uncle's wife, who I called my aunt, and two cousins were waiting to see me. We were all together in Jamaica not long ago, so it felt good to see them again and they made me feel very welcome. They showed me around the house. My younger cousin Patrick took me to his room that I would be sharing with him. He was excited to have me there, especially because we already built a bond in Jamaica. My older cousin Karen was happy to see me also. She was very quiet and laid back, but we had a good time in Jamaica. Once I got relaxed, my cousin started giving me the rundown on everything. He had his phone line in his room which he stayed on. He started putting me on the phone to talk to his friends. They would have trouble understanding me and likewise, I would have trouble understanding some of them.

When I got there, I started understanding better how it all happened so quickly for me to be in America. My aunt was the one behind it. When she was in Jamaica, she asked me about school and what I was doing. She even asked why didn't I try to leave and go to America. I did not pay any attention to it at the time. I didn't have any close family there, I didn't think my parents would allow me to do that, and most of all, I had no intentions of leaving Jamaica. I was very close to my mom. I had my room, but I still slept in my mom's bed. Furthermore, I felt very connected to my community. I felt like I was going to bring a change for the people. I was mad at my parents, but now that I was here, things started making sense. My aunt was on the phone talking to everybody trying to get me a job. She also wanted me to go to school. I had a 10-year visa but the immigration officer at the airport gave me only 6 months in the country. I was up for the work, but not the school thing because in the back of my head I was going back home.

My uncle did not talk much unless he was with his friends. He was very laid back. He was a mechanic working for a school bus company, and he would work on people's cars in the evenings and on the weekends. On the weekends, he had his regulars that would come hang out. My uncle loved music so he would be blasting the music, especially on Saturdays. I loved it. My aunt called up this guy who was one of my uncle's regulars. He came to the house, and we talked. He then took me to Burger King where he knew the manager. We talked and he told us what we needed to do and told us to come back and see him. Ten days after I landed in the country, I was working at Burger King. I worked the evening shift which started around 3:00 p.m. and went until closing. I had a hard time understanding what was going on and why my dad didn't want me working in Jamaica. Now I was here in America mopping floors and cleaning the Burger King bathroom. All that hustling I was doing before I left Jamaica had prepared me, so I did what I had to do and did it well. The boss liked the way I worked. My big sister who was already here living with a Pastor and his family in New York would come to pick me up to spend time with her sometimes when I had the day off. I remember one night she came and was waiting on me outside of Burger King. She was watching me through the window mopping the floor and taking out the garbage by myself after all the workers had left. All I was thinking is that I was going back home.

My sister took me shopping in New York to get me some winter things. It was exciting for me to walk from store to store on Fordham Road in the Bronx. I couldn't wait to make enough money to buy myself the things I liked. Not long after I got here, another family member that was in another state came to live with us. He was from a neighboring community in Jamaica, but I had never met him before. Now it was the three of us in my cousin's room. We slept together on the bed while my cousin slept on a cot. Things got more comfortable with him being there because we could relate to each other's circumstances, and he was very cool. He became like a big brother. His name was Esric. He knew most of the guys I was around before I left Jamaica and most of all he was a supporter of the Jamaica Labour Party, the party my community was aligned to. By this time, the election had passed, and we lost.

My cousin started taking me on the road to hang out with his friends from school. Even though I was older than them I still enjoyed getting out of the house to see the places and meet new people. For as long as I can remember, I was always traveling and meeting new people. My dad had taken us all over to go to different churches with my mom and going to school in a community some miles away from home, it came easy for me to interact with strangers. Most people would just take a liking to me. It did not take me long to start to know people and them to know me. I found out that there were some people I grew up around in my mom's church including my long-time Sunday school teachers. The church family was sometimes closer than the blood family. I would go visit them just to get out of the house. Little by little, I started learning about other people from my community and the surroundings that were living close by. It was winter so everybody was inside.

I was working at Burger King for three months, and they still hadn't given me a weekend off. My day off was always during the week. One Saturday my uncle was going to a cricket match in New York and wanted me to go with him. I told him I had to go to work, and he said, "Screw them, let's go." I was happy to hear that because I wanted to go to New York, and I was tired of the way they treated me there. I just didn't want to quit and have them think I was lazy and just didn't want to work. We went to the game, and I ran into some people I knew from back home which felt good. I did not go back to Burger King. Esric had gotten a job with this old guy cleaning houses, post offices, bars, and just about anywhere he got the job to clean. So I ended up working with the guy as well. Now we lived together and worked together. Even though this job got me dirty, I liked it. We were always on the road traveling from one job to the next. It was now spring, and everything started changing. It was like a different place. Leaves were on the trees now, people on the streets, and the place was not that quiet anymore. My uncle's driveway was now a big hangout. The time they gave me to stay in the country was getting close to expiring, and I wanted to go home for a visit and then come back. After all, I had a 10-year visa.

My parents said no I should stay which meant I would have to figure my way out. My mind was made up to go back home so we were going back and forth on the phone. They got my area leader on the phone to talk to me again. He told me that they lost the election, and nothing was going on for them. He told me that every one of the guys there wished they could leave so I should stay where I am. When I got off the phone, I thought long and hard. I missed home, especially my mom. Once my time was expired, there was no telling when I would see them again. The date came and passed, and now I was an illegal immigrant. I missed my family, friends, and most of all my home, but I pushed all that to the back of my mind and started to accept my new reality.

The honeymoon was over, and my aunt started arguing about everything. We would do everything to avoid her just to not start an argument. It did not take long to realize that it wasn't personal, it was just the way she was. She started reminding me of my grandmother, only that she did not drink. She would be the nicest person one minute and the next she would be a different person. Some days, it would get to me but for the most part, I wouldn't let it bother me. My uncle and my cousins had to put up with it as well. We got to understand some of the things that would trigger her and started avoiding them even though she would find some other things to argue about. Some people wouldn't bring their car to the house for my uncle to work on because they were scared of her.

I was always a people person, so it didn't take me long to start meeting a lot of people. One of the guys that always hung out with my uncle on the weekends while he was working on cars worked for the North American Van Lines Moving Company. My aunt told him my situation and that I was looking for a job. He brought me to his job and introduced me to the boss. The boss told me to show up, and he would try to find something for me to do. It was a situation where a lot of guys would show up at the office in the mornings and the dispatcher would assign us to different jobs. They would give work to their more senior guys first. Some days you would go back home after sitting there for hours. Thanks to my uncle's friend Dennis, who was a respected senior worker, he would always try his best to get me on his team. It didn't take long for me to build a name for myself. I was a very hard worker, and they liked the fact that I always showed up for work. We would have some long days, and some of the guys wouldn't show up the next day. I was always there. I rode a bicycle to work a few times because they asked me to meet a driver very early in the morning. The office was about four miles from my house. Sometimes I would meet the driver on the highway. I learned the ins and outs of the moving business, like packing household items, taking inventory, and packing the truck. The boss would drop a truck off at the house and give me a crew and I would pack everything in the truck. I would then call the office for them to come to get us.

At this point, I was the one looking out for Dennis. I would pick him for my crew and give him the easiest duties. While working with that moving company, I had a chance to go to Mike Tyson's Training Camp outside of Cleveland, Ohio. We had to pick up some equipment and bring it to Atlantic City where he was training for a fight. We also moved his stuff from his Bernardsville house after he sold it. It was the perfect job for me at the time. I was making money, meeting a lot of people, and getting to know the place. It was a very physical job, especially for an 18-year-old kid. I was an ambitious hard worker.

It got to the point where I started getting jobs for other people there also. A close friend of mine named Chino from my community in Jamaica moved to Morristown with his wife and I got him a job there. So now it was me and him on the road. Having him around got me more comfortable plus I was meeting a lot of other people. Some I knew from my community. I met a girl named Marie. Her mom was a good friend of my aunt. We would talk on the phone a lot and sometimes she would drive by the house. She was still in high school. My older brother Rohan came to Morristown to stay with my old Sunday school teacher and her husband. We knew them all our lives. They were our church family. He got married and stayed in the USA. He and his wife got an apartment.

I found out that the old councilor for my community in Jamaica and his family were also around, and they were close to my aunt and uncle. I used to go to the same high school as one of his sons and I played soccer with his youngest son Killa. Sometimes he would give us a ride home from school. I linked up with them and we started hanging out. Killa started introducing me to his friends. We started going to house parties. I was too young to get into the clubs. Esric was still working with the cleaning guy while I was at the moving company. Things were getting good with Marie. I got to meet her parents. Her dad was cool, but her mom was just like my aunt, always arguing about something. She didn't like me. Esric met a girl at one of the house parties and started hanging out with her. He would stay with her sometimes.

I got my driver's license, and my uncle gave me an old car he had been driving around. The body was rotted but the engine was in good condition. Now I started getting around. Chino and I started going to the Bronx to link up with some guys from our community back in Jamaica. They had a spot where they all used to hang out. It felt good being around my old boys. It was always a good vibe. I even linked up with some of my boys in Connecticut. I first went there to the Annual West Indian Day Parade. Back in town, I found out about a spot where these brothers had a sound system, and their backyard was a hangout for the Jamaicans. Sometimes I would stop by there. On Sunday evenings, the Jamaicans would play soccer at the park. That used to be a big hangout—car stereos blasting, drinking, smoking, and arguments over the game. I always looked forward to this hangout. I love the social scenes.

Esric was hardly ever home anymore. He stayed with his girlfriend Maureen most of the time. They decided to get married. It was both of us like brothers on a journey, so I was there by his side. Before the wedding, we went to the church to practice. I saw a girl walk in and I said to him "Damn who is that?" He said he didn't know who she was. I later found out she was the cousin of the bride, and she was one of the bridesmaids. I was attracted to her. Now I was excited about the wedding. On the day of the wedding, I started giving her some attention and found out her name was Natalie. At the reception, I got to dance with her. I was whispering in her ears all that time. We didn't have cell phones back then, so I wrote my cousin's phone number on a napkin and asked her to call me. I was still trying to get to know Marie some more at that time. After that dance at the reception, I was in love. I couldn't wait for the phone call. She called, and now we were spending hours on the phone. Sometimes my cousin would be on the phone, so I missed her call. Sometimes he would answer and tell her to call me back, and other times he would just ignore the calls.

One of our first times going out was to the summer fair at the Meadowlands. My boy Killa had a rental car, and he drove us there. She was in high school and had a part-time job at the mall. I would go there to meet her sometimes. She even started inviting me to house parties where I got to meet her friends from school. She did not live in my town, so I didn't get to see her that often. I was still talking to Marie and getting close to her. I found myself in a confusing spot. Marie was cool but her mom was not nice to me which made me feel like this was not going to go anywhere. I went there to drop something off one day and while I was still at the door, I heard her from upstairs calling me a derogatory name. She thought I had left. I walked away thinking to myself "why did my parents send me here to go through this abuse?" I knew these people didn't know how I was raised and the type of life I was living before I left Jamaica. As hurt as I was, I said nothing because I was raised to have and show respect to people, especially grown-ups. I paid her no mind even though Marie would take her on sometimes. Her dad was the coolest, nothing bothered him.

After Esric left the house one of my other cousins came to live with us. He didn't stay long. My aunt and he could not get along. He met this woman and went to live with her. Chino and I started going to New York more frequently to hang out with our boys. We also started going to Jamaican parties. There was a club in Newark that we would go to that didn't check us for ID. I wasn't 21 yet. Natalie introduced me to her sister that was working in a beauty salon in Morristown. She was very cool. I started stopping by there to see her all the time. Natalie started driving her mom's car to Morristown to see me, and we sometimes would go by her sister's. She brought me to her house, and I got to meet her mom. She was very pleasant to me which was surprising. Word started going around about me and Natalie which made the Marie thing shaky. Marie had a boyfriend at the time so even though I liked her I knew I couldn't be all in. Natalie was giving me all her attention and with all I was going through, it felt great. People started telling me to be careful because Natalie's dad was a gangster and had done all these things. I didn't care. I was never the kind to be scared of anyone. It got me motivated. I found out who he was, and I would see him around. He said nothing to me, and I said nothing to him. I remember one morning one of his friends came to the house telling my uncle to warn me because he said he would kill me if he caught me at his house.

Chino went to the beauty salon with me sometimes. He met Natalie's sister and they started talking. They would keep parties in the shop sometimes. My parents taught me to love and respect people, and now it was paying off. I was getting along with mostly everyone. Some would act funny for some reason but not because I was rude or disrespectful to them. I knew who I was and was firm about my beliefs. I was not going to be swayed by anyone. One night, there was a party, and everyone was there, even my aunt. After I left there was an argument between Natalie's sister and Chino's wife who was related to my aunt. She got up Sunday morning and started cursing me and saying that it was all my fault. At that time, I didn't know what happened after I had left the party. I was still lying in bed not paying any attention to the hurtful things she was saying as I always did. My cousin started shouting at her, telling her to leave me alone. My uncle was sitting in the backyard with the same friend that came with him to the airport to pick me up. He came inside and he said to her "Why don't you leave the boy alone?" My cousin was going back and forth, and he left the room with the door halfway open. She slammed the door wide open against the wall and was cursing at me saying I didn't buy any door here so don't close any door on her.

So much was going through my mind at the time. I couldn't believe I was being treated this way. She went into the closet and started throwing my clothes out in the hallway while saying I should get out of her house. I decided that I was not going to take it any longer. I got up, got dressed, and started picking up my clothes from the floor. I packed all my stuff in the car my uncle gave me that was parked on the street in front of the house. I then walked to the backyard to tell my uncle I was leaving, and I would check with him. I drove to Marie's house and used her phone to call my brother who was in New York attending church. I told him what had happened, and he asked where I was. I told him and he said, "Stay there. I'll come there as soon as I get back." When my brother got back to Morristown later that Sunday, I went home with him. It was a big relief being back with my big brother. It felt like I was back home. His wife was like family as we grew up together in the same community, went to the same school, and attended the same church. Her younger brother and I were close friends. We were both considered the black sheep in our family because we weren't following the traditional Christian way of life.

Before migrating, he also was aligned to the Jamaica Labour Party (JLP), so we were out on the road together with the same people. It was the best thing that happened to me up until this point. I kept in touch with my cousins and my uncle. My uncle was always outside working on cars so I would go there every chance I got to hang out. I always wanted them to know I appreciated all they had done for me, especially my little cousin. He shared his room with me and for the most part, he made me feel like he was happy I was there. He brought me everywhere he went, and he told everyone I was his cousin. He used to come by Burger King with his friends and I would hook them up when I could. It wasn't the first time my aunt had told me to leave. Only this time, she came into my room and was throwing my clothes out in the hallway. She had a way about her that right after she finished cursing she would turn around and be the nicest person to you like nothing happened. It didn't take long for me and her to get back on speaking terms. One day, I was in the driveway with my uncle and another guy, and she called me; the next thing she asked me to do something for her. The incident left me scarred but I was happy to get past it. We were family and I loved them.

Another one of the guys from my community migrated to Morristown. His name is Selo, but everyone calls him Lucky. He's the father of my little cousin and we were cool. Now Morristown was no longer feeling like a strange land anymore. There were so many people from my community and its surroundings here. I was not alone anymore. Chino was a known musician from back in my community. My other boy Lucky who just came up was also a DJ and he got a sound system from one of his family members. He set it up in his apartment where I would hang out sometimes drinking and singing on the microphone. There were two other DJs with sound systems that I would hang around and follow when they played at parties. I started loving the microphone more and more. I even started writing lyrics.

While working for the moving company, they would sometimes send me to the old Exxon headquarters in Florham Park, New Jersey to work as a porter moving office equipment and furniture from building to building. I met a Hispanic guy there that was involved in a television program called *Mi Casa, Su Casa*. They had a talent segment and he brought me on to sing. It was my first time on TV.

I bought a car from a guy I knew, and I fixed it up real nice so now I was driving as far as Connecticut to see my friends. Sometimes I would drive there just to party. I remember driving there to a party with a few of my friends. We stayed the night at a hotel. When we came outside that morning, there was broken glass everywhere. The car had been broken into. They took our clothes and shoes that we had left in the car. There was glass all over the seats. It took us a long time to clean up, and we taped up the window so we could drive home. A whole half of the guys I used to hang out with while in Jamaica were now living in Connecticut. On top of that, there was a big Jamaican community there. I loved the vibes in Connecticut. It was a nice getaway from New Jersey. There was a guy named Cumma there that was just different. He was a few years older than I was, but we grew up together. He lived next door to me in Jamaica until he migrated. He was like a brother not only because we were close but also because he looked like us. Some people used to say he was my dad or my uncle's child. The first time I visited Connecticut with my uncle and a group of others to check out the West Indian Day Parade, he came to see me at the house I was staying at. It was my first time seeing him since he left Jamaica which was a few years prior.

Later on, I linked up with the other guys from my community at a house they were hanging out at. Cumma was flamboyant, high-energy, and a loving kind of guy. He pulled up and the vibes changed. He immediately started planning something with the guys. It was parade weekend he said, "Get the fish and throw them on the grill. I'll get some drinks." He gave them some cash to get the stuff they needed. He said he couldn't stay but he would come back. We were close to the main road where the stores were, so before Cumma left he told us he was walking to the store to get an outfit to wear later that night. A few of the guys were saying, "Let's go with him because he'll show off and get us outfits too." I didn't like the way they said it. It sounded like they were going to take advantage of him, so I stayed back with the other guys. He gave me his number before he left and said to call him later to let him know where I was, and he would come to check me. We went to the club, and he came by to see me. I met him out front, and he gave me some money to buy drinks for my friends and me. He said he would see me tomorrow because he couldn't stay.

I remember an incident where I was hanging with Cumma, and he stopped by a crown and anchor game. He talked the guy into letting him bet a large sum of money. They agreed it was a one-time bet. I was never the type to gamble so I was very nervous. The man shook the dice in the cup then rolled them on the board, and when they settled, Cumma had lost it all. He tried talking to the man to bet him again. He was saying no but a little iffy. Cumma told me to ride with him to his place to get more cash. It was the first I was getting to talk to him. We drove to his place and back. When we got back to the game, the man decided he wasn't betting him again. I felt some type of way even though it wasn't my money. I was three hours away in New Jersey, but I kept in touch with him, and we would talk on the phone. Shortly after, something very serious happened with Cumma. I won't go into details but one thing I can tell you is it was my first real-life lesson that there was no loyalty in the streets. The same guys that we grew up with that were running around with him turned their back on him. As a kid growing up, I always felt that I was supposed to be there for my friends and family. I had the impression that they would do the same for me. What I saw happen to Cumma made me realize that it was far from the truth. I felt betrayed, let down, angry and stupid for not listening to some of the things my dad had told me. It got to the point where I felt like hurting these guys even though they were family and guys that I loved.

My parents used to ask me what I was looking for in the streets. They had given me everything, yet I wanted to be out there. It was simple for me. It was my love for my people. It wasn't money, politics, fear, power, or anything else. It was all love. On top of being disappointed and angry with these guys, I was feeling his pain and his very deep loneliness. Cumma is now serving the rest of his life in prison. He sometimes writes to me and encourages me to always do the right thing no matter what. He's always in good spirits and is hoping to one day win an appeal. The love in my heart for people was still there, but I had so many questions, especially about loyalty. I tried to understand what happened, learned all the lessons, and moved on.

I was now a regular in town. Everybody knew me or had heard of me. Natalie graduated high school and was now attending college in Washington D.C. We stayed in touch. Things got more settled with Marie. Her mom started treating me better and I was now welcome at the house. Marie was a feisty girl, but she was hard-working, independent, and I mostly loved the fact that she wasn't the outgoing kind of girl. Now that I knew all these people, there was always a house party or cookout somewhere and I was always invited. I loved to party so when I showed up, it was a vibe. One of my regular spots was at Esric and his wife Maureen's place, especially when Natalie was around.

I was still working at the moving company without papers so I was limited to the moves I could make and for sure was missing Jamaica. Marie and I talked about it, and we decided to get married. We did it without anyone there except for my brother. She filed papers for me to get my green card and after four years in the country, I got my papers. Esric knew everything that was going on. He was the only one I would share my business with other than my brother. Some things I wouldn't share with my brother out of respect for his Christian beliefs.

Chapter 3

Street Life

The Wrong Turn

One day I went on a job, and we had to move a baby grand piano. After taking the legs off and strapping it on the piano board, I was on the back end with two guys on each side. We did as we always did, count to three then lift. Something snapped in my lower back. By the next day, I was in excruciating pain. I couldn't even stand up straight. This was right before I got my green card. My boss sent me to the chiropractor. I went a few times over three weeks. Then he told me, he would give me a good recommendation. He couldn't use me anymore.

There was a Jamaican restaurant in town where the guys hung out on the corner or in the backyard. They would play dominoes, drink, hustle, and just hang out for fun. After my boss let me go, I started hanging out there a lot more. It reminded me of my old hang-out in Jamaica. I loved the vibes. Some of the guys were selling weed. Some were selling cocaine and some were selling both. I was there most of the time drinking with the boombox playing.

One day, one of the guys said to me, "Why don't you get a package? You're always here so you might as well make some money." I thought about it and made the worst decision of my life. I decided to give it a shot. I talked to my boy Scorcha who was a well-known hustler in town. He taught me all I needed to know to get started. I was hanging around long enough to already know the ground game. I've been a hard-working hustler all my life. Just never hustling anything illegal, especially not cocaine. I made a few moves with weed, but never on the street. I go hard with anything I'm doing so I was spending a lot of time on the street. We were making money, partying a lot, and playing hide and seek with the cops. On the weekends, we would be heavy in the local bars and then we would go out of town later. It got to a point where there were so many Jamaicans out on the corner making money, it cut off sales from the Americans who were further down the street which caused a beef between us. One night at the bar, it boiled over into a war. A young Jamaican kid got jumped by a group of them. A shot was fired while the whole thing was going on and cops came from everywhere. I went home and while I was getting ready for bed, I heard a knock on the front door. When I checked, it was the police. They said they were investigating a shooting at the bar and asked if I could step outside. I told them I had to get dressed. One of them came inside and walked with me to my room and watched me get dressed.

I stepped outside on the sidewalk. They told me to stand facing the street and that someone was coming to identify me. One of them got on his radio and told someone he was ready. A police car pulled up across the street with very bright lights shining on me. Someone in the car identified me as the shooter so they said they had to take me to the police station while the detectives did their investigation. They took me there and put me in a room. The room was so cold, I had to ask for a blanket. It was morning when they told me I was cleared to go and dropped me back off. Until this day I never found out who was in the car but at no point was I worried because I knew I did nothing wrong.

I even had a few confrontations with a few guys on the corner. I was always vocal about my feelings, especially when others were being mistreated. I am who I am, and I respect you for who you are. I'm not going to make who you are a problem for me. Love and respect always work in my favor. I have a major network of people from all walks of life because of the love and respect I show people. I know somebody from somewhere that can do something. If I went somewhere for the first time and was around people I had never met, before I left, I would have made a connection with someone. I have a lot of girlfriends for the same reason. It's just good vibes with me and no disrespect or trouble.

They started calling me Gotti. I could make things happen from the network of people I knew. It was all about community, people, and having a good time. Now I had all these people around, and I was always organizing something. If I went to the liquor store it was never to just go and get myself something. It was either I was going to get drinks for everybody or collect money from whoever was willing to contribute. We even organized regular barbecues in the park during the summertime. I was always preaching togetherness and it was working. When we went to parties, we would all go together. When we got to the door we would negotiate a package deal for everyone, and we would do the same at the bar once we got inside. All the promoters knew us and loved when we showed up at their parties. We started calling ourselves The Shinazz Crew. There was nothing organized about us. We were a group of friends doing our own thing. We were like family. A couple of the younger Jamaicans would hang out with us for the good times. It was always a vibe. With the good times also came the raids, the arrests, and the worst part, the not knowing when it was going to be you.

I would take the Amtrak train to Washington, D.C. sometimes to visit Natalie. She would show me around D.C. and introduce me to a whole new world. It was always motivating being around her. I would be on the train coming back dreaming big, especially after homecoming weekend.

When I finally got my papers (green card) I decided to make my first trip to the annual Caribana in Toronto, Canada. No one knew that I got my papers at this point except for my brother and Esric. My boy Lucky was talking about wanting to go so I organized it with three of my friends to take the trip. We drove up there and stayed with a guy from my community in Jamaica. He gave us a key to the house, showed us where everything was, and said "It's your home." One of my boys knew his way around Toronto so we partied all weekend, and then drove back down. The highlights from that trip was how well my boy treated us which was something different from the disappointments I experienced with some of my other boys and facing the immigration officers with my new papers for the first time. They took us out of the car and brought us into the building where we could see them through the glass windows searching the car thoroughly. They searched us, took our papers and we were just sitting there watching them search the car. One of the officers came in with a shirt and asked whose shirt it was. One of my boys said it was his and the officer told him to follow him. Now we were all frightened, wondering what it could be. They later came back, gave us our papers, and said enjoy your trip. I came to find out they found some empty plastic bags in his shirt pocket and wanted to know why he had them. Now that I made the trip to Canada with no problem, my next plan was to visit Jamaica for the Christmas holiday.

Also on the trip to Canada were my boys Shabba and Gramps. I had met Shabba and his younger brother a few years prior as young kids still in school. I showed them love but kept them at a distance because of their attitude. It seemed like they were always fussing about something and that was not my style. After school, Shabba would always hang out on the corner. He was closer to some of the other guys. After a while, I started liking him more and more. One of the things that made that happen was when I found out he was from a community in Jamaica that I knew was aligned with the Jamaica Labour Party (JLP). He was talking my kind of talk. He loved to drink and smoke so when he was around us, he was good. I started treating him like a little brother. Anywhere we were going, he was good.

Gramps, on the other hand, was my boy from my community in Jamaica. He was the true definition of streets. From the time I knew him, he was always around the sound systems, street mechanics, politicians, and what we called The Village Lawyers. These were the guys that would gather every day arguing about sports, politics, or any random topic. Everyone knew Gramps. He migrated a little while before me so when I got to New Jersey, he came to visit. He lived in New York so he would come through regularly. Gramps was one of the first people to give me a car to drive. Now that I was planning to visit Jamaica after almost five years, I started saving and packing a few barrels so I could bring some stuff for the people in my community. I even told Shabba to save some money for his ticket, and he could go with me. It was always the love of my people, community, and anything I felt a part of; I took loyalty very seriously.

After being here for a few years, I started feeling like a part of my new community. There was a beef between the east and west coast which was L.A. vs. New York. I was living on the east coast. Patrick Ewing was a Jamaican playing for the New York Knicks; Biggie Smalls was a Jamaican rapper at the frontline of the whole thing. With the mindset I was already in, I was taking this seriously. Until this day, the only teams I have ever supported are the New York teams. I wore a Celtics and Sonics jersey only for the green color back in the day. You will never see me in anything that says California or L.A.; it's just not who I am. In the middle of all this beef was the first World Trade Center bombing. It was devastating. I remember saying to myself, "What if the building falls?"

After a while, I started to feel a vibe coming from Snoop Dogg. I started seeing myself in him. He stands up for who he is and his beliefs while showing love for the other man and his beliefs. How can you not like a person who is blessed with the power to do that? The only way I know is to ride with my people, win or lose. If you're a Knicks fan you know how hard that is. I've never once denied Rio Bueno, Trelawny, the community where I am from. To make it clear, I have it tattooed on my arm. I wanted the world to know about the place I'm from so much that I even wrote about it:

Where I'm From

I'm from a different time zone
This life is moving express
Things that took hours to get done
Now only take a sec
I'm from a manual land
Everything in this place is hi-tech
From one weather I came
Into a new type of climate
Six months could easily pass
And I don't even break a sweat
I'm from the party world
By now it shouldn't be a secret
Where people party in the streets
And dance until they're wet
I'm from where life is a gamble
But on mine, I never stick a bet
I'm explaining where I'm from

There's Always A Light

Because you still don't know yet

I'm from a place where I came across
Many different spirits
From killers to prostitutes
With church people I worshipped
Impatient people
Trying to get what they want quick
Street hustlers are always planning
But nothing worthwhile they accomplish
I'm from a fire zone
That's controlled by government politics
Where the river and the sea meet
On one side of the district
The drug lords are always around
Controlling the airstrips
As the gangsters move around
With the heat on their hips
Get to know where I'm from
And you would be astonished

I'm from many different places
It's hard to call one spot my home
I'm from the real world
Where most time I feel alone
Strange voices speak to me
In a quiet whispering tone
I came across the desert
Where dogs don't even roam
Was so hard to find water
Think about finding a bone
I grew up in a stable of wise men
Now I'm pretty grown
Know the result of building on sand
Now I build on solid stone
Strong wind is never my problem
Tribulations don't make me moan
I'm from where a queen runs the palace
And embraces the king on the throne

Street Life – The Wrong Turn

I'm from where the sun gets really hot
And street thugs will burst shots
Where everybody seems black
Even the judges and the cops
Where my boys had my back
And they hold down the block
People party non-stop
And the parties are never whack
Ask me where I'm from
And I might tell you it's where I'm at

I had the privilege to travel from the time I was a baby which made me realize how special my community was. Most people are always quick to tell you they are from the city of Kingston. Because I know the geographic setup of Kingston, that type of talk never impressed me. I would sometimes conversate with people that lived in Kingston, and they knew nothing about the city but the garrison they lived in.

From an early stage of my life, I understood the chain of command on the streets, and I was never inspired to be a foot soulja. I was always close to the boss, the top man, the one that makes things happen. If you were a foot soulja and you were good at your position, I would run with you. So many didn't know the difference. They were the boss, a foot soulja, peacemaker, and everything in between which always made them their own worst enemy. I always try to find a way to work my way through it all while staying loyal to my teachings and my principles. The Book of Proverbs that my father gave to me before I left Jamaica was one of the best things he could have done for me. As a little boy growing up, I believed in my dad. He always would talk to me while driving and taught me about the road when I could hardly see over the dashboard. I remember everything and still rely on his teachings today. Even though I strayed from some of his teachings, the Book of Proverbs was my guard rail. Those words would convict me. They would be right there beating me when I was messing up. It was now my teacher. If there is one thing that I think people don't know about me, it is how much I pray. I would be going to do the worst thing and still ask God for guidance and protection. I guess that's what you call crazy but it seemed like he always answered. I'm always good even when I keep putting myself in the worst situations.

I spent the next four months getting ready for my return trip to Jamaica. I packed a few barrels with just about everything: clothes, shoes, caps, belts, underwear, socks, and lots of food items. Some were for our personal use. I also bought a few bicycles. I shipped them off in time for them to get to Jamaica before I got there. A few days before Christmas with two of my boys, Shabba and Glama, we boarded a flight to Montego Bay. The next thing I remember is walking through the doorway of the plane onto the step and the sunlight hitting me. The blue sky and the heat all together at once felt like I was in a different world. When I got inside the airport it was strange to see all the black police when I had been constantly around all-white police daily. The officers that checked me in and all the workers in the airport were black. It was something I hadn't seen in years. Driving home from the airport was surreal. It felt like a dream. It was a feeling I had never experienced. It was an overwhelming joy to be back mixed with the anticipation of getting back to my community.

We got to my gate and as customary, we first brought our luggage into the house, said a prayer of thanks, and greeted my family. After doing that, we took a walk through the community greeting my people. The whole community was happy to see me after all these years. It was a different kind of feeling when the older folks greeted me. There were hugs and kisses, and some even cried. I got the feeling that these people genuinely loved and cared about me. Until this day, no matter what I am going through or what the situation is, those moments remind me that life is about people and not myself. Bringing joy to a heart, a smile to a face, or comfort to one in fear is priceless. After greeting the ones we met, we went back home to eat and talk with family. Then we headed back out where the party began. The next day I opened the barrels I sent and started giving out some of the stuff. My boy Brent (Round Bread) helped me with who got what. I remember being at a party one night and almost everyone was wearing something I gave them, even if it was just a bandana or cap. I spent most of my time with my friends and family in my community.

We went to Kingston a few times where I spent a day in my boy Glama's community. Later that night, along with a group of men from his community, we went to the annual dancehall stage show called "Sting 93". This was where Beenie Man and Bounty Killer had their historic clash. It was one of the highlights of my trip. I was happy that two of my friends were getting to know the Mom I always talked about and the rest of my family. It was their first time meeting my family, and they welcomed them with open arms. They were treated as sons and brothers not only by my family but by the community, especially Shabba since he spent most of his time with me there. It was a reconnection to my people and some of my dreams and goals that I had lost along the way. My cousin, Robert, was our driver. He drove the rental car everywhere except when we had to take Shabba to his community to visit his dad. My dad insisted that he drive us there, so I agreed; after all, he knew the streets. It wasn't the most comfortable ride with the Pastor, but we went and made it back home with no problem.

One of our other boys, Flowa, was also visiting his people in Westmoreland, and he came to hang out with us in my community. As always for me, I met a couple of guys with some connections to people back in the States. I got some numbers for some of my old boys that migrated so now I would be heading back with a new agenda. The morning before I left for the airport, my dad reminded me to search my backpack before packing my stuff in it. While searching it I found weed in one of the smaller pockets on the inside of one of the bigger pockets. I have never put weed in my backpack, and it was not wrapped up in anything. I was surprised and pissed off. It had to be someone close to me. It came as a good reminder that not everyone close is with or for you as my dad was always beating into my head. My dad was upset with me most of the time I was there for that very reason. He thought I was leaving myself too open. As I later learned love can get you killed. I cleaned out my bag, packed my stuff, and said my goodbyes to my family. On my way out I stopped for one last drink and sounded the alarm about what had happened with the weed in my bag and how upset I was. I knew it was my fault, so I didn't let it cause any real fuss. I told them it was all love. I was sad leaving

55

them, but I was happy to get back to the USA to carry out my new plans with this new energy I had.

I got back and a few weeks later my grandmother died. I surprised my family by just showing up for the funeral. I stayed a few days. It was the first time in a very long time that I saw my aunts, uncles, and the rest of my family on my dad's side. Other than chilling with my boys at their regular hang-out spot, I kept it low for the few days I was there. Then I flew out, back to my game plan.

I had a renewed dream of my community and a clearer vision. I had planned to do a three-day course to learn how to ride a motorcycle. It was something I had wanted to do as a kid. Friday evening I joined a small group in a classroom with an instructor. We all had a textbook that was sent to us in a package with other materials and instructions before the class. We went through a part of the textbook and watched some videos. Saturday was all day. We started the day at 8:00 a.m. in the classroom. We finished going through the textbook and watched more video clips. Then we did a written test. In the afternoon we went outside in a parking lot where they first had us prove we could balance on a bicycle. They then assigned each of us to a motorcycle. We started practicing the shifting of the gears, accelerating, braking, turning, and all the stuff discussed in the classroom. Sunday morning we went back to where we left off Saturday afternoon.

After lunch, it was time for the road test. They set up different obstacles in the parking lot. Each one earned you points, and you only needed a certain number of points to pass. I made it up to my last obstacle and fell. I had enough points to pass the test, but once the motorcycle fell it was an automatic disqualification. My foot got caught in the motorcycle. When everything settled I was on the ground crying due to the pain in my ankle. The instructors and some of the students rushed over to me. I was sitting up waving my hand over my foot telling them not to touch it. I had my foot stretched out and was doing my best to keep it steady. The slightest movement would send a shocking pain up my spine to my brain. The ambulance came, and I would not let them touch my foot either. It took a while for them to talk me into letting them cut the lace of my boot so they could slide it off my foot. They also cut my pants' leg almost to the crotch. They slid a board underneath me, strapped me down, put me in the ambulance, and took me to the hospital. By the time I got to the hospital, my ankle was the size of a tennis ball and hard as a rock.

As always, my brother showed up at the hospital to stay with me until they did x-rays. They said it was a severe sprain, so they wrapped it and sent me home with painkillers. My brother helped me home and got me situated. Later that night, I got up to use the bathroom. I stood up on one leg and immediately that same shocking pain hit me, and I grabbed onto the TV stand. My bodyweight sent the stand, TV, and everything else crashing to the ground. My brother woke up and rushed to my rescue. He helped me back onto the bed. The pain I was feeling was so bad I was crying. My brother wanted to take me back to the emergency room. I refused because I did not want to move my foot an inch. After taking a pain killer, the pain subsided so I could use the bathroom and go back to sleep. The first few days were hard, and then I started feeling better. I started moving around on crutches. I was getting phone calls from motorcyclists from all over checking on me and encouraging me to keep riding. After about two weeks, I was out and about on crutches. I would spend most of my time on the corner or in the park. I even went to a few parties out of town while on crutches. There was always a lot of us so I felt comfortable with my boys around me.

Gramps was spending a lot more time with me in New Jersey, so he got to know everyone on the corner and in the Jamaican community. Gramps was the kind of guy that would get mad quickly, but he was very loyal and cool. Being around so many new faces in a fairly new place, it felt good having someone I grew up with around me.

When I was in Jamaica I got the link for my younger cousins that had migrated to Brooklyn, New York. I called them up and got their address. One day I went with two of my boys, Flowa and Ninja, to visit them. Most of the guys I got cool with were still in high school. I was a few years older than them. Ninja was a well-mannered, very humble kid that I took a liking to. We found the apartment building they lived in with my aunt. We chilled for a while and my cousin

Mikey decided he was riding back to Jersey with us. While he was getting ready, his younger sister, Kamara, said she wanted to go also. We talked about how I was living, and they didn't mind. I didn't mind, and I knew my brother wouldn't mind either. So they headed back to Jersey with me. I brought them to the apartment to see my brother and his wife. I showed them my room where they were going to stay. I gave them my bed and I told them I would be ok. After all, we were family. If all three of us had to sleep on the bed, that was what we were going to do. That's how I roll.

Not long after showing them our place, we went on the corner. There was a Jamaican restaurant on the corner, and we were cool with the lady that lived in the back. When we weren't in the store or on the corner, we were in the back chilling. Mikey was very good at playing dominoes, and there was always a game of dominoes going on in the back. It didn't take Mikey long to get in the games and start dropping six loves. Through the domino games and his personality, people started knowing him. After going back to Brooklyn, he started taking the train back and forth until he met a girl and started to stay in Morristown. Gramps was around and now Mikey was around. I started hearing words that there were complaints from some of the guys on the corner that I was bringing my family on the corner. I didn't pay attention to that because every man was doing their own thing. It was all love and open arms for me. No matter who it was. I was never the type to fear another or not share, even with a stranger.

Later that summer I went back to Canada for the Caribana Festival. I drove up there with Gramps and a few of my boys. Things went much smoother at the border than they had during our previous trip. We stayed with my boy, Jubby, who treated us like brothers. We had a great time and planned to make it an annual trip.

As time went by, I started getting deeper into the street life, drinking more, smoking every day, partying almost every day, and getting to meet more high-level hustlers. The deeper I had sunk into the underworld, the further I drifted away from my teachings. No matter what I was doing or where I was, it was always a good vibe that attracted all kinds of people, especially the girls. I loved being in the company of girls, especially the cool ones.

One night we were driving in the Bronx. It was Gramps, Scorcha, and me. Gramps was driving and he stopped at a traffic light. I looked over to my right and a guy was driving a car that looked familiar. While processing it in my brain, the light changed, and he sped off. I told Gramps to drive the car down because I know the driver from somewhere. Still not sure of who he was, Gramps drove, and I waved for him to pull over. We both pulled over on the side of the road. As soon as he got out of the car, Scorcha said, "Bobby" and it immediately came to me. I went to high school with Bobby. Scorcha was the type that was always in the streets, so the streets knew him. Everywhere we went, Scorcha knew someone and someone knew him. Bobby and Scorcha ended up getting shot at one point. Scorcha came back to Jersey to heal, and he never went back. This was the first time they saw each other since, and it was my first-time seeing Bobby since high school. We talked, exchanged numbers, and started to link up regularly. Scorcha became my righthand man in the streets.

Gramps didn't drink so he was the driver most of the time. We were all over the place. After linking up with Bobby, I realized he was very deep in the underworld; so deep, I knew I had to draw a line. I started learning more about the underworld of the streets from him, mostly what not to do and how not to be. He opened my eyes a lot. Now that we linked up, he linked me with some other guys in the streets. Some I knew and some I did not. I likewise linked him with some people, like my boy Killa. Bobby was a good soccer player and Killa was too. They played together back in their school days. We were from the same zone, northern Trelawny, Jamaica.

I always stuck to my spirituality. After all, for a while, I felt like it was just me and God. Even though I was around all these people, I was out in the streets alone and away from my family, my teachings, and everything I knew to be right. I started feeling like I was getting lost. I would regularly check myself and the people I was around. The way I was making money was the one thing I was not keeping in check. One of the links I got from Bobby was a cousin I never met that lived in

Connecticut. Marco was the kind of guy that was very ambitious. He was always working on some new plans. He was more laid back than a typical street dude but was well connected. His dad was one of the few that reached the level where he was at the top of the food chain before he got busted. He did some time in federal prison and then got deported back to Jamaica with nothing. Marco even introduced me to some of the O.G.s that used to run with him. In one sense, I was drifting away from who I was and heading in the wrong direction. I was sinking deeper into the underworld. I never used any of my friends or family to make a dollar. I was the kind of person that would break bread and share it with my circle. It was always the love and thoughts of my people that gave me the drive to climb the ladder. I was always trying to bring something to the table.

It was never about self for me nor was it about my immediate family. They were all in the church giving and always sharing in any way they could. They are the ones I learned selflessness from. They are the most selfless people I know, and that's 100 percent the truth. My parents would share the food that we needed to eat and even money that they did not even have. I've seen my mom borrow money to give to people that asked her for help. I used to get mad when I would see them doing this, and now that I am grown, I find myself doing the same thing. I would sometimes go check on Marco and his siblings. He would also come to hang out with me and my boys. Sometimes Bobby would ride with them when he was around and felt up to it. Bobby was an unpredictable kind of guy. That same year, my big sister, Maxine, who lived in New York got her green card, so we planned to visit Jamaica for Christmas and the New Year holiday. Maxine, her husband, and I went down to Jamaica. My boy Gramps came with us. It was my second visit in a year, so I was much more relaxed and in tune with the running of the place. This time I had more me time and spent more time with my family.

Marco's father, that I mentioned earlier, was there in my community. He was from my community. Like I said before, he got deported with nothing. He struggled and set up a shack on the side of the main road. This was where all the traffic traveling on the north coast of the island between Montego Bay and Ocho Rios had to pass before the new highway was constructed many years later. Most of the tourists that visited Jamaica would at some point pass through my community, so business was good for him. It didn't take this O.G. long before he constructed a place that attracted buses of tourists and locals that were vacationing or just passing by. It became a very successful business. It was a great story of a man that fell from the top, got back up, and started climbing to the top again. I've never had a conversation with this man. As a kid, we would hear people talking about him, and I got to see him on a few of his quick visits to my community. This time I knew I had to talk to him in search of some street knowledge.

One day, his nephew Brent (Round Bread) and I went to visit him at his business. This man is almost 7 feet tall and weighed about 210 pounds. When we walked up to him, the first thing he said was "Brent you have to leave, you know you can't come here without a shirt." Round Bread went to the car to get his shirt. I talked with him for a while. He was happy to share some of his knowledge with me about the streets. Most of the people talked badly about him and looked down on him because of the height he fell from. I knew he had some valuable lessons he could share with me. After all, he had been where I was heading. He gave me a blueprint to follow but I knew I was not going to follow it. It was not who I was, and I thought it was too serious for me at that time of my life. He also gave me some basics that I could use in my everyday movements. I had a good time hanging with my boys and the people in my community.

One of the best parts of this trip was having my big sister Maxine there. It was her first time back in Jamaica after many years. It was that original family feeling except that my big brother Rohan was not there. Natalie came down and we met up, so the trip was well rounded. It was January 1995, and we flew back to the U.S. together. I had so many plans in my head. I brought back a challis (bong) made from a coconut. I brought it to the corner where we would hang out. It was like a present for my boys. We loaded it and fired it up a few times. The cops pulled up and I stashed it on a column on the side of the building. It ended up rolling off and broke into pieces.

My cousin Byrdie migrated to Maryland to live with his dad. He called me and I got his address. Natalie was still in D.C., so I went down to visit her, and she drove me to the address. I stayed in D.C. for a couple of days. Byrdie came back to New Jersey with me for a visit. I showed him around town, hung out on the corner, and took him to a few parties. He got to see my brother and his wife, Mikey, Gramps, Uncle Leslie, and meet some of my boys. He had a very good time before going back to Maryland. Shortly after he returned to Maryland, he called me and said he wanted to come to New Jersey to live with us. I told my brother and like always, my brother and his wife had open arms. He said it was up to me because I would have to share my room and my bed with him. I would never say no to family, and he was more like a brother. It was all about my people in the first place, so I was happy to share my bed with him. My cousin Patrick shared his bed with me so now I got to spread the love with another family member. I thought it was a plus to have another one of my loyal boys around me. I wished all my cousins and friends I grew up with could have joined me.

Byrdie moved to New Jersey, got a job, and started to settle down in his new town. He was never a street type of guy like I was, but he loved to party. He would do his work thing and we would meet up to party. It was like we were back in the days of Jamaica again. My brother was our guardian. No matter what, we knew we had one of the most loyal people ever in our corner. My brother goes to church, work, and home. You can call him anytime and he is going to be there no matter what. After being around all these guys on the corner and seeing how bad they treated each other, it made me wish I had my brother on the corner with me to show them how it's done. I guess I had sunk into the dark underworld with a crazy thought like that. I sometimes wondered who some of these guys grew up around and who had they learned their habits from. This very thought inspired me to write what I called, "Who You Grew Up With".

<u>Who You Grew Up With</u>

I should have known better
All your styles are imitated
How can you keep it real

Street Life – The Wrong Turn

You're not family-oriented
Think back to who you grew up with
Picture it in your head
Should be feeling yourself
But feeling someone else instead
Wanna be a gangster
But telling gangsters what to do
Never take time to learn
From elders who you knew
Who showed you the tracks
You don't have a clue
On the streets for a minute
But to thug life you're new
Always stressing
Can't turn one into two
Who you really grew up with
The answer is probably you
Ask me who I grew up with
And that answer is easy
I grew up with the pits
The lions schooled me
Grew up in Sunday school
Always go to Bible study
Religion is up to you
But we all need spirituality
I grew up around thugs in Kingston
And killers in the country
With government officials
Stay close to the poor and needy
Still feeding on knowledge
I gather wisdom daily
Bits and pieces from everywhere
It could be from anybody
I'll use your experience
To save me the agony
I grew up around prostitutes
And soldiers from Germany

Wake up
I see you sleeping

There's Always A Light

You're lost
You need to do some soul searching
Trying to please everyone
You wanna be in everything
And that's impossible
We know where that's leading
Nowhere else
Than a bitter ending
You need to make a quick flip
Or a fast spin
Gambling all your life
And you still can't win
You never listen to the lions
Or take heed from their teachings
I can see through you
Your mind is so thin
I'm not saying you can't make it
But your chance is very slim

My boy Scorcha hooked me up with a connection in Spanish Harlem, New York. We would go there to buy the coke and resell it in New Jersey. Scorcha was one of the best joint rollers in town so I would watch him—step by step until I was competing with him. I learned a few things about the streets from him. I started going to get the coke by myself after the Dominicans got to know me. Looking back now I see how lost I was. I would pray before I left and thank God when I got back. I would always pray before I left for a party. It got to the point where I wasn't reading the Bible anymore, and I would only pray when I was about to put myself in danger or when I was already in danger.

I was moving around the streets more seriously now, taking more chances and losing the morals and values I once had. A few of my friends in Connecticut came to see me and asked me to help them out so they could make some money in the streets. These were the same guys I was mad at for the way they treated my boy, Cumma. A few years had passed, and I started to see it differently. I realized everyone is not going to be as loyal as I am. So I let it go. My love for them had not changed; I was just mad at them. I helped them; it was only a favor. I was not making any money from them as that was not my style. After doing them that favor, months went by and it was one excuse after another. After a while, I started calling it a loss and knew that was it for dealing with them regarding anything concerning business.

I was still meeting up with Bobby and my cousin Marco. I was hearing all kinds of crazy stories about Bobby, but he was still my boy from school, and I felt like I needed someone of that caliber in my corner. Marco told me that he knew a man that could protect me in the streets, and he was the one protecting Bobby. I did not give it any thought as I was not the type of person that even believed in the horoscope. I had never gotten my palm read or called any psychic hotline. I grew up in the church. My belief was in God and it's God alone who is in control of all things. He was the one who had been helping, providing, and protecting me all my life. I have a huge church family that I know is always praying for me. I thought God must be protecting me as people around me were getting arrested and I was not. Bobby was out in the streets playing Russian Roulette and he was never scared or nervous about anyone or anything. I agreed to meet the man. Marco took me to see him. He told me to come back with a sum of money, and he would give me something to carry around in my pocket and I would be safe from the cops or any harm. I brought him the money and he gave me a small heart-shaped pendant to carry around in my pocket.

About two months later it was Friday, July 1st and the first of the month was the biggest money day, especially on the July 4th weekend. I had no product. There was nothing around and we were calling it a drought. Gramps and I left early in the morning for New York to get some product. I was driving Gramps' car. When we got over there, Gramps stayed in the car while I was getting the coke. For the first time since I had been going there, no one was out, and everywhere was closed. I walked around from one spot to the next and found nothing. All I was thinking about was the money I could make if I got this product. I ran into a guy that took me into the basement of one of the buildings. All he had was an ounce so I had him split it into two halves so I could share it with my boy. I still needed to get something for my other boy because that's how we had been doing it for each other; whoever went to get it would get it for the other. I kept searching until I found another half ounce. This was a place where if you want a few kilos, it was never a problem. Something didn't feel right, but I wanted to get this product, get back to town, make the money and enjoy the July 4th weekend.

On our way back now with the product in my underwear, we crossed over the Hudson River on the George Washington Bridge on Interstate 95. I was in the middle of traffic when a state trooper pulled up beside me, looked over in the car and then turned his lights on. The car behind me slowed down and the trooper came behind me and pulled me over. When he came to my car door, he asked me where I was coming from and where I was heading. He then asked me for my papers. He went back to his car, came back, and then asked me to step out of the car. He patted me down and put me to sit in the back of his car while he searched Gramps. After searching Gramps, he came back to his car and came to the side of the car I was sitting in. He had one hand on his gun and opened the car door with his other hand. He told me to slowly bring up whatever was in my pants. I took it out and gave it to him. He asked me what it was and if there was any more in the car, and I told him no. He asked for permission to search the car and we gave it to him. He then put Gramps in the car with me while he searched the car. When he got done with the search, he came and sat in his car, and started asking me more questions. I told him Gramps knew nothing about the drugs. He wanted to seize the car and arrest Gramps also. I kept telling him Gramps did not know I had the drugs on me. He decided he was going to take both of us to the state trooper barracks where I had to sign papers that the drugs were mine and Gramps did not know anything about it. He said Gramps would then be released.

While driving to the barracks, he told us that it was a sting that we got caught in. He asked me if it was my first time being arrested, and I told him yes. He said he loved the fact that I didn't give him any trouble and if everything I told him was the truth, he would talk to the judge and get me to go home that day. The Monday was going to be July 4th holiday so the courts were going to be closed until Tuesday so I would have to wait in the county jail until then. The trooper asked

Gramps if he would do the same for me. He kept asking me until I told him it seemed like he wanted me to lie about my friend. We got to the barracks, and he took the cuffs off Gramps and left him in a room. Then he took me to another room where I sat for a little while until he came to get me. He brought me to what looked like a courtroom. He put me to sit in front of a microphone, and he was asking me questions from where the judge would usually be. He told me the whole thing was being recorded. Afterward, he gave me a paper to sign admitting that the drugs were mine and Gramps knew nothing about it. I signed it and he then released Gramps. He took me back to the room I was in before and chained my foot to an iron bar that ran along the bottom of a concrete bench. Then he took the cuffs off my hands. He told me he was going to do the paperwork and talk to the judge to get him to release me on my recognizance. The car was towed off the highway, so Gramps had to wait for someone to pick him up. After a long time waiting, he came back and said, "You're going home." Those were the best words I ever heard. He even gave me his name and told me to reach out to him if I needed a recommendation for the judge or anything else he could help me with. He said he could tell that I was a good kid that made some bad choices.

When I walked through the door, it was just in time to see my boys pulling up to get Gramps. We went to pick up the car and came home together. Riding home in the car, I started reflecting on the events of the day. There were so many signs right in front of my face, but my mind was on the money which blocked the view of everything else that was going on. I felt relieved getting back to town. It felt like I had left all that trouble behind me. Other than a few of my boys, no one in town knew what had happened. I went back a week or two later for an arraignment at the Teaneck Municipal Court. I pled not guilty. Now I had to wait for an indictment and a court date. My mind was now in a different place but as time went by, my thoughts came together.

It was summertime so I was outside on the corner or in the park chilling again. I loved being in the park. It was very relaxing. The river that runs along the outer boundary reminded me of my community. We had a barbecue grill that we used regularly; we drank, smoked, and listened to music. Some young Jamaican girls would come to the park to hang around us. They were family and friends of my boys. It was the culture they were used to, and they could identify with. They even called themselves Shinazz girls.

My uncle's friend, Craigie, that had come with him to pick me up at the airport always had family barbecues and would invite me. His brother-in-law who is also my uncle's friend had introduced me to his brother Duke who lived in New York at the time. Duke had now moved to Morristown to live with him. I welcomed him with open arms. He was a cool guy who knew a lot about the streets. It's love that drives me, so I never feared the new guy since there was no reason to be suspicious as long as he didn't give me a reason to be. I started introducing Duke to my circle. He was very easy to get along with.

That same summer, Uncle Leo who I called Dread, got shot in Philadelphia where he lived. Dread is my Uncle Leslie's brother. After he got out of the hospital, he came to stay in Morristown to be around family while he healed. He is a Rastafari, the coolest guy ever; nothing bothered him. Dread was someone I could reason with all day. He always kept it real with me. Despite the fact of getting shot multiple times, there was never a day that he wasn't in good spirits. I used to feel hurt just seeing him that wounded and knowing that someone almost took his life. All kinds of evil thoughts would go through my mind, but I knew it wasn't the time for that type of talk. Dread couldn't even walk without the use of crutches. One day after Dread was healed, I asked him what we were going to do about who shot him. To my surprise, he said he had to leave it alone. It was a beating from Jah (God). He was saying it was a debt he paid for a wrong move he made. I am a spiritual kind of guy, so I understood exactly what he was saying. It was the most powerful thing anyone had ever said to me. I knew it took a different kind of strength to get to that state of mind. After digesting it, I knew I hadn't reached that level of consciousness yet.

I knew I had to get a job before I went back to court so I talked to Esric's wife, Maureen. She was a supervisor at the Mennen Company which had been bought by Colgate-Palmolive. She told me to sign up with a temp agency which is what I did. They called me and I started working with her. It was in the middle of the Colgate transition, so we were moving office furniture, painting, setting up cubicles, and doing just about anything they needed to be done. It was an easy job for me, especially after working with the moving company for four years. It also helped that Maureen was my boy's wife, Natalie's cousin, my friend, and the mother of Natalie and my goddaughters. Byrdie was also working with her in the mailroom, and then Dread also started working with us. I worked there because I needed a job and needed to show the court I had a job, but I was still running the streets. We would go out some nights and then go to work with no sleep. We would hide and take a nap at work sometimes.

I started spending a lot of time with Dread. It was always a good vibe around him, and he was a guiding light in my dark days. Byrdie and I got an apartment in the same building my brother was living in. The boys that I was close with would come over sometimes. Even the girls would come by to hang out. I got cool with them.

Things got crazy for me when my best friend Esric and my cousin Byrdie got into a conflict over Maureen. I was caught in the middle and was trying to stay neutral while dealing with my issues. It was tough for me. I was the one that brought Byrdie around and even though I had nothing to do with it, I still felt bad. The good thing was that Esric knew that. I did my best to keep a good relationship with both of them while they figured it out. Both of them were like brothers to me.

There were two sisters among the girls that were cool with me. They were the sisters of one of my boys from the corner. They were always around with the other girls, but they stood out to me because of their attitude. There was an American girl always hanging around that was always dancing to reggae music. You would have thought she was Jamaican. They called her Flacka, but we called her "Goodie Goodie". When they came around it was a good vibe.

Things were happening around me on all sides. In New York, where my boys had the spot, Danny's younger brother Chris was shot and killed. Chris was the quietest and most humble of all the guys on the block. Shortly after Chris was killed, his sister Carol was shot and killed. Jimmy, the older brother who I grew up around, was falling apart due to all the pain. Jimmy was the only one to ever give me something and said to go make some money. Until this day I still don't know what happened, but it was a dark moment. Inside I was very hurt, but everything was a mystery, so I kept it in. Danny decided to move back to Maryland and started a restaurant. My boy Chino was a really good chef, so he moved to Maryland to be the cook at the restaurant. After all that happened, my boy Cubba from New York started coming around to see me regularly. He had been hustling over there, so I put him on to a few people so he could start making some money. Anything I could do for my boys I would. That's just who I am. Cubba was going back and forth every day. I even hooked him up on some other things.

With all this going on, Marie and I were still on good terms. She had done something for me that I could never forget and will always respect. There were a lot of arguments because of the way I was living and sometimes it was just her attitude. I wasn't a bad person but from the time I met Natalie, there was a special feeling in my heart for her. It was a constant fight in my head with the situation. Natalie finished school and was now living in New York where she worked. I would go visit her sometimes. Despite living so close to the city, it was Natalie that introduced me to the city. Most of what I know about New York came from Natalie showing me.

My cousin Presly (Cubby) was always moving around. He would be living in one state and before you knew it, he was in another. He's very intelligent and street smart. He knew everyone and everything. Anything you wanted to know you could ask him and he would know. He's a family member I have a lot of love for. He called me up one day and said he needed to leave where he was, and I told him to come to stay with me. We had a space where he could stay. Once more, another one of my family members was in town. Cubby fit right in. He knew about street life, loved music like me, and was always ready to ride. One thing that was different about him was that he had a very bad cigarette habit. He would wake up just to smoke a cigarette and then go back to sleep. If he didn't have any cigarettes, he would walk to the

24-hour store just to buy some. Even though he wouldn't smoke in the apartment, it would still smell like cigarettes in there. He smoked so much, he had the smell of cigarettes coming through his pores.

Duke started going out with a girl named Julie. I had grown up with Julie in Jamaica and was very close with her. Duke was now considered family. Julie was what we called a Soulja. She got along with everyone. She and Duke moved in together so I would go hang out at their apartment all the time. I was welcome there at any time no matter how late at night it was. Duke still had his family and friends in New York so I would go with him to visit and party. Duke was not driving so Julie would drive everywhere. She was like one of the guys.

We couldn't talk about the streets and not mention Big Mikey. Big Mikey was just as his name says, a big guy. He stood at around 6'6" and 300 pounds with a bad boy attitude. Big Mikey was an icon. He had been in town for a long time before most of us, so all the Americans knew him. He was respected in the streets. I got close with Big Mikey. I used to love it when he came out to parties with us. He looked like a natural leader especially when ten or more guys were around us. He was more of a gentle giant and was always clowning around. I remember driving Big Mikey to the airport. He said he was going to Jamaica for a visit, but he never came back. He stayed there until he died a few years ago.

There was also Chinkie who I had met while I had been living with my uncle. I would hardly see him but that changed when I started hanging in the streets. Our relationship was not tight because he was not always around. Sometimes I wouldn't see him for a while, but we were still one crew. There was also Geefus who was Scorcha's younger brother. He was the one that first started calling me Gotti. Geefus had strong energy and was very confrontational. Once I expressed that thought to him, it caused a rift between us. It was all out of love. I just wanted love and unity between us. There were a lot of us on the corner. Some were there for a short stay. It was a Jamaican thing for me at first. For some, it was just a hangout.

My relationship with Byrdie started to become strained due to what was going on with Esric and the way he was acting toward me. He became more like a roommate. He would just come and go. I hardly saw him anymore, and when I did, it was like a stranger next door. We had been very close all of our lives, so it felt strange. One day he complained about my television being too loud and that he couldn't sleep because of it. He did not come to talk to me about it but rather argued about it. I thought of him as a brother. Now I was thinking this can't be the same guy that I shared my bed with and everything else with. I already knew where he was coming from with it, so I was thinking whatever you feel like doesn't matter to me. One night Cubby and I were sitting in the kitchen chilling, and he came in. He immediately started with Cubby. He was complaining about all types of problems he had with him. The way he was speaking was disrespectful which made me mad. I stepped in and told him to stop being disrespectful. Then he started going off on me. We ended up in a physical fight and that was it for our relationship. After a few days passed I felt bad for losing myself and letting it get that far but my anger outweighed it all. This was the family that I had inconvenienced myself to help accommodate that was behaving this way. I couldn't understand it, but I kept on moving forward with Cubby.

My other cousin Mikey was now living in town and working as a barber which was something he had been doing since he lived in Jamaica. He was now officially in town and was doing his own thing. My brother had filed for my parents a while ago, and now they were finally able to move here and move to Morristown. They were staying next door with my brother. Now that my parents were around, I tried not to let them see that other side of the life I was living. There was so much going on that summer. Now when I look back on that time, it was like I was losing my mind. Bobby was still coming around to hang out with us and he was always scoping out a hustle.

We used to party in Paterson a lot at a spot called Zenas. We had a good relationship with Momz, the lady that was running it. It became one of our favorite places to party. We were cool with most of the street guys down there. They all knew who we were. Scorcha was "the man" down there and he was very close with Momz. Bobby went there with us one night and Scorcha introduced him to Momz. He told Momz that he had connections with some major Jamaican artists, so they planned to meet again and set something up. Bobby came through with two artists that were hot at the time. He talked to Momz and got a down payment for a performance to be scheduled for another date. One of the artists found his way back to Brooklyn and he left the other one stuck with us at the apartment. My sister had come to visit so when she was leaving I asked her to drop him off in Brooklyn. My sister and her husband liked him. He was a funny guy. Bobby never came back to see Momz or contact her. We felt betrayed and disappointed because Momz was very good to us. We were not about that kind of life, and it was good that she knew that.

Ninja's aunt and two kids came to live in town from Jamaica. I believed that if I was rolling with you, your family was my family. Ninja's little cousin was in the park with us one day. He was new in town, so I welcomed him with open arms. I tried to make him feel safe and secure around us. As usual, we were singing lyrics when he chimed in. He had a nice vibe. From that day I started calling him DJ and I took him under my wing. He started going out with Lucky's stepdaughter, Tina. Tina, Ninja's sister (Tracey), the sisters (Theresa and Shereka), Flacka, and a few other girls used to hang out with us sometimes. Theresa's friends were always telling me that she liked me. We would hang out sometimes. Shereka was different from them. She was more laid back, mature and she mostly hung out with the American girls. She was always respectful which I gave to her in return. Both Marie and I and Natalie and I were in an on and off kind of relationship because of the way I was behaving. I loved being around females even though my feelings for both of them were genuine in different ways.

The whole thing with Byrdie and Esric got worse. Esric was now always out, sometimes on the corner with us trying to tell me what was going on. I always tried to make time for him because he was my friend from day one. Now that Esric knew what happened with Byrdie and me, he felt more comfortable talking. It was a rough time for him, and I tried to be there without getting into what was going on. I had my plate full at that time. After a little more than a year, I got a letter in the mail from the Bergen County Court saying I was indicted on the charges. It was a very hard time for me, and I was trying to digest what was happening. My parents were now living here. I still didn't tell my brother and I didn't know how to. He had heard something and asked me. I played it off like it wasn't anything. I decided not to say anything to them hoping I wouldn't get any jail time. At this point, I was out of control and living dangerously. I was fearless. It was like I was in a blackout state.

Killa was a friend and brother that I had a heart of love for. He was good to me from day one. He was a smart, charismatic, humble, and spiritual guy. He was now living in Somerset, New Jersey which was about 45 minutes from Morristown. He was running a sound system there and had a whole crew around him. He brought them around, so I got to know them, and they got to know me. It's open arms. If you are running with my brother you are my brother too. We would go down there to party with them, a good way to show them his strength. Everyone loved and respected Killa. It was all about good vibes and getting paid. He was a loyal Soulja, the type that was going to be there. His right-hand man down there was Gaurdy. Gaurdy was a very cool dude that I got to know very well. I would ride with them and for them anytime. If Killa called on me, I was going to be there.

I went to court in September, and they offered me a plea deal for three years. My lawyer and the Prosecutor talked, and they set up a new court day for October for us to decide if we were going to take the deal or go to trial. I pled guilty on the day I was arrested so there was no way I was going to go to trial. After talking to my lawyer and looking at the facts, I decided to take the three years. This meant I would be eligible for parole after nine months. The Judge had the final say so there was a possibility that I could get a break. Scorcha kept telling me not to take the deal, but he could not give me a reasonable reason why I shouldn't take it. I knew I had done something wrong, and I wanted to pay my dues and put it behind me. At that time, Scorcha had a few open cases against him. He kept getting them pushed back and was buying more time but had no plan in place to beat the charges.

I was always an independent thinker and an informed decision-maker. I went to court in October and accepted the plea deal. The Judge told me to go home and enjoy the holiday; then come back for sentencing on January 10th. The pressure I was feeling at this point was heavy and was mostly due to not having told my brother what was going on. I felt like I got myself involved in it, so it was my responsibility to handle it. At times I would feel the need to tell him, but I couldn't do it. I had strong mitigating factors on my side so I started hoping the Judge would give me probation instead of jail time, and then I wouldn't have to tell my brother.

I was drinking and smoking more than usual. I was partying hard trying not to think about it all. I was as far away from being my true self as I had ever been. I remember going to a party in Paterson right around Christmas with the whole squad from Morristown. I had some words with one of the DJs which was something that happened all the time. A few days later I got a call from Killa. He told me to be careful because he was at a spot where he heard some guys talking about me. They were saying they were going to kill me that night in Paterson but there were too many of us around. I knew who he was talking about, but I didn't know where he was from. At the time we got along with most of the street guys in Paterson.

Lucky went to Jamaica for the Christmas holiday and had left his car with me. I knew they were always in the downstairs of the club gambling. That night after a couple of drinks, I decided to go find out what they were saying was all about. I got this girl to go with me. When we got there, a group of men was there just like I thought they would be. Most of them I knew including the guy that was running the spot that night. He was also a DJ. I first talked to him about what I heard, and he then brought the others into the conversation. The DJ wasn't from Paterson, and they were surprised about what they heard. They knew nothing about it. As long as they were good with me, I was good. The other guy I could care less about. I then ordered a few rounds of drinks for all the guys down there. We drank for a little while and then I left. Knowing he wasn't going to see me again for a while due to my court date, I told him I would pay him the next time I came through. I was good for that with him.

Lucky came back from Jamaica, and we went out on New Year's Eve to a club in East Orange. We were partying hard and the next thing I knew Tafari was in Lucky's face arguing with him. Tafari was my boy; he was one of us. He was a Rastafari that I had love and respect for. The first time I went into a Superior Courtroom was to be a witness on his behalf. For someone on the street, what I did was a no-no. It was putting a target on your head. If I roll with you, I'm going to ride with you; that's the only way I knew. His lawyer didn't feel the need to call me to the stand and he was found guilty. He did his time and when he came back it was like he never left. Lucky was my boy from my community in Jamaica. He was not the street type, but he knew the streets. Now I was in the middle of a family situation with my two brothers about to fight. Tafari was the one that had come up to him, so I told Tafari to chill and leave him alone. He left and then came back wanting to fight again. I got in between and talked him into leaving again. I was getting mad and was feeling like he was disrespecting me by trying to fight my boy right in front of me. He did not seem to care about what I was saying to him. I knew he had a lot to drink so I was looking at it like it's just the alcohol. I had never seen him behave that way before. He came back again and that time it was him and I. I got in his face and told him to back the F up. The security and others that were around us got involved and squashed it.

It was now days away from the date for my sentencing, so I made a phone call to my lawyer's office. I will never forget when he told me to walk with my toothbrush. That was when reality had hit me. After running the streets for over three years, it was looking like it was time for me to pay up. I was still praying and hoping that God would give me one more chance even though I wasn't behaving like I deserved it.

Chapter 4

My Road to Damascus

A Divine Journey

On the morning of January 10th, I woke up and the first thing I did was pray. I asked God to go with me and to make things work out in my favor. I showered, got dressed, got my paperwork together, and was ready to go. I think I told my brother I was going to court, and I would see him later. I was hoping I would see him later. Marie and Esric drove me to the Bergen County Superior Courthouse in Hackensack, New Jersey. The courthouse was a few miles from New York City. When I walked into the courtroom, it was a surreal feeling. I was in a different world. I went and sat beside my lawyer. He didn't say much and was occupied with a device he had in his hands. The judge called my name, and we both walked to the front of the courtroom to face the judge. It went nothing as I had thought it would. It was quick. The judge read the charges and what I had pleaded guilty to. He asked me if it was correct, and I told him it was. He then asked me if anyone had forced me to accept the plea and I told him no. He asked a few more questions and then went on to read some rights that I had and some other things. At this point I was numb. He asked both the prosecutor and my lawyer if they agreed with the plea. They both agreed. The judge then sentenced me to three years in state prison with parole eligibility after 9 months. He kept on talking for a while, but I wasn't hearing anything he was saying. I was in shock. When he was done talking, the court officer walked up to me. He told me to put my hands behind my back and he cuffed them. I turned around to look at Marie and Esric before having to walk away to the holding cell.

There was one other guy in the cell at that time. It seemed as if he was there waiting on me. He was a big guy, tall and muscular. He seemed very relaxed. He was calling the officers by their names as they walked by. The conversations made me realize that he was a regular visitor. He started asking me questions as if he had the feeling it was my first time. He asked and I told him it was my very first time in a cell. The day of my arrest I made bail before having to be put in a cell. This guy walked me through the journey I was about to take step by step. I felt like he was giving me a manual. He told me they would send me to see a psychiatrist and that would be who determined the condition and kind of treatment I would receive for the duration of my stay in jail. He told me to be brave, not to present myself as if I was nervous or scared. I should tell them I wanted to work and go to school. I was a state prisoner so I would be transferred to state prison, but I should tell them I wanted to sign a contract to stay at the county jail. He also told me there was a drug program in the jail and I should apply to get into it because if I completed the 90-day program, I could apply for a reconsideration of my sentence and possibly get released earlier. He added that there were other advantages to the program like access to a phone, microwave, pillow, clean bathroom, refrigerator, computers, and a much safer surrounding.

After talking to this guy, I was out of my state of shock and started to accept my new reality. Since it was a sentencing day at the courthouse, other inmates kept coming into the holding cell. Some of them knew this guy I had been talking to. They brought us sandwiches for lunch and he told me to take an extra one or two because by the time I got to the county jail I might miss the dinner there. After a few hours, they called out our names and drove us to the county jail in a van. I never saw that guy again. Everything started just like he said it would. I spoke with a psychiatrist, and I told him everything the guy had told me to say. He did ask me if I had ever contemplated suicide and asked how I was feeling about being locked up for the first time. I told him I was there to do my time and put it behind me. I even joked with him by telling him if I was scared I wouldn't have shown up for my sentencing. The conversation went well. He said he could tell I was a good kid that made some bad choices.

After a while, I realized that jail was just like another town on the outside. There are different wards, only that in jail they are called blocks or pods. The psychiatrist was the one that determined which you would reside in. Some of the things they took into consideration were the nature of the crime you committed, affiliation with a gang, and your background. There were some other deciding factors like race and who you knew and who knew you. When they took my clothes and handed me a jumpsuit to wear I knew I was officially a prisoner. I will never forget the strip search. It was so humiliating. My first stop was Pod-C which was the receiving block. Everyone goes there first while they decide your next move, or you get bailed out. It had two tiers of cells on the outer perimeter and was shaped like a horseshoe with what they called a bubble at the open space. That area is where the officers were so they could see everything. In the center were tables and chairs connected and bolted to the floor. There was a TV and payphones. Whenever we were not locked down in our cells, that was where we were able to hang out. While there, I got a better understanding of what the guy had told me while in the holding cell. There were inmates in paper suits instead of jumpsuits. They had no sheets on their mattress and they were under 24-hour suicide watch by other inmates. I got a cell on the upper tier. I was by myself the first night and got a cellmate the next day.

The first phone call I made was to my brother. It was a hard call to make but I relaxed quickly. My brother just wanted to know that I was ok and what he could do to get me out. He didn't understand why I didn't tell him so he could have possibly helped me avoid jail time. After talking to him I felt more relaxed and all that pressure was gone. I did my best to comfort him that would in turn comfort my parents.

The first two days, I pretty much just slept. I had been drinking, smoking, partying, and stressing before my sentencing so I was dead tired. Things weren't as bad as I thought they would be. I was a people person and the type of person that adapted easily. My cellmate wanted to play cards and I told him I couldn't play. He told me he would teach me. I told him I didn't want to, and he got mad. He said I was boring, and asked the officers to switch him with someone and they did. My new cellmate was cool. We talked a lot. Just about everyone there smoked. I quickly realized that cigarettes were the currency in jail. One inmate bet that I would start smoking before I finished my time. I thought, we'll see about that. The weekends were busy in Pod-C with people getting arrested and people getting bailed out. I was in Pod-C for a little over a week. One night, a few officers called out a couple of names, mine was one of them. They told us to get our belongings and follow them. They led us to a cage where there were stacks of mattresses. They told us to each pick one up and continue following them. I walked with a plastic bag full of my belongings in one hand and a mattress over my shoulder on what was called a catwalk in jail. Inmates were escorted by officers, and you were only allowed to walk within the boundaries of the catwalk. There were lines painted on the floor. If there was more than one inmate, you had to walk in a single file formation. That was how we were walking while carrying our belongings and mattress. The officers were watching over us, and it felt like a scene from a slavery movie.

When we got to our destination, I was devastated. Two dorms were facing each other. They were separated by iron bars with a gate on each side. There was a hallway in between with an iron cage at the entrance between the two dorms that housed the officers. On one side was 1 East and the other side was 1 West. I was put in 1 East which was mostly Hispanics. 1 West was mostly blacks. This was the ghetto of the jail. It was rowdy and very dirty. There were bunk beds on one side and a table on the other. My Bunkie, the inmate I shared the bunk bed with, told me to sleep with my shoes under the mattress by my head; otherwise, they would steal my shoes. There were plastic bins that we put our belongings in and pushed underneath the bed. Anyone could go in your stuff when you were sleeping or using the bathroom. What finally broke me was the bathroom area. It was an open space in the already open dorm. Everyone in the dorm and the officers could see you. On one side, there were toilets and on the other were the showerheads. There was no partition. It was the most humiliating feeling I had ever experienced. The next day, I called my brother and told him he had to get me out of there. I was broken to the core. I remember after talking to my brother, a group of officers looking like a swat team ran into both of the dorms. They put all of us to the side. Some searched us while others searched our belongings, under the mattresses and everywhere else in that place. I later found out it was what they called a shake-down.

My brother had talked to a lawyer, and he needed my papers so he could see what my situation was. I gave him my lawyer's information so he could get the papers from him. In the meantime, he must have prayed because the next day the officers came and called my name, and I was on my way to my next stop. I didn't care where I was heading. I knew it had to be better than where I was. My next destination was H-Pod. It was much smaller. It seemed as if it was a big metal container. Everything was metal including the floor. I quickly found out, it was the residence for the workers. Everyone in the block worked. I was told it would take a little while for them to assign me to a job. Most of the guys worked in the kitchen, and they had to wake up very early in the morning. It was a friendly atmosphere. Everyone was getting along very well. I always had cigarettes with me after I found out that you could trade them for anything. I started ordering them on my commissary. I traded them for packs of soup, extra trays of food, Ensures, and just about anything. The workers were the ones with the connections. They were the ones that moved things around, even a message to someone on another block. They got to go to different blocks to drop off and pick up trays or they knew someone that did. Some worked in the laundry room, and they were able to move around as well. Now I was around the hustlers. Everyone was what we called "living good" in there. I was one of the few that wasn't working at that time, and I contemplated if I wanted to be working when I would hear the 4:30/5:00 a.m. wake-up call.

After about a week of waiting for my work assignment, the officers called me to tell me that I got accepted to the drug program. They told me to pack my belongings and that an officer was coming to escort me. He also told me that I couldn't bring any cigarettes or matches with me. I gave what I had to my cellmate. Later that Friday night around 7:00 p.m., they took me to the drug rehabilitation center known as DRC. When I got there, they searched my belongings and then took me to the bathroom to be strip-searched. I got blue scrubs to change into. After I got dressed, I was shown the bunk and locker I was assigned to. I put my stuff in the locker and was taken to meet my Big Brother. My Big Brother showed me around, explained how the program worked and what the expectations were. It was a dorm that was divided into sections. Each section had two bunk beds on either side and lockers on the back wall. There were two meeting rooms with TVs, two offices, a bathroom with shower stalls, a storeroom, and a section where the computers were. It was immaculate just like I was told it would be. There was a refrigerator, microwave and we had pillows. The walls around the dorm area were painted green and white. I loved it. I got to meet some of the guys before going to bed. Saturday morning when I woke up, I met the rest of the guys. They informed me that the weekend schedule was much lighter than the weekdays. They went over all the rules of the DRC with me. I started wondering if I had made a bad decision even though it was what I wanted. I shared my intentions with some of the guys I met before. They all asked if I was serious and why would I do that. Some of them told me that I should go to a state prison where there was more freedom. I was thinking the only freedom for me is outside. I felt as if I was in the belly of a beast, and I was trying to stay close to the mouth so any chance I got I could slip out.

The idea of going to a state prison felt like I would be going deeper into the mess, only to come out like feces. At this point, I wasn't reading my Bible or praying anymore. I was mad at God for not saving me from jail. For the few weeks, I had been in regular population, I had already met a few higher-ups in the food chain and made plans for the streets. That's the type of person I was. They found out my story and were attracted to my loyalty. Some had warned me about the strict rules of the program and if I were to get kicked out, it would be harder for me to get out on any program. I thought hard about it and decided that I was up for the challenge. There were just about 30-35 inmates in the program. We had to be out of bed by 7:30 a.m., dressed, and our bed properly made before inspection at 8:00 a.m. No one was allowed to be on or in their bed before 8:00 p.m. which was after our last meeting for the day. You had to attend and participate in meetings, counseling sessions, computer classes, meditation sessions, and exercise classes. Everyone was assigned a job that was expected to be properly carried out.

Every two weeks, they would put the job titles written on small pieces of paper into a jar for everyone to pick from. The inmates were the ones that maintained DRC. We had no contact with anyone else in the jail except for the officers, counselors, and the people that would come from outside to speak at the NA and AA meetings. There was also a teacher from the Bergen County Community College. We had to keep an updated diary that they would randomly ask to see. They wouldn't read it, but they wanted to know that you were writing in it. The rules were no cigarettes, no eating in the dorm area, no talking after lights out which was at 10:00 p.m., no fighting, and no stealing. We were also required to be properly dressed at all times between 8:00 a.m. and 8:00 p.m. Every morning after breakfast (chow), we started our day with meditation. We all had a meditation book that had a word for each day and a few supporting paragraphs. We would read it and discuss it. After the meditation, we had group meetings. There was nothing else until our night meeting. That was the weekend schedule. There was visiting on the weekends as well.

Monday morning came, and it was a different atmosphere. The officers only work at the DRC. They do not go back and forth between the other sections of the jail. The sergeant who only worked on weekdays came in first followed by the counselors. There were three counselors: Joe, Ellen, and Barbara. The director's name was Patrick. Joe introduced himself as my counselor. There was a full schedule for the weekdays. It consisted of group therapy, meetings, computer classes, gym time, meditation, and sometimes one-on-ones with my counselor. Some of our sessions would be broken down into different groups. Each counselor was responsible for a group. It was a 90-day program with a 90-day curriculum. We went over different topics that we would each get worksheets for. It was designed in a specific way that gradually broke things down as if you were on a journey; it could be called a journey of recovery.

While I was there on my journey, my brother was doing everything he could to get me out. That phone call must have touched him. He got me a different lawyer and brought my paperwork to him. After going over my case files, he suggested that the Intensive Supervision Program (ISP) would be the quickest way to get me out. The lawyer came to visit me and explained the program to me. It was very strict, but I decided to apply for it. He filed the paperwork with the court and then we had to wait for a court date. I also had the reconsideration of sentencing as plan B. The first job I got was to wipe down the walls and doors. It was a very easy job since the place was spotless. I went into the program with my intention which was not about recovery but after the daily meditations, therapy sessions, AA, and NA meetings, and working with the counselors, I started seeing things differently. I started feeling like I had been before the drug dealing. I started learning some computer skills. I signed up for the G.E.D. class, and I started to love working out. Most of all, I started realizing how cruel it was to sell cocaine. At that point, I started accepting my punishment.

I started to read my Bible and pray again, asking God to forgive me and for help with what I was going through. I started paying more attention to everything that they were teaching us. There was a Sunday service which was optional. I started attending the Sunday service where a chaplain would come in to lead the service. Someone from ISP came to talk to me and notified me that I was accepted into the program. However, after hearing what I was required to do, I declined to enter into the program. One of the requirements was going to Sussex County three times a week to see my officer. I was disappointed but I felt I had made the right decision. I shared with my group how I was feeling, and their feedback helped me to deal with the stress.

I missed my family and friends and wanted to go home. We used the same lawyer to file for the reconsideration of my sentence. The lawyer filed the paperwork and now I had to wait for a court date. In the meantime, I had taken the G.E.D. exam and was waiting on the results. At the same time, I was getting certified in different levels of Microsoft Word and Excel. I started to get along well with the officers. They all told me that I had good people in my life that loved and cared about me. They also told me to learn everything I could and go home to my family.

My brother came to visit me almost every weekend. When I first got to jail, I didn't feel like talking to anyone. I just wanted to forget about the outside world and get my head wrapped around what was happening. When my brother came to visit, he asked me why I wasn't calling. He said he wanted to hear from me. The news of my arrest had spread, and people were asking him about me, and he didn't know what to say. It made me realize even more how special my brother was. Other inmates were complaining that no one would take their phone calls.

One night my big brother in the program suddenly got sent to state prison. Everyone was surprised. I got worried because I was also a state prisoner, and I wasn't sure if the same would happen to me. It was a constant roller coaster ride. One day I would be in the best mood and the next, I was stressing about something. The first time I saw someone get kicked out of the program was scary. Officers just came and got him at night, no questions, no explanations. The counselors, director, and sergeant made the decision and left the order to be carried out by the officers. I was doing very well in the program so these incidents didn't affect me for long. My court date for the reconsideration kept getting postponed which was stressing me out. The support I was getting kept me focused. I called my brother one day and he told me that the results from my GED exam had come in the mail, and I passed. He brought me my diploma and the score sheet. It was a great feeling. I shared the news with everyone. My teacher was happy and asked me to help the other guys to study for the exam.

After finishing the 90 days, I had a choice to go to a block that allowed me to work with fewer restrictions or stay in the program. I chose to stay in the program. My brother was pushing my lawyer to get a court date and the day finally came. I went to court and the judge offered me time in an inpatient program upon being released with a five-year probation. I turned down his offer. It was now July and when I had seen the parole board earlier, they gave me an estimated release date of October 10th. So I decided to just wait the three months. I was very disappointed again. I was mad at Patrick, the director, because he was the one that recommended I continue treatment on the outside. We talked about it in my group session, and everyone helped me to see it positively. Now my next expectation was to be released on parole in October. One of our previous lessons was about commitment so the counselors told us to think of something to commit ourselves to. We were in the yard working out and one of the counselors, Barbara, called me to the side. She asked why not choose exercise to commit to because it seemed like I enjoyed doing it. I told her I loved her suggestion and exercise will be my commitment. I've been working out since then and continue to this day. The exercise was my best therapy then and it still is.

I missed a lot of people and a lot of things, including the sunlight. I remember writing up a medical slip to go see the nurse not because I was sick but just to go for a walk. Of all the things I missed, I missed my mom the most. I always hoped and prayed that my mom was not worrying too much about me that could cause her to get sick and even worse pass away. I would call her and my dad to let them know I was okay. Even when I was stressed, I would reassure them that I was happy where I was.

The sergeant gave me a book, *Underboss: Sammy the Bull Gravano's Story of Life in the Mafia*, to read. He said it would help me. That book was life-changing for me. I could relate to most of what he was talking about. I was experiencing some of it at that very moment. I knew then I had to reassess myself, my lifestyle, my loyalty, my priorities, and the people I associated with. After reading the book, I realized that I was on a journey that was not complete yet. I wasn't ready. I started looking back on my behavior that led up to the day of my arrest and the time between then to the day of my sentencing. It became clear to me that my prayers were being answered. I was heading to a point of no return. Everything had gone exactly as the guy I met in the holding cell at the courthouse had said it would. Of all the jails in New York and New Jersey, I was locked up in Bergen County which at that time was the only county jail with a drug rehabilitation center. It had only opened less than two years before I got there. I started to see all the signs that God ordained the process of change for me, and I wasn't going home until God saw it fit. It was hard to accept that reality, but I was grateful for the understanding of the situation. It was a burden off my shoulders. I had blamed the police, the system, informants, and what I should have done better which had caused a build-up of anger, animosity, and stress.

It became clear to me why some of the guys I knew kept going back and forth to jail. They always thought they had a better way of doing the same thing that got them into trouble in the first place. That's exactly how I felt for the first couple of months being locked up. I just wanted to go home to do things differently. Now I knew the only way to do things differently was to stop. It was more than getting locked up for me. It was the constant fear of getting locked up that never left. Whether in bed at night, on the streets, in the mall shopping, or driving on the highway, I suspected everyone of being a cop or an informant. Then, there was the fear of getting robbed or even killed. Either you didn't buy anything of value with the money you made, or you bought it and didn't enjoy it. I knew guys with expensive cars that would only drive them out of town; guys with houses in other people's names. Money was given to family and friends to stash which never ended well; killings over drug money. It was a life of constant hide and seek. The worst of all was the part you play in the destruction and possible deaths and the effect it had on families, friends, and society in general. Realizing all these things reminded me of what Dread had told me after getting shot—that it was a beating. Now I was realizing that jail and all that I was going through was a beating I had to endure for a chance to start from a clean slate. It felt as if it was good to get it over with. I always knew it was coming, just didn't know when.

My parents had just migrated to Morristown, and I knew the way I was living was not safe for them. This had to be God's plan. I started speaking more in the group sessions and sharing with the other guys the way I was seeing things. Some would say I was brainwashed. They called me Mr. NA, junior counselor and some would even get mad at me. It didn't matter to me. I knew it was the right thing to do. I got to meet the sheriff of Bergen County, Jack Terhune. Shortly afterward, the director, Patrick Hughes, asked me to go along with two of the older guys to share my story with some kids. I was happy to go. They gave us fresh orange jumpsuits to wear. It was the first time seeing the outside in eight months. We went and spoke to the kids at a government facility. It was a Saturday, and it was part of their punishment for the trouble they had gotten into. I was nervous at first but after I started I got comfortable.

The next week, the parole board came to see me, and they gave me a release date of October 15th. This date was only a month away, the best news I had received since I got to jail. I started to see the light at the end of the tunnel. It was a feeling I can't explain. Now I started getting worried about the INS. I only had a green card and with a felony charge, they could detain me. I talked to the director about the situation and asked him to check if there was any detainer against me. He checked and told me there was not. This calmed my fears, but it was still on my mind. I knew it could pop up at any minute.

We had to say the serenity prayer everyday so now I was practicing it in my life:

God grant me the Serenity to accept the things I cannot change,
the Courage to change the things I can and the
Wisdom to know the difference.

I knew I had no control over that and from all I was experiencing for the last eight months, I was convinced that God was with me on my journey. The director asked me to go share my story with the kids at Lodi High School. He told me the undersheriff would also be there. I went and there were three different groups. After speaking to the first group, I got comfortable. They got to ask me questions. They expressed much sympathy for me. It was a long journey for me but more so for my brother. He had come to see me every weekend except when he went to Jamaica for the church convention. He had been working on some kind of way to get me out up until I got released. My time was getting shorter, and it was a joyful feeling. Four days before my release date, they asked me to go along with one other guy to speak to some kids. The officer that was driving us stopped at Dunkin' Donuts. To our surprise, he said let's go in. It was the weirdest feeling. People were staring at us as if they were uncomfortable. It was good having donuts and being in society again even though it wasn't the best situation.

We went and shared our stories with the kids that were also in a program. I was much more relaxed knowing I was going home in a few days. It was hard to see inmates come and go, and I was always the one that was left behind for eight months. I saw quite a few guys pass through the program. Most graduated, some got kicked out and some asked to be returned to the regular population. If you completed the program, they would have a graduation ceremony for you before you left. A day or two before you left everyone would gather in a circle including the counselors and the director. One by one, everyone would say something to whoever was leaving. Then the director would hand that person a certificate. A few days before my date to leave, my brother came to visit and I asked the sergeant for permission to send most of my belongings home with him. I had kept all my worksheets, my diary, meditation book, pamphlets, and certificates I received from the different levels of Microsoft Word and Excel. I sent these home with my brother.

Finally, it was my turn to graduate. It was very emotional. All the guys that were there saw me when they came. For a few months, I was the most senior guy in the program. I had helped them get settled, shared tips with them to make their jobs easier, and always encouraged them. They all thanked me and expressed how much they were going to miss me. They encouraged me to do the right thing and never come back. One of the counselors gave me a coin which I still have to this day. On one side is the serenity prayer and on the other side is an image of twelve steps with the words one day at a time. He told me that before I go back to my old ways to swallow it. Later that night before bed, we had our get-together. We made noodles from packaged soups with eggs and chicken we had saved from Sunday's dinner. We also ate chips, crackers and had Tang to drink. We gathered together, ate, and talked.

After what was my best day since I got to jail and it was almost time for my last night's sleep there, I found out no one had come to sign me out. I went to bed stressing and wondering if it was because of INS. I got up early the next morning, Wednesday, October 15th, hoping and praying that someone would come to sign me out now! I had breakfast which I hoped was my last meal there. When the director came in, he told me everything will be ok. I'll get to go home soon. They came and signed me out, so I called my brother who was ready and waiting on the call. We knew the process would take a while, but I didn't want to have to wait around after being released. I stripped my mattress and emptied my locker. I gave away the food and toiletries I had left. They called for an officer to escort me to the front for checkout, so I said my final goodbyes. The times when I left to go speak, I used a side door with direct access to the DRC, so this was the first time in nine months

I was seeing the place where I entered the jail. They gave me a bag with the clothes I had on when I came, and I changed into them. After waiting for a while, they gave me my release paper, opened the door, and I was finally free. My brother was waiting so I went to the car, and we were out of there.

Chapter 5

Life After Jail

The Reset

The parole board gave me a few hours after being released to report to their office in Clifton. We drove straight there. When we got done there, we drove to Morristown. I will never forget the moment I walked through the door. My mom hugged me and as soon as my dad saw me, he started to cry. I had the greatest feeling of being home. Everything was different on the outside, but the air was the first and most noticeable. In the back of my mind, I had a fear of going back, especially for something silly. I was home but still had to do eighteen months of parole which had its own rules. I wasn't worried about the rules they gave me. They were nothing I couldn't handle. I was more concerned with getting into a fight with someone from the past with old grudges or just something from the past that caught up with me. Some of the rules were 90 AA or NA meetings in 90 days, no alcohol or drug use, steady employment, report to a parole officer as scheduled, no traveling out of the state without permission, random drug tests, and no involvement in any criminal activity or association with anyone that does. I met my parole officer (P.O.), and he went over all that he expected of me. He had a very good personality which made me feel comfortable. There was a place down the street that I lived on where meetings were held so that was an easy one for me.

At the first meeting I went to, I realized it was all people I knew from the neighborhood. Some I sold drugs to, and some were other dealers I knew that were probably on parole or probation. I did my 90 meetings and continued to go randomly until I stopped. I called up Maureen and asked her about my old job. She told me to check with the temp agency to make sure I was up to date in their system, and she would get me back in. I took care of it, and I was back on the job. One of the parole rules was that you must inform your employer that you are on parole. The temp agency didn't care, and Maureen already knew the situation. When I got home, my brother and father were working there. They had been hired permanently. Byrdie had been hired permanently as well. I worked with Maureen through the temp agency for four months, and then I got hired by Colgate permanently. It was a great feeling to tell someone the truth about my past and they still gave me a chance. I started on the night shift with both my dad and brother. We worked from 11:00 p.m. to 7:00 a.m.

One of the reasons for the strict sleep schedule in the program was to prepare us for the typical nine-to-five job. It turned out to be the total opposite for me. The reconditioning process was hard for me, but I fought through it. My P.O. was happy with the way things were going with me. Byrdie and Cubby were gone when I got home. My mom and dad were there. My P.O. came there and met them. He adored my parents. Everything was falling in place for me. I had no issues. For a long time, my mind would keep going back to jail. It was much more than my sleep time that I had reconditioned myself to. Everything was a routine in jail, not much of anything ever changed. It was like you were programmed to do the same thing day after day, week after week, month after month. It's one of the reasons people end up going back or have a hard time in society. It was a blessing for me that I spent almost my entire time in a program getting counseling. I was also blessed to have the support of my family and friends.

When I was in jail, I had many people that visited me other than just my brother. My brother's wife and baby Olivia would visit sometimes. Marie would come to see me. My big sister and her husband, Paulie, my sister and her husband and kids came to see me while visiting from Jamaica. Natalie and I were not on good terms when I went to jail, but she would still come to see me and encourage me. Esric, Dread, Gramps, Lucky, Parky, Killa, Wendy, Brother Beris, Sister Velma, Denise, Simone, Nadine, and Mr. Blackman were some of the people that came to show their love. Others would just send me a message. There was one lady from the church that I grew up around in my community in Jamaica that was now living here. Everyone called her

Sister Cinthia. When Lucky visited me, he told me Sister Cinthia gave him $20 to put in my account. I was very surprised. It touched a part of me that was never touched. It was the act of kindness and the thought. No one had ever given me money other than my dad. This lady was a struggler. She came from Jamaica to work and help her family back home. I knew she was just breaking her bread with me not because she thought I needed it, but because of the kindness in her heart. It reminded me of the kind of love I grew up around in the church. I will never forget that feeling of being truly loved.

When I got back to town, everything was different. I was now wondering if it was a part of God's plan. The building on the corner that was the Jamaican restaurant where we used to hang out was demolished. If you hadn't known, you never would have known a building had been there less than a year before. That would have been a temptation for me even just to hang out sometimes. My living situation was different; it had been me, Byrdie, and Cubby. Now it was me and my parents. It was almost nine years since I had lived with my mom in Jamaica, and I never really lived with my dad. He had worked in Kingston. He would come home for most weekends and sometimes for an extended stay but never day-to-day. It was a great feeling not only to be home from jail but to be back in my home. I had been missing my mom for years. There are a lot of things happening right now but if you are following you should now see that it's all coming together to make sense.

I talked about my relationship with my dad earlier. Now that we were back together, and I was more mature I asked him for some time to sit down and reason. I shared with him some of the things I learned in the program that helped me to see a lot of things differently. I felt like it was the right time for me and Pops to reconnect, but it didn't go that way. My dad was saying everything that was happening was God. It had nothing to do with counseling, meditation, the books I've read, the speakers I've listened to, and even the videos I watched. I said it many times before. It was divine intervention. God's plan, God's leading, and that I think is the spiritual side.

Then there is the physical side. All the people he used—the police that pulled me over, the guy I met in the holding cell, the counselors, the people that came in to teach us how to meditate, the guys that came in to share their story with us, and of course my brother. The conversation I was trying to have with my dad was the one I had with my brother every time he visited me. Jail brought me and my brother's relationship to a level that only God would know. My brother was and still is like a father to me in so many ways. He is the best example to me of a righteous leader, brave, humble, kind, forgiving, understanding, faithful, truthful, very spiritual, smart, and slow to anger, although I have never seen him angry. I could keep writing about my brother, but I think you understand what I am saying, and you'll hear more about him later. My dad is a very good father, but he looks at everything through his religious beliefs, and I see things very differently.

Some of the guys I used to hang out with weren't around anymore. A few were locked up while some had open cases, and most of them were still around. I would run into some of them around town while I was on the move. There were those that I was very close with that I would visit from time to time or talk to on the phone. For me, it was work, meetings, home, and I would go by my uncle's to hang out sometimes. My parole was smooth sailing. My P.O. told me not to let him down because he was bragging about me at the office. After hearing people complaining about their parole and probation officers for years I felt good to hear those words from mine. I knew I had let a lot of people down, especially my family. I wanted to now make them all feel proud of me. I went from seeing my P.O. every two weeks to once every three months in no time. The last time I saw my P.O., I had more than three months left on parole. He told me good luck, take care of myself, and just call him to sign out. The time came, I called, and I was done with parole!

I had mixed feelings about my relationships when I came home so I had a whatever attitude. Marie and I weren't that close anymore. Natalie and I were cool again. I wasn't treating her right before I went to jail, and she overlooked that and gave me her support. Even though some bitter feelings still existed on both sides, the door was opened. I would talk to Theresa sometimes on the phone. After a while, we started hanging out again. Shortly after I got home, Shereka had baby Quba. We were cool so baby Quba was my little niece.

I mentioned Cubba earlier before I got locked up. Cubba was my boy from New York that I brought to the corner. He came to see me and told me he was doing some business down south and he wanted to help me because I was the only one ever to do anything for him. I talked to my boy Scorcha about it because I didn't want to do anything with him. Scorcha said to get him some money, and he would deal with it. After Cubba left, he didn't call, and he stopped answering his phone. It was hard for me to understand why someone I grew up with and did so much for would do such a thing. I felt betrayed. I called the guys from Connecticut that I helped out and never got paid and told them I was home and needed some money. They sent me to Western Union three times back-to-back and still, there was no money. Once again guys that I grew up with, that I risked it all for, betrayed me again. I later ran into them at a party in New York and approached them. Their excuse was that they were gambling to win some money to send to me. Why would you send me to collect the money you didn't send? Now I was feeling disrespected. It was my boy Parky's party and my boys that were with me calmed things down. I reminded myself that it was a lesson from the past. Years later I saw them, and I told them to forget the past and that I still loved them.

Scorcha had a few open cases that he kept delaying. They were cases that he had long before I got arrested. He turned down all the plea offers until it was time for the trial to start. He ran and it wasn't long before he got caught. The trial he ran from was tried without him there and he was found guilty. His sentence was somewhere around sixteen years. So when they caught him, it was time to pay. He went to prison for a very long time. Then he was deported back to Jamaica. There was so much evidence all around me that selling drugs never ended well.

I developed a liking for working out while I was in jail which has now become an addiction. When I first came home, I was doing mostly pushups, dips, and some abs at the house. I would even get it in at work sometimes. After I got hired full-time and started receiving benefits, I had access to a gym that my company had an agreement with. Later on, after I got off parole, I started working out with some guys I knew from the streets, a few of whom I had past issues with. I always had a love for people, but being in the program helped me to express it and spread it beyond my circle. I told you how my love for the color green started. Now it represented more than just a political party or the people in my community. The color green for me now represents the love of all people and not just one group, race, nationality, religious belief, or class. I realized my love was for all mankind and I should treat people accordingly. Most of the negative energy I was attracting came from my behaviors. With that understanding, I started making changes that would bring unity, peace, strength, happiness, courage, calmness, and boldness to create a fertile environment for love to strive in. All the fuss and fights about whose corner, who is stopping who from making money, which cop is cool and which ones are trouble, and who is an informant were gone with the decision to stop selling drugs.

It was now over a year since I had talked to my cousin Byrdie. A little voice in my head was telling me to leave him alone. He should have visited me while I was locked up but the love in me was much louder and stronger. One day I went to him, and I told him to put the silliness away. We are brothers and I have nothing but love for him. I knew he loved me likewise. It was a reconnection of love, family, and a great relief for both of us.

I always had a passion for music. Whether it was listening to it, dancing to it, or singing it. I started writing lyrics when I was locked up. Music was one of the tools I used to relieve my stress. During my free time between my last meeting and bedtime, I would exercise and listen to music. On Friday nights we had a later bedtime so most of the guys would be watching movies in the meeting room. During this time, I would get dressed in a fresh suit of scrubs, put my street shoes on, grab some snacks, put my headphones on and head to an empty cubicle in the back of the dorm where I would listen to music and even dance. They would mess with me sometimes asking me if I'm about to hit the streets. They taught us in meditation that with our mind, we can be in any place we choose. We practiced a kind of meditation called guided imagery. While we relaxed with our eyes closed someone would talk to us as if they were leading us somewhere. The person would describe the sounds and the surroundings to make us feel like we were actually in that place. I started practicing it on my own and that's what I would do on Friday nights.

My counselor suggested that I start putting my feelings on paper. I started writing songs, poems and sometimes I would just write. When I got home I started taking my lyrics writing more seriously. One of the things I started to realize was that selling drugs completely takes you away from your true self. It becomes an addiction. I've been business-minded since I was a kid. I was always looking for something to sell for a profit. I was on a good path until I started dealing drugs. Now that I had stopped, my passion for the business was now coming back. I started promoting parties. I started a record label called Shinazz Entertainment and started going to the studio to record some of the songs I wrote. One of the trainers at my gym told me he had a studio at his house and invited me there. I went to see the recording studio he had, and I was impressed. He started teaching me the process of recording a song. From there I started inquiring about recording studios. I started meeting more people in the music industry. I remember meeting a guy with a reggae program on the local cable channel. He invited me on to the program. I went and we spent some time talking before I performed. That was my second time performing on TV. One downside to the music business that my counselors were concerned about is that drugs are usually involved. In my case, it was weed so I wasn't concerned. My thought was if I'm not selling it, I'm good. I was still concerned that it was illegal.

I was off from work on Friday and Saturday nights so that was when I would hang out. I was everywhere. If I was cool with you, I would support you, and I was cool with everyone around town. From birthdays, weddings, baby showers to funerals, I was going to show my love. I linked back up with Ninja's little cousin Ricky (DJ). I loved his musical vibes and his humble personality. We would get together sometimes to sing, talk music, and money. He started to know the lyrics of my songs. I would share my dreams and goals with him. He always encouraged me.

Chaka Demus and Pliers performed in a club close to Morristown. Ricky came on stage with me to open the show. The club was packed, and the reception was good. That performance cemented our relationship. I was around Ricky a lot and started spending more time with Theresa again. She was friends with Ricky's girlfriend, Tina, and his cousin Tracey. We would hang out in the park all the time, even some nights. Since I wasn't hustling drugs anymore, I had a lot more time to chill out. Working the graveyard shift gave me time to be outside in the evenings. Sometimes in the summer, I would stay out until it was time to go to work. On the weekends, I would party. We would go to the local bars and from there, we would go to either a reggae party out of town or a house party.

At my job, I was working on a production line that made deodorant. My primary duty was running the machines that put the labels on the bottles. The machines pretty much ran on their own other than when there was a jam, or it was time to change the roll of labels. I was mostly sitting around watching the machines. After doing it for a while, I would know when any of the machines stopped by the change in the sounds. I would keep myself busy by writing most of the time. Sometimes, I would read. It was against the rules to be writing or reading any material that had nothing to do with my work duties. We weren't even supposed to sit down, but on the night shift, there was only one boss and one or two team leaders, so it was much more relaxed.

The day shift was much different as there were many levels of bosses, supervisors and sometimes people would come in for a tour of the factory. My supervisor caught me so many times. She would just warn me or give me some type of work to do that she knew I did not like. I was a good worker. The main goal was to keep the machine running so we could make our production numbers which made everyone happy. My team and I were good at doing that so for the most part she usually let me slide. I was there but I wasn't there. Just like I had learned in jail, I used my mind to take myself places beyond the walls of the factory. It reminded me of jail sometimes because there were no windows, and the doors were always shut. Once you were inside you wouldn't know anything that was going on outside. You couldn't even tell if it was night or day from the inside. I think it was designed that way to keep our minds inside on the job. Thanks to meditation, I was traveling places while doing my duties. I spent a lot of time at work thinking about all kinds of stuff. That's one thing they could not stop me from doing. Sometimes I would have to hold my thoughts and write them down on my break or when I got home. The first time I wrote my thoughts down on paper was in jail. This was what I wrote…

Real World

Real world, real life
It's a breath and a heartbeat
Real world, real life
It's just a two-way street
Your way or my way
From the west or the east
It's a journey we have to take
At death it is complete
Be understood or understand
Who is right or who is wrong
There are always disagreements
In most conversations
Who is of God?
Who is of Satan?
Who is of themselves?
Or things in their possession
Why is there a war
Between all these religions?
Who is going to hell
Or to the Promise Land
The Jews or the Christians
The Muslims or the Rastaman
It doesn't make a difference
A man is just a man

There's Always A Light

Real world, real life
It's hard to keep it real
Real world, real life
Speak the way you feel
Some think you're soft
Always need a shield
When others are so sure
Your heart is made of steel
Lord, let me know my friends
If I have any
Give me the sight to see
Those who are my enemies
Locked up in jail
Knew I had to pay a penalty
Joked about it for a while
Then I had to face reality
My brother asked me about it
I gave him a story
Couldn't keep it real with him
The burden was too heavy
I'm on the phone with my girl
Stressing and feeling lonely
Feels like I'm doing life
In some strange country
She asked if I'm thinking of her
And I told her not really
Didn't want to lie to her
Cause I love her dearly
Doing this time ain't no joke
I have to take it easy
Don't wanna think too hard
This place will drive me crazy
Thought she would understand, instead
Keeping it real made me lose my baby
Real World, real life
I have to make this decision
Real world, real life
I'm at an intersection

Where should I turn
Which is the right direction
Lord, I need your help
In making sure I choose the right one
Here I go again
A fight between two of my friends
Help me, dear Lord
Not to lose any of them
Now both of them are mad at me
Which way to turn, Lord let me see
I'm fighting with myself
Because I don't know
I'm at another crossroad
Which way to go
Is it working nine to five
Or hustling on the street
Anytime I'm hungry
I'll do whatever just to eat
It's a real world
And I'm thankful for life
I've made a lot of decisions
Not all of them were right
In the dark places
Lord, please be my light
It's a real world
And I'm gonna live my life

Some of these things were in my thoughts for a long time before I was locked up, but with counseling, meditation, and lots of time to think, I started feeling more confident about who I was on the inside. Growing up in the church, I had a belief that Christianity was the only righteous religion. Before leaving Jamaica, I had the chance to meet some Rastafarians that made me start wondering about this very topic. Some of these guys were saying the same things I was hearing in the church. In the church, it was Jesus and for them, it was Haile Selassie. Both groups believed there's a God. On one of the political motorcades, I watched a group of men corner a Rastaman asking him which side he was on. He told them he was not on any side as he was not involved in what he called politricks. He was begging them not to hurt him. One of the men hit him in the face. He raised both hands and all he kept saying was peace, peace, peace. The men were talking to themselves and then walked off leaving the Rastaman standing there. It was my first time experiencing that level of humility.

I came to America and got exposed to people from different places, races, and religions. The one thing I realized is that if they didn't identify themselves with a particular religion, I could not tell the difference. I now know and truly believe that it's what is in a man's heart and his actions that make him righteous. One of the questions I ask myself sometimes is why is it that where a person is born and raised influences the religion that person believes in? So is there a geographical aspect to righteousness? No, can't be! Think about how hard it was to write this. Imagine having a conversation with someone like my dad. I tried when I got home from jail, and it didn't go anywhere. He shut me down. It's very hard sometimes to tell another person how you feel. Mainly because of a type of fear within—fear of their reaction/response, fear of rejection, fear of losing someone, fear of hurting someone's feelings and so much more. Think about how many times you told someone their cooking was good when you thought otherwise. Or how many times you told someone they were right about something that you really thought was wrong. How many times have you told someone you didn't have it to give to them when you know you did? I know it's hard to keep it real in this real world.

When I pray, I ask God to give me the strength, to be honest, kind, forgiving, humble, and courageous. I learned a lot in the program and from the whole experience of being locked up. There were things that I was still struggling with though. I was working while pursuing music, and I still had a lot of connections in the underworld, especially in the weed trade. Some of my friends knew this so they would sometimes ask me to link them with my connections. I once linked one of my boys with a weed connection out of state. He got the weed but kept giving me stories about the people's money. They were calling me about their money, and I was telling them whatever my boy had told me. All I did was a favor, and now I was caught in the middle of the back and forth. It got to the point where they started threatening me, so I told them to do whatever they had to and don't call me back. That was the end of that situation. I picked up my pen and wrote about it.

I was very inspired by DMX. The language he was speaking was very clear to me. I grew up around dogs, so it all made sense. He was very spiritual like I was. He was like a preacher and a teacher to the lost souls in the streets like I was. Here are some of my thoughts, feelings, and experiences that I wrote down during that time.

Why Are You Calling Me Your Dog

Why are you calling me your dog
Like that you don't know me
A dog is a man's best friend
So how come I'm so lonely
You don't know how I live
Or what I eat when I'm hungry
You only want this dog around
Just for security

Be roaming the street
With nowhere to sleep
Didn't see you around
When I had thorns in my feet
You need to watch your speech
Before you feel my heat
When you call me your dog
In your mouth I wanna reach
I'm always outside
You ain't never let me in
Didn't get your help
When ticks were in my skin
Sent me to the races
You know I always win
So when I got back
I gave you everything
You supposed to look out for me
Instead, you gave me not a thing

There's Always A Light

Your man put you on
Now you acting shady
Supposed to make me eat
But keep saying you'll see me
Before you break me bread
You're trying to own the bakery
Just cut me a slice
I need something in my belly
Must be from the Promise Land
Couldn't be from Jersey
Cause every time I see you
It's a different story
Been around me for a minute
And you know I'm not lazy
You know how this dog get
Anytime he's hungry
Now you getting bread
You wanna be greedy
Greedy dogs lose their bone
And taking yours is easy

Where all the big dogs at
I know you heard me
All the dogs around you
How come there ain't no puppy
They must have starved to death
Or bounce when they were hungry
Young hustlers stay around you
They'll never make no money
I'm gonna stretch it till it reach
If you're my dog you're gonna eat
Drink milk and swallow meat
If I get food we have a feast
You're calling me your dog
But to me, you're like a leech

I had so many experiences with close people that I shared with, defended, and even helped to get their own that turned their back on me when they got a break. I've also watched people experience the same. Pay attention to the lines that said before you break my bread you're trying to own the bakery. Some people just never have enough to share. The more they get, the more they want. While they keep telling you to give them some time, they got you. They're saying I need to save ten thousand before I can afford to give you one hundred even though you need it.

Now I've seen parents do that to their kids, especially fathers. Telling their kids they don't have it to give to them but they're spending it on women, alcohol, clothes, jewelry, friends and some just have it in the bank while their kids struggle. I've also seen parents spend their all on kids only for them to grow up and turn their back. The streets are like the Promised Land. As soon as one of your boys gets a break, the promises start, and it usually continues until something bad happens or they just stop coming around. They'll buy drinks and give you enough to smoke but nothing to help yourself. Kindness to your family, friends, and close people is when you have a dollar and can give them fifty cents, and in some cases the whole dollar. I pray for strength to have that level of kindness. Nothing is too small to share. There are some people you can never call to ask for a favor; no matter how small, they always have an excuse as to why they can't. If you're my dawg, I'm gonna ride with you and for you and that's my word.

You're Gonna Be Proud Of Me

To all the dogs I played with
When I was a puppy
We played after school
Summer was a big party
Got older to realize
I have to face reality
So I took control of my life
Deciding my own destiny
To the offspring of my bloodline
And soldiers in my army
Good people that I met
Somewhere along my journey
You're gonna be proud

There's Always A Light

For all the things you taught me
I'm at the drawing table
Setting up a bakery
That will bake so much bread
You won't be hungry

Got me ready for school
Made sure I had food to eat
Kept my clothes clean
Mom, you taught me to be neat
Couldn't miss Sunday school
In church I watched you preach
From your arms to your back
You carried me when I had problems with my feet
Always want the best for me
You taught me how to speak
Now people asking themselves
How come he's so deep
Still have a lot of self-discipline
Even when I'm off the leash
You told me to be humble
You showed me how to be meek
Mom, you'll still be proud of me
Even though I love the streets

You ain't heard from me in a minute
But that's how it is
A dog has to eat
If a dog wants to live
Been through many tunnels
Now I'm setting up a bridge
So you can cross over
And set up your own biz
The reason you haven't seen me
I'm in the cut getting big
Or probably in the marketplace
Putting in my bid
Trying to stock some food up
So I have enough to give

Not much time to see my people
Working this night gig
But I know they'll be proud of me
For getting up after I slid
If I never get to see you
Stay hot and be safe
You are a shining star
Never lose your faith
You taught me a lot
You put food on my plate
All the habits I caught from you
Not one went to waste
Taught me a lot about love
You added flavors to my taste
Was a source of energy
That can never be replaced
The power that you left me with
I'm still lighting up the place
If you get there before me
Stay close to heaven's gate
Sophia, you're gonna be proud
To see the way I escalate

When I wrote those words I was feeling detached from some very close people, mainly because of the life I was living and all the different things I got caught up in. The love of people was always my driving force—my family, the people in my community, and those who believed in me. I was going through some changes and trying to find my way, so things were very different in my relationships with people. Getting locked up was a setback and a big disappointment to a lot of people who were rooting for me. Those words were a message to them, letting them know that I was good, and I will never give up. I loved and appreciated them, and I would make them feel proud of me.

Let The Doggy Out

There's always good and bad
And two sides to every story
I have a dog in me

There's Always A Light

That could get really dirty
Heads or tails you ask
Before you flip the penny
On my flip side if you check
You probably see Lassie
Or depending on the vibe
You might just see Spotty
The type that plays with kids
And moms treat like a baby
I keep a pit bull in my cage
In case things get rowdy
What could be the outcome
If you let them roam the party
Just let the doggy out
If that's what's gonna make you happy

There's a dog in everyone
But some still don't know that
So it's caged up all their life
The type that's always laid back
Never let him out to walk
Or send him to the meat shop
Never take him to the vet
For a checkup or a wash
Got him growing in the cage
With the gate always locked
And all the other dogs you meet
You're always ready to attack
When there's more dog in you
Than Snoop Dogg and the Lox
Let your doggy out to walk
And he might never come back
Excitement would have him wilding
The type that doesn't know how to act

I watch dogs play around
Without hurting themselves
With chains making sounds
Just like jingling bells

Life After Jail – The Reset

Let your dog out on the sand
So he can play with the shells
Good way to keep him healthy
Make sure he's doing well
Let your dog out in the club
So he can walk around and smell
He'll probably sniff an enemy
Or find where the poodles dwell
She might lead you to Ryo
He might lead you to Michelle
Where your dog might lead you to
It's very hard to tell
I let mine out in a party
And we end up in a cell

Who let that dog out
Take responsibility
We'll give you a deal
If you'll plea guilty
I was only trying to eat
First of the month I was hungry
For the pleasures of this world
For power I was thirsty
So I let my doggy out
To feed in New York City
Crossing back the bridge
He had a comfortable tummy
Enough food to start the game
With the devils of New Jersey
He got bit in the first round
We end up in the county
It was all my fault
For letting my dog out in a hurry

It's a great feeling being oneself. The fear of what others might say, think or do can cause us to hold back from things we want to experience or express. It's a different level of freedom and emancipation when someone finds enough courage to overcome their fears and do what makes them happy. Doing something might not produce the results you anticipated but it's the only way to find out. I realized that a lot of people who criticize others for being themselves are jealous of their freedom of expression. We all have things we want to do. Some we want to try at least once: skinny dipping, singing your favorite song at karaoke, walking up to someone you've been admiring and letting them know, having a few drinks, and heading to the dance floor. Recently I met an older lady who was probably in her 70s, and she told me that she would love to have sex in a red pickup truck. When's the last time you heard someone having a good laugh out loud in public? Come on people, let your doggy out!

After getting out of jail and being on parole, I pretty much kept low, stayed away from the hood, and avoided most people. It was one of my parole restrictions to stay away from people and places that involved any kind of illegal activity. So to avoid any problems for myself or with parole, I stayed away. Now that I was off parole, I was working, going to the gym, and was on a schedule. The one thing that was missing was the interaction with the people in the community. I was born that way. It was the people first, before the politics, drugs, and parties. I started driving through the hood and depending on what things looked like or who was outside, I would stop and chill for a while or just say what's up and keep it moving. It was a constant assessment of the surroundings as things could change quickly. Some days would be more relaxed, especially when I was hanging out with the old guys or chilling with some girls and close friends. Other times, I was at the spot where the super love sound system was based. It was much different there because it was Jamaicans doing what they do, playing music, singing, playing dominoes, drinking, and smoking.

Some days, I would be in the park. Sometimes the hustlers would have people meet them in the park or people would be drinking alcohol or smoking weed. Here I was still chilling with people around these circumstances because it was who I was. I would always share my newfound knowledge with the hustlers. I was always the type of person who had a special love for the younger youths. I was always cool with them, sharing hard truths with them. On the other side, I would be drinking and smoking with them when I was out there. Some girls were always around, and I loved chilling with them. One thing I noticed since I was a kid is that most people despise the poor, the ghetto, or just disadvantaged people. Some move away and never come back. Some come by only to show off and point fingers, and some never leave but act as if they are different from everyone else. It was all these things that I was thinking about when I wrote what I called a Thug Stop.

<u>Thug Stop</u>

Every so often
In the hood I stop
Where me and my dogs roam
Or might just kick back
Every place I go
There's always a spot
Where the big dogs gather
To politic or relax
Smoke in the air
From weed, cigarettes, or blacks
Young thugs around
Getting familiar with the straps
Ready to do it all
To put their set on the map
Hot girls around
Some you be calling hood rats
Ghetto movie stars
Girls that know how to act
Waiting to be discovered
By a thug that make a stop

Making a thug stop
Can get really crazy
With your boys on the block
Still getting money
With the ride or die chicks
Representing the community
Enforcing thug laws
Coming up with new strategy

There's Always A Light

No one babysitting you
So to eat you have to study
And come up with ways
To get food when you're hungry
With police always around
They're like our biggest enemy
You might be making a thug stop
And get hit with a conspiracy

If I have to make a thug stop
To holla at a shortie
I'll pull up on her block
No matter how it's crazy
If I have to make a thug stop
To get what someone owes me
I'll make it in a minute
With the Shinazz posse
Some leave never to return
Only to meet their calamity
Some come back for a funeral
Where the casket bears their body
Old friends gather to mourn
Oh no, what a pity
He could have made a thug stop
Before last stop at the cemetery

What a thug stop really is
I have to make it clear
It's chillin with your people
Let them know you still care
A thug stop can be made
Anytime anywhere
Some won't do it
Because they're filled with fear
Thinking they'll be pressured
With more than they can bear
Or they just don't have that love
Never was sincere
Lying about where they're from

While family is still there
I'm gonna make a thug stop
For my team I have to cheer

I got to realize that we're all individuals connected by blood, marriage, friendship, associations and are bonded by love. Many times, our differences cause frustration, arguments, breakups, and sometimes fights. With all that our differences cause us to go through, the bond of love will never be broken. I had some real-life experiences with people that I loved and who also loved me. My behavior and actions put loved ones through pain that would sometimes frustrate them which led to arguments. My personality, spirit, beliefs, attitude, and boldness sometimes caused others to challenge me negatively. Even my love of the color green would cause a bad vibe with some. I started understanding these differences and got better at accepting others and also became more forgiving. I mentioned earlier about arguments and fights I had with family and friends that I made peace with, and I'll be talking more about that later on.

If I feel like you genuinely hate me and are trying to hurt me, then we have a problem. That's rarely the case though. An open conversation sometimes solves the problem. Other times you might have to leave it alone for a while and with respect for each other, the bond of love will work it all out. After all, we're one same bloodline. I wanted my people to know how I was feeling so I picked up a pen and started writing. A simple way I like to put it is that people will put themselves on whatever shelf they would like in your life by the way they treat you. Not everyone is going to be a top-shelf friend. Those are very rare and as good of a person as they might be, they still can't be a top-shelf friend to all. We all have shortcomings, bad ways, and secret faults. The better we understand them in each other, the better the relationship could be. Some of us keep running around looking for top-shelf friends when we are not even a friend on the floor. Remember we are all part of a bigger puzzle, one big picture.

The Same Bloodline

I'm from my Mom's bloodline
But I keep my Pop's spirit

There's Always A Light

She couldn't understand
From where I get my habits
Couldn't believe it's me
The baby she used to cherish
Hate to see me in pain
Or taking a beating from life's whip
She always said if I didn't change
There's no way I can make it
Many sleepless nights
Sometimes I pushed her to the limit
When she would shake her head
Sometimes she bit her lips
At times embarrassed me
But on her, I couldn't flip
We're from the same bloodline
And our blood is very thick

It's all good, dog
Even though you made me bringle
Couldn't know the outcome
But I knew you were in trouble
I'm from a strong bloodline
So I was ready to rumble
Until I found out
You were my man's people
A real soulja that I run with
A lion from the jungle
So on the strength of him
I have to be humble
We're from the same bloodline
Though I'm not in your circle
I'm holding it down out here
You're frustrated by the struggle
Try not to cross my path
Cause I'll do what I have to

A lot of days passed
She was messed up in her brain
Thinking to herself

Is she really insane
We're from the same bloodline
And that was very plain
How come I'm so different
To her, no one could explain
She said I always have it easy
But go against the grain
The type that learns the hard way
After feeling some serious pain
She showed me a path to take
Still yet I refrain
So she told me to go my way
And she'll stay in her lane
We're from the same bloodline
So we'll both meet up again
We're two different people
That don't mean I'm messed up
We're two different people
Drinking from the same cup
I can't be like you
You can't be like me
We're two different people
That's just how it be

Sharing my story with you is the next hardest thing to the experience of living it. As I pray right now to God for strength, to be honest with you, back then I prayed some days when I felt weak and empty. It was around this time of my journey that I wrote down this prayer, and after I'm done writing I'll move on with my story just like I did then.

I Will Follow You

Show me where to go
And I will follow
Let me reach my destination today
And start a new journey tomorrow
Show me the right turns
Let me see the arrows

115

There's Always A Light

Lest I stray
Onto a path that is too narrow
Which leads to destruction
Pain and sorrow
Give me the mind to repay
Everyone from whom I borrow
Give me the strength I need
To control my ego
Use me as a vessel
Let me be your hero
Show me the way
Lord, I'm ready to follow
You showed me the right turn
Still, I went the wrong way
Keep giving the feeling
That lets me know when I stray
You are my shepherd
Don't let me become a prey
You tell me to move
Sometimes I delay
Sometimes I leave
When you're telling me to stay
For spiritual sight
Dear Lord, I pray
I see your footsteps in the sand
But I can't see them in the clay
Decisions I have to make
The tuff parts of the day
Tell me what to do, Lord
I'll follow what you say

To do things your way
Sometimes come with pain
Then right thereafter
Showers of blessings like rain
Meet me at the crossroad
Hear me when I call your name
When I call on anyone else

Seems like it's always in vain
Only feel good outside
Inside my sorrows still remain
Lord, please be my head coach
Teach me how to play this game
Win, lose, or draw
Help me not to complain
But keep following your teachings
Let them stick in my brain
Lord, I'll follow all your plays
Just make them clear when you explain.

It was over two years now since I got home from jail and even though my mind was in a much better place, the struggle with some things continued. Things with Marie and I fell further and further apart. The good thing was that we always maintained a good relationship and mutual respect. She was now like family and a good friend. I was cool with her whole family, even her mom. One day she told me that she was going to file the papers for a divorce. I told her I was cool with it. It went through very smoothly. It even seemed like things got better between us with time. There wasn't any reason for the occasional arguments anymore. We had a good understanding. Natalie and I got much closer since I had gotten home. There was a connection between us that would always pull us back together. She was now living in New York so I would visit her, and she would always come to Jersey.

Esric and Maureen had two daughters which were our goddaughters. It was only right since we met at their wedding and most of our courting took place around them. We would hang out at their place all the time. I was still working nights, so I only got to party on Friday and Saturday nights. It was mostly Esric, Ninja, Gramps, sometimes Duke, and me. Duke wasn't the type to come out to the bars but if we were going to a party, he would ride sometimes. He hardly missed the house parties. He was more of a drink-in-the-house type of guy. He loved when I stopped by which I did regularly since he was right in the hood. Sometimes when I left his place, I would just walk across the street to check Ricky or just to hang out with whoever was out chilling. Sometimes I would link up with Lucky when he got off from work.

Theresa was always around Ricky with Tina, Tracey, April, and a few others. They were always around somewhere. I started hanging out with Theresa more. She was cool, but when she drank it was trouble. I didn't like that. Her sister, Shereka, was the opposite. She was always cool no matter what. I got along with all of them. I knew a few DJs. Everyone knew me and I knew a few spots so I would promote parties. I loved music and some of my boys were also into it. Chinkie started his own sound system called Ghetto Rock. He and his brother Raka were the DJs. My boy Parky, who was in New York, also had his sound system called Traction Sound, and another one of my boys, Kiwi, had a system called Love Vibration. I had the two original big sound systems, Super Love and Unity Sound. They were more for the bigger dances. When I promoted a party, I would do my best to make it fun even if I didn't make a profit. I was happy if it was fun for everyone.

Chapter 6

The New Millennium

Here Come the Babies

It was now the year 2000. God didn't come, the computers didn't crash and none of the crazy predictions happened. No one could have predicted all that was about to happen in my life. To start the year off, my boy reached out to me because he wanted to make a movie in Bermuda, but he didn't know anyone there. He knew I had a cousin living there so he asked me to link him with my cousin who already knew him. I set it up and he flew to Bermuda. He was staying at a hotel where my cousin went to visit him. While my cousin was there, the police ran down on them and arrested both of them. They ended up charging my boy for drug smuggling, and they released my cousin since he didn't know what was going on. My boy got bailed out, but he couldn't leave the island until the case was over. There was also a girl involved. She was the one that implicated my boy. While all this was going on, I was here losing my mind because I was not sure what was happening. I couldn't make any phone calls, and I felt like I was the cause for my cousin to get caught up. I wasn't sure if I was caught up in it myself. To make matters worse, my boy had a baby boy back here. He was his first child, and they were very close. I knew that being away from him was hurting him more than anything else.

Next thing, I found out that Theresa was pregnant with my baby. My head was now spinning. I was thinking everything from I wasn't ready, she's not ready, what if I was deported, how was Natalie going to feel since things were getting good with us and I didn't want to hurt her, what was Theresa's mom going to say. The most serious part was the fact that I felt like I was not going to be able to live up to the standards my dad set for me. With time, I started feeling better. Dread was still around showing me the positive side like always. I talked to her mom, and she was very cool and respectful. That took some weight off me, and the one thing she asked of me was to be a father to the baby. That was not an option for me. I wanted to be the best dad. I had pressure building up in my head. When Natalie found out, that pressure exploded. I was hurting for her, mad at myself, and found myself in a mental breakdown. It was like getting hit with a wave of a rip current and getting disoriented for a little while.

When I came back, and the smoke cleared, Natalie was gone. There was nothing I could say or do but wish her the best and cherish the love I had for her. Now it was me and a baby girl that I was looking forward to meeting one day. As if enough hadn't happened in my life already, I introduced a girl I was very close with to this Jamaican guy I knew. He sent her to Jamaica and gave her some drugs to carry back to the U.S. She got busted at the airport and was now in jail in Jamaica. Now it was all over town that I sent her, and it was my drugs that she got busted with. That was the last thing I needed in my life at that point. Everyone was talking about it, but I knew the truth and kept my head high. I kept pushing through. I got into a fight with the guys after I asked one of my friends that she knew to visit her while he was on vacation in Jamaica. I found out they were not helping her, so I had to step in. I was constantly thinking about it when I was awake. When I went to sleep, I would dream about what was going on in my life. One day, I picked up my pen and started writing.

What's Going On?

What's going on in the world
Everything seems like a mystery
Heads up waiting on God to come
Some still worship Hailie Selassie
All the things they did to Cuba
Castro still standing with his army
All the bad things that I heard
Some of his people still seem happy

The New Millennium – Here Come the Babies

What's really going on
With the sanctions against Gaddafi
And I'm still trying to find out
Is Sadaam really our enemy
Or it's just a political warfare
So he's fighting for equality
If love is what the world needs
Why they fought against Bob Marley
Or it's because they couldn't understand
The harsh words of reality
What's going on around here
Can anybody tell me

What's going on in my life
Only God knows
Ain't nothing happening
Everything is moving slow
Is it the hills getting steeper
Or it's my energy getting low
Feels like I'm begging all day
And all I'm hearing is no
I've been hustling for so long
Thought by now I'd be a pro
Every day brings something new
Another pain another woe
My life is like a river
Always on a constant flow
So many different episodes
Like I'm starring a cowboy show
The good, bad, and the ugly
Me and my boys searching for dough
One of my seeds already sprung
Now it starts to grow
I have to find out what's going on
I never came this way before

Somebody tell me what's going on
I'm getting confused
Always been a winner

There's Always A Light

You know I hate to lose
Never was the type to stress
I call that self-abuse
The quickest way to kill yourself
Easiest way to blow a fuse
People are going out like that
But for me I refuse
This experience has me bugging
Every day is bad news
My head is just above water
I can't afford to snooze
From your view, it's looking good
But put yourself in my shoes
Then you'll probably realize
Life is not a steady cruise
I need to know what's going on
Why am I paying all these dues

What's going on
Can somebody tell me
My boy got bit in Bermuda
Trying to bake bread for the family
Can't make his visits
Because of immigration policy
I'm here feeling his pain
I'm suffering his agony
Feds trying to smoke Scorcha
They got him in the county
Waiting for sentencing
On charges he thought was petty
Trying to find out what's going on
And I heard some other story
My girl got bit in Jamaica
Now she's in the penitentiary
I'm here fussing with these cats

To at least look out for her baby
What the hell is going on
My world is going crazy

At this point, I was just living in the moment. My mind was all over the place. Working on the night shift was even more stressful since I wasn't getting enough sleep during the daytime. I pushed through one day at a time. I started focusing more on my baby girl entering the world. Theresa's sister, Shereka, stepped up to help me with understanding the journey I was about to embark on, and she helped me with communicating better with Theresa. Not too long before, she had her baby girl so she was there to share her experience with her sister which was a blessing. She was my go-to person with everything concerning Theresa and the baby. She never got tired of me. With time, things got better. I started feeling excited to meet my baby girl. At times, I would feel bad for Theresa as a young new mother bearing a child in a less than preferred situation, but with the help of Shereka, her mom, and some of her friends, she was getting by. Late one evening I got a call that she went into labor. I rushed to check on her. She was doing fine and was in good care. They told me it would be a while before she had the baby so I left to call my job and let them know I wouldn't be coming to work that night. I also let my brother and my parents know what was happening. My mind was running all over the place. I was wondering if the baby was going to be okay and if Theresa was going to be able to handle the pain. My biggest worry was if I was going to be around long enough for my daughter to know me. I went back and waited. Just like all the other times, Shereka was right there too.

Shortly after midnight my baby girl, Deedee, entered the world and with her, I felt like I also entered a new world. Both she and her mom were doing good which took a lot of pressure off of me. After the excitement calmed down, they took the baby away, and Theresa went to sleep. Shereka and I left together. It was now early in the morning and before I dropped her off, we sat in the car and talked for a while. It felt like we had gotten to one destination and immediately started another, but at that moment it was a celebratory mood. After I dropped her off, I went home to get some sleep. So much was going through my mind that I couldn't fall asleep.

From a very young age, I got to understand life and death. In Sunday school and during church services, they talked a lot about death and being ready to go to heaven. The thought of death used to be so scary that I would do anything not to think about it. As I got older I started understanding and accepting the fact that death was inevitable, and it could happen at any moment. Now that I had a newborn daughter, there was so much I was wishing for her. If I only had one wish it would have been for both of us to live long enough to have a conversation. Like I had been doing, I decided to write a message to her expressing what I was thinking so I picked up my pen and notebook.

> To my daughter Deedee,
> 4:25 a.m.

I will do my best to give you the energy and strength you need to walk the path of life. I will do anything possible and within my belief, including putting my life on the line for you. I'm walking my path and sometimes I get weak or lazy, but I call on my higher power, which I choose to call God, for strength.

On this day in November 2000 at 12:39 a.m., you came into this part of the world and I'm truly thinking there's something very special about you, a true star that will shine in any place that you're present. I will help you to search, find and nourish all the brightness in you. Always remember luck won't do it. You have to practice and work toward anything you want and it's possible.

Do not blame anyone or anything for your disappointments. Search for the lessons and try again. Also, know when to let go. If I should be sleeping when you grow up always remember Daddy loves you. Don't mourn for me, live and enjoy yours. Keep in touch with the one who sent you, your Creator. Search yourself for him. He will be with you. One way to do it is to pray and read your Bible. I hope and pray that we will get to sit and talk about some of these things. Think Big!!! Stay hot!!! Keep focused!!! Be safe!!!

Daddy loves you

Later that day after I got up I got some flowers and balloons, and with my letter in hand, I visited them. When I got to the room there was another girl that we knew in there with her baby she had sometime after I had left earlier that morning. I read my letter out loud to baby Deedee and I later got it printed on paper, along with a picture of me holding her in the hospital. I framed it and gave it to her mom. It was now a new day in my life. I always had the strongest love and loyalty to give but no one had tested the depth of it up until now. After being betrayed and let down by close people time after time, I got very cautious with my love and loyalty. When my daughter was born, I felt joyful that I could now express all the love and loyalty I knew I had in me to someone that was the blood of my blood.

My dad sat me down and he could not have said it better. He told me the little baby girl belongs to God. He's only asking me to take care of her for him here on Earth. He told me to do my best and that I would be greatly rewarded. He also said if I didn't, how could I expect him to take care of me. As a very spiritual person, I understood him loud and clear. I vowed that I would never let anything, or anyone come between me and my baby girl. I've raised baby birds from being a few days old to see them fly, lay eggs, and have baby birds themselves. I've raised hundreds of baby chicks to see them lay eggs or used for meat. I took care of goats, piglets, and puppies. I was pretty good at taking care of all those animals and I didn't doubt that I would be a good father to my baby girl.

Working at night gave me time during the day to take her to all her doctor visits. I took her to get all her shots. I would pick her up every morning and drop her off at the babysitter's and then pick her back up in the evenings. I would drop by sometimes during the day. I remember going to pick her up one evening and the babysitter met me at the door. The babysitter was a Spanish lady and all she kept saying was "Papi, Papi, Papi" with a look on her face. I started wondering what was going on. She made a phone call and gave me the phone. It was her daughter, and she explained to me that my daughter had fallen and split her bottom lip. I walked into the room where she was sleeping in the crib. My heart was broken when I saw her lip. She opened her eyes as soon as I picked her up, but she did not give me her usual smile or excitement. For a few days, my daughter did not smile. No matter what I did, she wouldn't smile and that was not like her. She was always happy. Her lip was swollen, she was getting a fever at night and her nose was running. The look on her face had me in pain. I was at work thinking about her and started writing.

I'm Gonna See You Smile Again

My baby ain't smile in a few days
Feels like it's forever
Crying with a runny nose
Roasting from a fever
Cold on her chest
She has diarrhea
Not a smile on her face
Serious as a monster
Not used to seeing her like this
It hurts to watch her suffer
Even though it could be worse
Things need to get better
It's not a blizzard or a storm
But it's still bad weather
I need to see her smiling face
So what it looks like I can remember

Can't smile now
I know that you're hurt
Experiencing a drought
You're crossing a desert
Put a lot of time in
But things didn't work
If there's nothing to smile about

Just let me get a smirk
Only if I could show you
How much your smile is worth
And how much you're really valued
All the times you smiled since birth
For anything to make you smile
I'm in constant search
I'm gonna see you smile again
For now, I'm staying alert

Smile for a while
And give your face a rest
You're frowning too long
Do what you do best
From a sad situation
Bring out the happiness
Don't matter whose fault
You're already in a mess
Another experience
It's probably just a test
But you're taking it too hard
I hate to watch you stress
If not before the day breaks
It might be before sunset
I'm gonna see you smile again
What time, I don't know yet

It wasn't long before my baby was smiling again. She brought a kind of joy I never felt before. I was on cloud nine. I wanted to know where she was, who she was with, and what she was doing at all times. My over protectiveness caused her mom a lot of stress, but at that time I didn't know better. I just wanted my baby girl to be okay. It was stressful at times for her mom, but she had a strong family support system. Her mom, who I call Nana, was there and Shereka too. My mom was always there for baby Deedee. One of my wishes was for Deedee to grow up to experience the type of person my mom was. Telling her about her grandmother could never be the same as having her own experience with her. They met at the hospital the day she was born. That was very special for me. It was the start of a great relationship and the first step of my dream come true.

I was with my baby girl every chance I got. She went everywhere with me, and I mean everywhere. I loved holding her in my arms. I hardly ever used a stroller because carrying her in my arms was the best feeling. Sometimes, I would just walk around with her instead of driving. One day I was walking down the street with her, and a car pulled up next to me. It was Natalie. It had been about a year since I had seen her. She asked if she could see the baby and I said sure. I opened the car door and sat in the car. I handed her the baby and she talked and played with her for a little while. It felt good to see her smiling again and showing my baby love. I immediately felt relieved of the pressure I had been carrying around knowing how much I had hurt her. When she drove off, I was singing and dancing with my baby girl down the street. We started staying in touch again. It was like we picked up where we left off.

My daughter was now my biggest motivation. I wanted it all. I was writing more, and I was anywhere the music or studio was. I was trying to learn the process of writing and recording a song. I didn't know anyone that was into recording music, so I had to find my way. I was meeting a lot of people in the music business, and I bought a couple of books to educate myself. I got connected with the host of a show on the local cable channel called Real Reggae. He invited me to the program in May of 2001. At that time, I had a song that I had written but hadn't yet recorded. I decided to talk about that song on the program with him because it was a message to the street youth. The title of the song was *Everywhere is Dawgs*. What inspired me to write that song was the fact that all my life, I had been listening to people in the streets talking about where they were from as if it made them more gangster than another guy from another place. I was hearing it in Jamaica and hearing it here in America. It starts from this street or that street, uptown or downtown, my town or your town, the city or the suburbs, town or country, eastside, westside or southside, this state or that state, this region or that region, this gang or that gang. I began to realize that none of that mattered. There were gangsters everywhere. I met them everywhere I went, and I wanted to send the message to those who didn't know.

<u>Everywhere Is Dawgs</u>

Dawgs are fighting in the streets
The cities running red
Dawgs are in the suburbs
So the war starts to spread
Government strengthen defense
All the churches beg
Pitbulls are involved
So it's a lot of bloodshed
Dawgs that don't take shorts
They'll give it instead
Never let them get the feeling
Like it's you have the edge
That's when they'll get nasty
And wet you up with leads
I can hear dawgs barking
From the prison beds

Dawgs are in the west
I run with dawgs in the east
I've seen dawgs up north
And in the south like beasts
Different race, different place
Dawgs from different creeds
Different names, different colors
Dawgs from every breed
Dawgs with three legs
From wounds, dawgs bleed
Dawgs are fighting
Cause of envy and greed
With all that hate in them
How can there be any peace
Dawgs are fighting
The war is at its peak

There's Always A Light

You're not the only dawg
Out here on this route
Cut your speech, shut your mouth
What you're talking about
Dawgs are all around
Listen to the sound
Out in L.A.
They keep dawgs in pounds
Pitbulls are in the east
Roaming the city streets
Some dawgs are getting weak
Can't find nothing to eat
Biting without teeth
Is like burning without heat
Every day in this war
For real dawgs, I have to seek

My dawgs ain't here
But I'm gonna keep it gangsta
Calm as a lamb
With the spirit of a gorilla
Only trying to eat
Was never a troublemaker
Plead guilty from the door
Didn't even need a lawyer
Your boys ain't around
So you're talking to the prosecutor
Promise to hold them down
But you turned an informer
Dawgs are everywhere
You should have known better
Now you're on the run
Trying not to get murdered

I talked with the host of the show about the message in the song for the first half of the program, and then I performed. There's a saying that goes: "It's not where you're from but where you're at." For me, I learned to show respect to everyone no matter our differences. Respect hasn't failed me yet; it works.

My brother and a few other members use to hold church in a house and travel to New York on some Sundays to attend church services at a church that was part of the body of churches we belonged to in Jamaica. They later rented a place to hold worship. My brother was now an ordained Minister just like my dad was. They were both Pastors at the church. It was another special experience for me and my family when they both officiated the christening of my daughter. I was a son of the church and having my friends, family, and church members around was a blessing. Some of the church people knew me since I was as small as my daughter was. It was a historic moment that I knew my daughter would grow up to cherish. We got together later that evening and celebrated my way with food, music, and lots of drinks. A few weeks later, the whole world changed.

I came home from work on the morning of September 11, 2001, and like I usually did I ate, showered, and went to bed. I would watch the morning news while getting ready for bed. I always said my prayers before getting into bed. On that morning, I muted the television before kneeling beside my bed to say my prayer. When I opened my eyes I saw breaking news across the television screen with the picture of the World Trade Center. One of the towers had smoke coming out of it. I unmuted the television to find out it was a plane that flew into the building and the rest started to unfold. I was watching when the second plane flew into the other building. At that point, I felt like it flew into my heart.

I mentioned earlier in the book what New York meant to me. I couldn't explain how I felt even if I tried. I got up, put my clothes on, grabbed my backpack with my notebook and I went to the park. I still wasn't sure what was happening, but I was numb, lost, angry, and very hurt so as I've always done, I poured my heart out onto paper. I didn't know of anyone that may have been in the city at that time. Natalie was still in New Jersey after visiting for her grandmother's funeral. On my way to the park, I ran into one of my friends and he followed me there. We sat on the grass under a tree and talked for a little while. He used to live in New York, so he was sharing how he was feeling. After he left, I sat there for a little while before I started to write. I felt a dark gloom over me. I kept looking up as if I was looking out for planes and with tears running down my cheeks I wrote…

I'm Feeling Your Pain New York

I'm feeling your pain, New York
I'm feeling your pain

New York, you're at the front line
Holding it down for many years
Representing all people
Through blood sweat and tears
I know that you're not sorry
I know you have no fear
All your people are with you
People from everywhere
You've blessed many nations
So many lives you've spared
New York, you are the greatest
You've just made it clear

I'm feeling your pain, New York
I'm feeling your pain

It's daytime in the city
But it's like midnight
Sky overcast with death
New York is paying a price
You never go to sleep
But this time you just might
There's one thing that I'm sure of
You'll never lose your life

Stay awake New York
I'm with you in this fight
Your war is my war
Cause when I bark you bite

I'm feeling your pain, New York
I'm feeling your pain

Smoke in your air
Dust carpets the earth floor
Water mixed with blood
Disaster is on your shore
Open arms to many nations
Now you've closed your doors
Only for protection
And to keep yourself secure
You've helped a lot of people
And you'll still be helping more
The Lord promised to bless those
Who look out for the poor

I'm feeling your pain, New York
I'm feeling your pain

What you're going through
Is just to make you stronger
Even when you're hurting
They still can't take over
You took a big loss
But it's still not over
The nation is around you
Like a crutch under your shoulder
New York, you set the pace
You are the trendsetter
I know you'll be around
As long as the Hudson River

I spent most of the day in the park. In the afternoon, people started to gather around and everyone was sharing their story of the day and their feelings. Theresa even dropped Deedee off to me. The country was pretty much in lockdown all day, so I figured I wasn't going to have to work later that night. I was wrong. It was late in the evening when I found out that I had to go to work. I tried to get some sleep before I went, but I wasn't able to. I pushed through at work.

During the days and weeks following those tragic events, I found myself in a deep state of anger especially after seeing the aftermath and the rising death tolls. I was so angry I felt like I wanted to join the Army if I was allowed to. As I mentioned earlier, it was only a few months since I was on the Real Reggae television program. I called the host to tell him about the song I wrote and how I was feeling about the attacks. There were a lot of different sentiments floating around at that time. I felt like I wanted to make mine clear, so I asked him to bring me back to the program. He was excited about the idea, so we set up a date and time for an in-studio recording. By this time, everyone around me knew my views on the attacks and some already heard the song I had written.

I shared with my friends and family the upcoming appearance on the program to speak on the events of September 11th. It seemed like everyone was living on edge from all the different information that was circulating in the media. Everyone was looking up at every sight and sound of a plane. Some were looking at people from the Middle East as the enemy. Some people were very vocal while some were scared to express their true feelings. My mom thought it was a bad idea to speak on the television. She felt the terrorists could be among us listening. I didn't care if the host himself was one; I went. We spoke about the attacks and the aftermath. I shared my feelings with TV Land and then I read the words I had written. It was a great relief to let out most of what I was feeling inside. I was also closely following the wars that were going on and then something else happened.

God gave me my most challenging assignment yet. Natalie was now pregnant with my son. My daughter Deedee was not even a year old and my relationship with her mom was already challenging. Now it was a constant battle. I knew I was responsible for the situation I found myself in, and I didn't want to cause any pain for anyone, but I did. That bothered me a lot. With all that was going on, the one thing I knew was that I was not leaving my daughter. I had no idea how it was going to work but I knew it had to. One good thing was that Natalie had accepted my daughter and always welcomed her with open arms. As time went on, Theresa calmed down and she never let anything get between my baby girl and me. It was one day at a time with ups and downs, but the joy my baby girl brought into my life was all the strength I needed to keep going. I had no idea how I was going to be there for two babies in separate homes, but I was excited for my son to join our team. Natalie was very strong, responsible, and caring which gave me great comfort for my baby son. She always showed love to my baby girl, even during her pregnancy.

One evening, I was driving in the car with a friend, and I got a call that Natalie was in labor and heading to the hospital. I told my friend, he would have to go with me, and I would get him a ride home. We headed straight to the hospital. When I got there it wasn't as crazy as I thought it would be. Natalie was calm even though she was in some pain and discomfort. After she got settled, they told me it would be a while so if I had anything to do or if I wanted to get something to eat, I could do that. My friend was still there so I left to drop him off, get something to eat, and let my family know that my baby boy was on his way to meet us, and that Natalie was doing good. Natalie's mom who I called Grandma was there with her. I will never forget watching them insert the epidural needle into her back. I was feeling the pain for her. I had to turn my head away. After it was all set up, and when I saw that she was okay, I felt some relief. I knew the real challenge was ahead. That long needle so close to the spine caused me to think the worst. We were now into a new day and my baby boy was still not born. I was a little disappointed because I thought he was coming on my big brother's birthday. But, he and God had their plan. It wasn't long after the new day of May 2002 at 1:02 a.m. that my baby boy, Danny, came into this world. Two hands, two feet, ten fingers, ten toes, two eyes, two ears, a nose, a mouth, and all were functioning properly. If there's one time you want to hear a baby cry, it is in that moment. It's like he was saying I'm here and I'm good.

Mommy was exhausted and in some pain, but joyfulness was paramount. They cleaned up baby Danny, weighed him, and did their routine before taking him away so mommy could get some rest. It was another glorious day in my life. With a baby girl and now a baby boy, I felt blessed. A lot was going through my mind driving home that morning but the one thing that I was most excited about was for my daughter to meet her brother. I couldn't wait. Later that day I got up, kind of in a new world, and took my mom with me to visit baby Danny and Natalie. I knew challenging times were ahead of me, but at that moment I was joyful and excited that my baby boy was here, healthy and blessed. His mom was also doing great. Baby Danny came home, and the real work started. The time and attention I was giving my baby girl now had to be shared with her brother. I told myself that I was not going to dwell on the past and the way it should be, but would focus on what I had to do going forward. I wanted to do the best for both of them. I was still working the night shift which worked out better for us. I had time in the days to be there for all the doctor visits, drop off and pickups, and for whatever I was needed for. Some days, I had to sacrifice my sleep, but I knew that was a small sacrifice compared to what their mothers had to go through.

I took Deedee to meet her baby brother, and it was something like love at first sight. It was more of a divine connection. Deedee was only a year and a half old but immediately claimed big sister status. She just wanted to hug him, feed him, and take care of him. Thanks to Natalie, she had already been introduced to her little brother while he was still in the womb. It was like she had been waiting with us. My one biggest worry was that they could grow apart from each other and not be as close as I wished. I have three siblings that I did not grow up around, and the connection is not there like it is with my siblings that I did grow up with. I love all my siblings, but the connection is different. I knew I had to do everything to keep the babies as close as possible so they could build their relationships with each other. I wanted them to have a steady memory of their times together. If there is anyone that believes in family ties, it is me. That's how I was raised. Now I had my own family to keep together despite the circumstances. Peas of the same pod—that was how I felt about my babies and me. They were me and I was them and that could never be changed. All three of our names start with the letter D so I came up with the name D-Pod to identify us as one. I wanted to declare them as part of me to the world.

As they got older, my actions would make them feel secure and loved. I changed the record label name I had started from Shinazz Entertainment to D-Pod Records. They were now my main source of energy to pursue my music, so I felt like it was only right to include them in the building of the foundation. As I wrote earlier, I always watched Channel 11 news while getting ready for work. Then in the morning, I would watch the morning news on the same channel. After the morning news, *The Maury Show* would come on and I would sometimes watch part of it before going to sleep. I didn't like seeing men and sometimes their family members criticizing babies and young children who sometimes turned out to be their child, grandchild, niece, or nephew. I planned to make sure that my kids never felt abandoned, alone, left out, not loved, or felt like they didn't belong. I was going to be at the doctor visits, games, teacher meetings, concerts, and all the milestone celebrations. They were living in separate homes in different towns which were miles apart. I was the bridge that linked them together.

Some days were really hard especially when I was being pulled or pushed to one side, but my love for both of them would never allow that to happen. I made all my decisions and choices concerning my kids out of pure love and not what seemed equal or fair to their mothers or anyone else. I always asked God to give me the strength to put them first before my feelings. If you know me you're going to know I have two kids. If you're just meeting me, not long after you're going to know I have two kids. I started mentioning them in songs and I would even mention them on flyers for the parties I threw. I would take Deedee to visit Danny all the time, and she was always excited to see him. It didn't take him too long to start recognizing her. We spent a lot of time together. Eventually, we were hanging out every Friday evening. It was our together time. I wasn't the stroller-pushing kind of dad. We were always walking. Most of the time, I had Danny in my arms and Deedee was walking next to me. She was a very understanding big sister, but she would get tired sometimes, and I had to pick her up also. Even though my arms would get tired, it felt good being close to them. When they were in their car seats behind me in the car, it sometimes felt uncomfortable for me. I didn't like that I couldn't interact with them. Taking them into New York City by way of the train was one of the most challenging things we would do. Some of my best memories are from these times.

I was still working the night shift from 11:00 p.m. to 7:00 a.m., writing and recording music, throwing parties, and partying. I took my kids to an event in the park on one Saturday. There was a young man there who was in his teens playing a keyboard. I stood there watching and listening to him until he was finished playing. I knew most of the kids in the neighborhood, but I did not know him. I went up to him to congratulate him on his skill and introduced myself to him. He told me that he played for the local Baptist church, and he lived up the street from me. I briefly explained some of the ideas that I had that I thought he could help me bring to life. He was open to my ideas so we exchanged phone numbers. I called him up and went to meet him at his house. His grandparents, his mom, and his little sister were there. I went over some lyrics I had written and explained to him the sounds I was looking for. He was willing to try so we started working one key at a time, time after time, song after song. I had about ten songs that now were alive and had a beat to them. I realized that I had met a musical genius. Even his baby sister was running around trying to sing and dance while he was playing. I brought Deedee with me one evening so they could play while we worked. I will mention more about the songs and the project I worked on with this young genius later on in the book. Before I move on I want to tell you about one song that had a heartbeat from the time I wrote it. This kid gave it life. This song was inspired by Natalie, the mother of my son. These lyrics are the original lyrics to the song I wrote. The title of the song is Pitbull In A Skirt.

Pitbull In A Skirt

She's a pitbull in a skirt
I don't know how much she's worth
All I know she bites, she bites
She's very down to earth

I heard she been like that since birth
All I know she bites, she bites
A pitbull in a skirt
Her name is Sophia
This thug girl I know
Her people are from Jamaica
Her mom is the church type
And her pops is gangster
Born in the U.S.
Mix with a Caribbean flavor
Stand tall in strong wind
Never crumble under pressure
The type that you meet
And will always remember
Defend what she believes in
Protect it if she's the owner
A pitbull in a skirt
She a true battle soldier

Straight thoroughbred
Top-class quality
Held it down through school
Books she loves to study
Break bread with her people
She was never greedy
Very independent
She gets her own money
And all the dogs she run with
Is strong, big, and healthy
A thug dream girl
That could raise a good puppy
The kind that would bite
Although short and fluffy
She's a pitbull in a skirt
That shows her integrity
The most complete girl
I ever came across
With a perfect attitude

And qualities of a boss
Always hold it down
No matter what the cost
Probation or time
She will without remorse
She knows the rule of the game
When playing up north
That without proper gears
You'll get bitten by frost
No rematches
A loss is just a loss
She's a pitbull in a skirt
Hot pepper sauce

She's a pitbull in a skirt
Believe me, I know that
Looking for her?
Check where the big dogs at
Love to ride with her
I know she'll have my back
It's always good for her
A castle or a shack
She's a ride or die chick
But real laidback
The type that goes to church
And sings while she claps
But if on her way home
Another dog should attack
She'll let her doggy out
To eat that as a snack

You'll hear much more about this song later in the book. Every day was something different in my life as you'll see by the time you finish reading this book. There was excitement, sadness, and everything in between.

It was now time for my son to be christened. I felt like I was in a perfect world. Just like they did for my daughter, my dad and my brother officiated the christening. It was another blessing and the greatest feeling to have my family, friends, and my extended church family present for such an important day in my son's life. I know God comes first in our lives followed by family and friends. I truly believe it takes a village to raise a child, and the more contributions there are the stronger the foundation. After the ceremony, we gathered at a hall to celebrate. It was joyful and a display of togetherness. Even Natalie's dad that I was not getting along with came and it was all love. Danny was the man of the moment. He had a host of kids celebrating with him especially his big sister who was talking non-stop and running around. Other than my parents, it was an honor to have the two wise guys there that picked me up at the airport when I first came to the United States—my uncle Leslie, and my adopted uncle Craigie.

They got to watch the relationship between Natalie and me blossom into this baby boy. One of the highlights of the whole thing was how everything was falling into place with me being able to keep these babies together. This was in part thanks to Natalie for opening up her arms to my daughter. I was very protective of my daughter. We were all so close that you would not know we were not all living under the same roof. After all, togetherness does not mean you have to live under the same roof or be present in person. This one was the connection of the hearts which was the greatest of them all.

A few months after my son's christening, my uncle Leslie passed away. During the last couple of years of his life, he would go to Jamaica every December. He would stay there for a few months and return in the spring. As I mentioned earlier, he had a major problem with his heart which led to a heart transplant. He had to be on medication for the rest of his life. He got sick right before he was to return to the United States and died in Jamaica. He died in the community where we are from so he was around family and friends. He was a mechanic all his life. He did work for a lot of people especially the people that couldn't afford to go to the car dealer or a regular garage. Most of his family and friends were here in the United States where he lived and worked for many years. His death truly hurt me. I was sad that neither my daughter nor my son would have the opportunity to get to know him. The family decided to bury him in Jamaica. I couldn't travel there at that time which brought me more pain. We got together to celebrate his life before they left for the funeral in Jamaica. This did bring me some comfort. My uncle Leslie will forever be part of my life. May his soul rest in peace.

At this point in my life, it was all about my babies. In everything I did, I thought of them. They brought me joy that I had never felt before. They became my biggest motivators. I was more determined to succeed. Due to my situation with immigration, I cherished and appreciated every day that I got to spend with them. In between all the good days were some bad days. There were days that I was tired, frustrated, lonely, hurt, or confused but I always found a way to fight through those feelings and keep going. There were days that it was one or both of my kids that were sick, cranky, mad, or just not in the mood, but I got better at understanding it was all just a part of our journey. I was always a compassionate person, but my kids brought me to a higher level of compassion, especially when they were sick. It would hurt my heart to see them sick. I could never forget the changing of the diapers, especially when we were on the road. I would have to make sure one was safe and comfortable before changing the other. The men's room would never have a changing table in it, so my daughter was a different type of challenge. I must say people were always offering their help to me. The older my daughter got, the more challenging it got because I didn't feel comfortable taking her into the men's room anymore. I would sometimes ask strangers, women, to take her in the women's room while I waited by the door. We made lots of friends on our journey. It was the sweetest thing to get the smiles, thumbs up, compliments, and the random stranger walking up to us to start a conversation.

I will never forget taking them to Rockefeller Center in New York City to see the Christmas tree. If you have any idea what Times Square is like the day before Christmas, you know what a challenge it was for me and with no stroller. I'll just say it was very fun and adventurous. By the time we got back on the train, I was exhausted, so I relaxed while they were next to me playing. My daughter came over to me and said "Daddy, tell Danny Santa Claus is not real." I said no in agreement with her. A lady was sitting across from us, and she yelled "Don't tell him that." But we continued our conversation. When the lady was getting off the train she walked over to give my son a dollar and said Merry Christmas kid. It was a very weird moment. My daughter looked at me while I was looking at them and then we laughed at the whole thing. I was thinking to myself how dare this lady tell me how to raise my kids and then give a dollar to one as if she was mad at the other. It was not that serious for her to do that, but it was a learning moment for me. We are all different people. My daughter kept bringing it up for many years afterward.

Chapter 7

Trouble Strikes Again

Always Something

I was still involved in the music thing, working, and hanging out with my friends as I loved doing. Like I mentioned before, at times I found myself between two friends. I hadn't seen my old friend Tafari since the incident I had with him. One Saturday evening I was at a barbecue that a friend of mine was having on the street I lived on. Natalie was also there with my cousin Patrick and me. We stayed there for a while and were drinking and having a good time until Patrick and I decided to go to a party at a hotel in East Orange. Patrick was driving, so I told Natalie to stay at the house and we would be right back. We planned to just go by the party to give the promoter that we knew our support, have a drink, and head back home. Nothing went as planned. As soon as we got to the party which was on the second floor we stumbled upon Tafari who instantly was in Patrick's face saying something. I stepped up closer to him and told him to "leave the man alone" and we kept walking to the very crowded bar. While we were trying to get a drink, there was Tafari again pushing up against us. I was already feeling good from drinking earlier, so I was not playing. I said to him "didn't I tell you to leave the man alone, back up!" He started saying that we couldn't come outside, and then he walked away.

We stayed at the bar until we got two bottles of Heineken. After standing around at the party for a few minutes I said to Patrick, "We should go now." We went downstairs to exit the place. As we were headed to the car, Tafari walked toward us talking. I said to him, "Why are you still talking? Didn't you say we couldn't come outside?" While I was talking, I started splashing some of my beer on him. He and I then started to fight.

A plainclothes police officer was sitting inside the doorway. He ran outside toward us, and as soon as we saw him, Patrick and I ran back inside down the hallway to another exit. The cop was running behind us. Tafari was running on the sidewalk toward the back exit. As soon as I exited, he threw a bottle and hit me in the back of my neck. The cop pulled his gun and told us to get down. All three of us got down on the ground. We were immediately surrounded by cops. They arrested all three of us. When the bottle hit me, it made a minor cut on my neck. They took me to get it bandaged, and then put us in separate holding cells. They said we couldn't get bail until we saw the judge on Monday, so we stayed in the holding cell for the remainder of the weekend. We went to court that Monday and the judge released us. Neither one of us pressed charges so the judge dismissed the case. After reflecting on the situation, I knew that if I hadn't been drinking, I would have handled it differently. It was a lesson learned and that was now behind me.

My good friend Ninja had more family who migrated from Jamaica to Morristown. I consider my friends' family to be my family. I took his one cousin Kirk under my wing. Kirk was also Ricky's younger cousin. Even though Kirk was in school, he would always hang out with us. One night Duke had a party at his house with family and friends invited. There was an argument between Shabba and Ninja's cousins, and Shabba hit Kirk in the face with a bottle. The bottle broke and cut him pretty deeply. There was a lot of anger and disappointment amongst everyone since it was all close family and friends there at Duke's house. Kirk had to go to the hospital to get stitches. The police got involved and Shabba got charged. Shabba was like my little brother and Kirk was now like family. I felt like Shabba could have handled it differently knowing that he was at Duke's house, and Kirk was Ninja's little cousin who was also his very close friend. I understood how our judgment is affected when we are drinking, so I tried to not hold it against him. I was trying to bring peace between them.

One day, I was sitting across from the park we used to hang out at, and I was trying to get Kirk to drop the case against Shabba. I looked up and saw that Shabba was in the park. He walked over to where we were and started threatening Kirk. I told him to leave the man alone. "You cut him in his face and now you want to fight him again." He didn't like what I said so he started threatening me too. I got really angry because he was trying to fight this kid that he already violated, and I was there pleading his case. I would not stand around and allow anyone to do that to a total stranger without trying to intervene. I ended up telling him that I was not going to stand by and let him do anything to this kid. We went back and forth for a while until he left. Before he left, he said he was going to get me. I was now aware that our relationship would be different going forward. From that day, it became a constant back and forth with him threatening me every time I saw him. I knew what he was about, so I didn't give him an ounce of attention. I knew he wanted us to get in a fight that ended with the police getting involved; he had nothing to lose. He already had a lot of cases where he was going back and forth to jail. That was the very reason I was begging Kirk to drop the case against him.

For me, on the other hand, I had two priceless babies, parents that I loved dearly, a whole village in Jamaica on my mind, dreams, and goals that I was trying to achieve. It was a constant test of my strength. I started looking at it like it wasn't even the Shabba I knew. It was the devil working through him. The more I ignored him, the angrier he became. Things took a turn when I ran into him one day at the corner store. I had my baby girl with me. He started calling me a pussy and saying I was soft. My daughter wasn't old enough to understand what was going on. I respected her and myself enough to know that he crossed the line. After that day, I started preparing myself mentally for what could happen. My biggest fear was getting deported and having to leave my babies behind. I decided that if that was what was going to happen, he was going to pay big time. The next time I ran into him was in a local bar. He came up to my face talking, and I was amazed as to how many people confronted him. I was just there watching it all occur. He mentioned that it had been a long time since he wanted to kill me. I knew he was either drunk or just talking as usual. He knew where I lived, and I was always out and about, but I did take his words seriously.

The next day, I went to his house. I knocked on the door and someone came to the door. When I asked for him, the person said he didn't live there and was living with his child's mother. I knew the family very well so I said I would go there. I left and went to his child's mother's house who was a good friend of mine. I knocked on the door and her cousin, who I knew very well, opened the door. I asked for Shabba, and she said he wasn't there. I then asked for his child's mother. She said she was upstairs, so I asked to speak to her. She told me that she would be right down, and I could come inside to wait. I turned down the invitation. I was thinking that if he and I were going to get into something I didn't want it to be inside the place he lived. His child's mother came to the door, and I told her what was going on and how I was feeling. I let her know I had had enough. She told me not to pay him any mind and that she would talk to him.

I don't know what happened, but after that day he never said a word to my face again. He was still running his mouth to other people, but I could care less what he was saying. He allegedly even started spreading a rumor that I was gay. I guess that was supposed to make people in the community look down on me. It was a joke to me because I knew who I was. I was never the kind of person who cared what another person thought of me. I took it as a sign of defeat. There were already defeated ones that were happy to join the rumor mill. I used all that energy to keep shining until they got tired and started feeling silly and petty. Even now when I think about it, I thank God for the wisdom, knowledge, and understanding he continues to give me and the strength to control myself, especially in a situation like that. I have seen too many people fall for petty stuff. Some things are serious so it takes good judgment to make the right decision. When we make the wrong decision, we have to own it, learn the lesson, and keep going. It's like playing a video game and continuing to get stuck in the same spot. We are going to be presented with obstacles along our journey. If you can avoid them or maneuver around them, great. If you can't, then put up your best fight. The goal is to get to your destination. Get around them and they will just take on the other guy behind you.

I already knew my situation, but the experience with Shabba opened my eyes to how vulnerable I was. I was not going to let the fear of being deported allow anyone to harm me or my family. I decided to use my time to show love to my loved ones and be better prepared for the worst-case scenario. I had the instrumentals that went along with the lyrics for about ten of the songs I had written thanks to the kid who had recorded them for me. The instrumentals were pretty basic so I now needed to find a producer to work on them so they would be of industry quality. I had been playing around with music for many years, but now I was ready to give it my best shot. What I knew about writing and recording up to this point had come from buying studio time here, there, and everywhere. I had always heard people say it cost to learn and now I know what they meant. I was much more knowledgeable than when I first started. I bought books and magazines to read about making music and the business of music. I had the lyrics of the songs and the instrumentals. Now I had to find the pieces to the puzzle to put them together into professionally recorded songs. The first thing I started to do was arrange the lyrics of each song to fit their beat. Then I practiced singing the lyrics with the instrumentals. While doing all of this, I was also making calls, asking questions, and trying to meet people in the industry.

While working on the music, I had also ventured into modeling. I felt like it was all part of the entertainment business. I did a couple of photoshoots with different photographers. I even did a few fashion shows. After spending time and money, I concluded that music was where my passion was, and it could be the gateway to modeling. I got a referral for Ed Robinson who was a Reggae artist and producer that owned a recording studio in Brooklyn, New York. I called him, and we talked about what I was looking to do. We scheduled a time to meet at the studio. After meeting him, I felt like he was the kind of producer I needed. He was very humble, patient, and fun to be around. The surroundings felt safe. His wife was his business partner and was very nice. The part that stole my heart was that his baby boy was always in the studio with him. Not many established producers are willing to work with an amateur artist like me. He agreed to work with me. The plan was that I would give him the instrumentals to work on in his spare time, and when I was satisfied with the beat, we would start recording.

I was one step closer to my goal of recording an album. In the meantime, I was to arrange the songs how I wanted them, find the voices I needed for features and practice, practice, and practice some more. The more prepared I was, the smoother things would go in the studio. I spent a lot of time in the park by myself going over the lyrics, singing, and even dancing; it was something I loved doing. If I stayed in the park long enough, some people would join in. Eventually, I would have to put my stuff away as there were too many distractions. Some of those distractions would become inspirations due to the vibe.

My close friend Ninja's mom had moved to a house across the street from me along with his sisters. Kirk and his friends were downstairs in the basement. They had a sound system (DJ equipment) down there. Attached to the house was a patio where the older guys would get together to play dominoes, especially on the weekends when there would be a larger crowd. It was a hangout spot for Jamaicans mostly. I was very close to the family and the Jamaican community in general. I was like family to them, so I felt very comfortable there. We would play music, drink, smoke, and have a good time. My nights off from work were Friday and Saturday. At some point on my nights off, I would stop by even if it was just to say hi. Some would say I love the streets not knowing it's the people that I love. I learned from an early age in Jamaica that the separation of people is the cause of most of our issues as humans. If you are doing well, you move away and stay away. If you join a religious group, you find new friends. If you get married, you pull back from family and friends. I could go on endlessly about all the ways that separate us as humans, not to mention race and religion.

When I was growing up I was always drawn to the community and those that serve to build it. Bringing people together can be from bringing two total strangers together to two nations in conflict. We should all strive to build relationships. We tend to follow those before us who tell us what and who we should be. I feel like as long as you know who you are, what you stand for, have morals and values that guide you, and have boundaries, you will be headed in the right direction. Know your direction! Know when to turn, when to stop and when to just keep moving. If you know and practice all these things, there's no reason to fear man.

One of the people I met in my community who was fearless in that sense was a guy called Tyrone. This man was not originally from the community, but he loved the people. He was a barber in one of the only black barbershops in the community. He later became the owner. From there, he built a base for the community; it was much more than a barbershop. He taught young men the skill of barbering because he was a true mentor. He loved and supported the sport of basketball so he made a court in the back parking lot of the shop that kids could play on at any time. He started an annual get-together every summer for the kids where he would have games, music, food, entertainment, motivational speakers, dance contests, awards, and gifts for back to school.

It was also a platform for local DJs and performers to show their talent and build a base within the community. I became a regular performer there. There was a garage in the back where he had a gym set up. He had everything you needed to get and stay in shape. He gave me and people in the community access to use the gym equipment. He told me I could come by anytime and if he wasn't there, I could get the key from one of the barbers in the shop. Tyrone would support anyone in the community even with their issues. He was a genuine person that had a love for people. He had a barbershop that served mainly black people, but there were also Hispanics, whites, and all different races that would come to the barbershop. Tyrone and I became very close friends. I admired his love for people and realized that came with great sacrifices that didn't deter him from showing love to even those that made him vulnerable.

One afternoon while I was working out in Tyrone's garage, a young white boy came out of the barbershop. On his way to his car, he stopped by the garage. He was standing in the driveway watching me.

I said hi to him, and I started talking to him about working out. I asked him if he wanted to join me. He said he had to go but he would love to work out with me another day. He spoke with a very low-toned voice. I could hardly hear him when he was speaking to me. He seemed very shy. I tried to make him feel welcomed and comfortable with me. This was how I already treated any of the kids that were in the gym trying to learn. He asked me what time I usually came there to work out. At that time, I was working out at a local boxing gym which was open between the hours of 5:00 p.m. and 8:00 p.m. Some days they would close to take the fighters to other boxing gyms to spar with other fighters. It was days like those and the days I had something to do in the evening that I would go to Tyrone's garage to work out. Sometimes I would go there in the mornings after work if I had the energy, and that was usually the time Tyrone would be there working out as well. The kid's name was Jay, and he was about 18 years old. We exchanged numbers, so I called him a few times when I was going to Tyrone's, but the timing was always bad. We never got to work out, but we became friends.

Sometimes he would come to town to hang out with me in the park or come on the weekends to grab a six-pack of beer. I took him to the basement and introduced him to Kirk and my other friends. He even got to know my babies because they would sometimes be in the park with me when he would come there. He was a very cool kid and even came with my daughter and me to eat one time. He was a very cool kid. He said that he and his family would vacation in Jamaica every year, so he was very comfortable being around me. He said the only times he saw his father and grandfather smoke weed was when they were in Jamaica, and the last few years he joined in with them. He loved to smoke. I was working on my music so we spent a lot of time talking about that, or he would just listen to us singing or talking. He didn't talk much, especially after he smoked. He would come with his weed. He thought the weed we smoked was garbage. He was from a wealthy family and had a twin sister. He told me that his dad would buy damaged or rejected clothing like t-shirts, underwear, tank tops, and socks in large quantities and ship them to third-world countries. He would express how badly he felt for our struggles and even shared ideas with us about how we could make money.

One day he asked me if I knew anyone he could get good weed from. I told him I knew a guy in East Orange. I called to let the guy know that I was bringing this white kid with me to see him. I didn't want to be in the middle of any deal/transaction. He said he was ok with that, so I took the kid with me to see him. The weed he had was not good enough for the kid, so we got something to smoke and left. I told him I would check with another guy that I knew might have what he was looking for. All this time I was thinking I would like to help him out, get the sale for one of my boys, and I would get a portion for me and my boys in the basement. At that time, I would smoke a joint, then write, sing, or go to the studio or I would bring it with me to the studio to smoke it there. Sometimes on the weekend, we would smoke, drink, and play music to create a party vibe. I had given up hustling years ago so for me, it was not about making money from any drug transaction.

I had become close to another white kid that I worked with and took him to meet my daughter when she was born. He gave her a blanket that his grandmother had knitted. I would sometimes hang out at his house, and he would come out with my friends and me. He also loved to smoke and would bring me weed sometimes. I started feeling the same way about this kid, Jay. The only thing that was different about him from my other boys was the fact that he was white which came with disadvantages. A white boy hanging out with all these black Jamaicans in the park, in a basement with a lot of people coming and going, would automatically become suspicious. Even some of my boys were concerned that he might be a cop. I didn't feel that way about him nor did I care because we weren't doing anything other than hanging out, partying, and playing music. The only thing I was doing that was illegal was smoking weed. At that time, weed was not legal in New Jersey. I set up a time to bring this kid to meet with one of my other boys.

The day before he came to meet me, he called to ask if he should bring the mula (money) and I told him yes. When he came, I had him park his car across the street from the park where we always hung out, and he rode with me. I took him with me because I did not want to be in any kind of drug dealing, not thinking that by facilitating the transaction I would still violate the law. At that time, I innocently didn't feel that way. We went to East Orange and met up with my guy in the parking lot of a shopping center so he could check out the type of weed he had. He didn't like what he had but my boy wanted the sale, so he was trying to talk the kid into buying what he had. The kid knew what he wanted so he wasn't going for it. He was looking for weed without seeds. My guy didn't know anything about weed without seeds. Back then exotic weed was rare and very expensive. I got impatient and told them I had to go because I was meeting my daughter and her mother at a modeling agency in a town that was 15 minutes away. I was running 5 minutes late, so I was very irritated. I got on the highway and like a flash of lightning, I was at the place. My kids come first, before anything else, including me.

He came inside with me and sat in the meeting. On our way back, I told him that I didn't know anyone that was going to have the weed he was looking for. I had heard him say to my guy that if he were to find the type of weed he wanted, he could make him a lot of money. Now I was starting to feel uncomfortable. The only thing on my mind was my two babies who I couldn't afford to leave, especially for going to jail. I told him to forget it and that I couldn't help him. He came around a few more times just to hang out because he liked being around us. One day we were talking on the phone, and he brought the subject of weed up again. I got mad and told him I am into music, and I didn't want to be associated with any kind of drug dealing so don't call me regarding anything to do with weed again.

I was still working at night, and sometimes I would sleep for a few hours then drive to the studio in Brooklyn to work on my music. The studio was usually busy at night with more established artists so he had time in the afternoons to work with me. If I went to the studio, I would only have a little bit of time to relax before having to go to work, but I was determined to record these songs. My supervisor would catch me nodding off sometimes because I was so tired. On the weekends, I was still going to the basement to chill and share my recordings. I would stop by with some drinks and chill for a little while before going out.

Ninja's mom was now getting ready to move which meant the end of hanging out in the basement. At this time, we started to notice some suspicious activities at and around the house. Strange people were coming there asking for drugs. One night on my way down to the basement, I met a known drug addict at the door. He said he was looking for someone named Kirk. Right away, I knew something wasn't right. I went downstairs and told Kirk. When Kirk went to the door, the dude told him someone sent him to buy weed and that he should ask for Kirk. We already knew it was a setup. There had never been any drug dealing going on there, so it was a joke. Detectives were constantly driving by and would sometimes park across the street and watch the house. Ninja's family had to move by the end of April. On a Friday night two weeks before they were scheduled to move, my friend who worked the 2nd shift got off at 11:00 p.m. He called me to see if I was around and wanted to do something before he headed home. I told him I was in the basement, and he came by. There were only a few of us there. He asked if we had anything to drink. We had beer and rum but nothing to chase it with. He went down the street to buy something to chase the rum with. We started to wonder why he was gone so long. When he got back, he told us the cops pulled him over and asked where he was coming from. When he told them, they asked why he was there and what he was doing. After all their questions, they let him go on his way.

That confirmed what we already thought, but we didn't care because we weren't doing anything illegal. A week later, everything was out of the house due to the move. The only thing left in the house was the sound system in the basement which we planned to use for one last party. The party was planned for Friday night before they had to be out. Friday evening, I stopped by to see what was going on and if the party was still on. We were sitting there talking, and I said to them that if the police were going to show up it was probably going to be that night. I thought this because it was the last night before they had to move out the sound system and turn over the keys to the landlord. I kind of said it jokingly because there was nothing illegal going on, but the activities of the police for the last month suggested they were thinking otherwise. I went home for a while. After I took a shower and got dressed, I went to the liquor store to get some drinks before they closed. I had told a few people about the party, so I wanted to make sure I had enough drinks for them and any others that showed up. I dropped the drinks off, hung out for a while, and then left to stop by a local club for a while since it was too early for the party to begin.

When I got back, the party was in full swing. The basement was crowded, and more people kept coming. It was all friends and family who were drinking, chatting, dancing, and just having fun. Sometime after midnight, there was a loud bang, and there were police everywhere. They were wearing masks and riot gear like the swat team usually does. They told us all to get down flat on our stomachs. Then, they used plastic ties to tie our hands behind our backs. After everyone was secure, some of them stood guard while others searched the whole place. One of them was standing directly over me with one foot on my back. I had difficulty breathing, and I remember saying to him, "I can't breathe."—the very same words that Eric Garner said before his death years later. Eric Garner's death was caused by a prohibited chokehold while being arrested by New York City police department (NYPD) officers. The policeman told me to wait a while and it wouldn't be very long. He was a black officer, and I again said to him, "Why are you treating me like that bro? Like I'm some kind of animal." Two detectives came down into the basement with laptops in their hands. They told the officers to have us sit up. There were about 25 – 30 of us, and there was a guy that worked with Kirk who was about 400 pounds. They had a hard time picking him up.

After searching the place, they did not find anything illegal. All they found were a couple of 12 packs of Heineken and a partial bottle of Hennessy. The detectives then said they were going to check our identification before letting us go. Before they started checking IDs, I heard them on their radio saying to bring the van. When he got to my ID, he looked at it and then turned to the other detective and said, "Look who is here. Ask Jeff if he wants him." The detective left the basement and went outside. Meanwhile, I was there thinking about what they could want with me. He came back down, and I saw him bow his head to the other detective. My boy Ricky was next to me, and I said to him "Damn, di bwoy dem want mi, a muss di white bwoy." What I said was "Damn, they want me; it must be the white boy."

They handcuffed me and took me outside, and had me sit in a van. When I got outside, there were police and police vehicles everywhere. There were also a lot of people outside watching, some of whom were on their way to the party. I was there waiting for a while until they came with another one of my boys. He told me that when they ran his name, it came up that he had a warrant for missing an anger management class that had been ordered by a judge due to a dispute he had with the mother of his child. They must have been expecting a lot of arrests because they had a patty wagon (police van) there. When they finished with their big operation, there were only two of us that got arrested.

On top of all the detectives, swat team, and regular police officers that had been at the house when we got to the police station, it was like a 10:00 a.m. weekday at the courthouse. It was now 2:00 a.m. Saturday morning, and there were prosecutors, clerks, and more officers who were ready to start the booking process. They were expecting a patty wagon full of defendants which they were referring to as bodies. One asked the officers that brought me in, "Where are the bodies?" He made a gesture with his hands toward me as if he was saying "that's it!" Another asked, "so what were they doing?" He pointed at the two twelve packs of Heineken and the partial bottle of Hennessy while he replied "Drinking!" It was a while after my arrest that I thought to myself, "Why did they confiscate the alcohol? There was nothing illegal about adults drinking at a private home." After sitting at the police station for some time, they told me I was being charged with conspiracy to possess and distribute marijuana. It was then that I knew it had something to do with the white kid. I said to myself, "Damn!"

Everything I had said to him about not wanting to be involved with any kind of drug dealing started running through my mind. My mind then turned to thoughts of my babies. I just wanted to get out of there. I found out that they took my car that was parked in the driveway at the house. They later took me to the county jail. When I got on the block, I saw four white kids sitting at a table talking. I recognized one of them who had come with the white kid to hang out with us once before. I walked over to them. He already recognized me when I walked in. They started telling me all these things that had been happening for the last few days. The white kid, his dad, and some of his friends and associates were arrested. Everything became clear. I didn't know them, I didn't trust them, and I didn't have anything to say to them.

My bail got set at $50,000; no ten percent. I made a phone call to my brother. He had already heard of my arrest from Natalie. She had been at the party and had gone to her car right before the police stormed the party. She ran into them when she was outside, and they kept her by her car until they finished their raid. My brother and Natalie worked on getting me out of jail. They paid a bail bondsman ten percent of my bail, which was $5,000, to get me out of jail. The process took a while, so it was now Saturday mid-morning. I didn't even make it into a cell. In the middle of all this, I found happiness and something to be thankful for which was the fact that God gave me the strength to resist the temptation of the money I could have made if I had indulged with this kid and his activities. I knew I had a road to cross, but I felt confident that God was with me, and he would work things out the way he saw best for me.

When I got home, I took a shower and went to sleep. When I got up I called a few of my boys and let them know I was home. There was a party at the local club in town which happened to be next to the jail I had just been at hours ago. My boy Ninja said he was coming to town to check on me. Ninja, Ricky, Kirk, and I went to the party. We got to the parking lot at the front of the club, and the same detectives that arrested me less than 24 hours ago were standing there. They looked surprised to see me. They were looking at me while talking amongst themselves. I looked back at them as my friends and I walked by. We went into the club and had a good time. I felt free and at peace with myself knowing what happened with the white kid and me. I was ready to put up a fight. I'm not preaching religion, but at that point in my life, I was convinced that God was with me. If you don't see or believe that at this point in my story, I hope you will before the end. After all, it's the reason I tattooed Psalm 27 on my shoulder. When I got to the club, some people were surprised to see me because they heard I was locked up. Others hadn't heard the news yet. It was a long, stressful, and active Friday night. I wanted to have a good time and not think about it for a little while. I knew that I had a big fight ahead of me.

Sunday night, I was back at work like nothing happened. The $50,000 bail was so extreme, but that's just a way of having you sit in jail because you can't afford the bail. Being stuck in jail causes you to lose your job, and all your other responsibilities come crashing down which puts you at a disadvantage to fight your case. It's a system that many never recover from. Thankfully, I was home, back at work, and surrounded by a strong family. I've learned that there is always something to be thankful for, even in bad situations.

A few days later, it came out in the local paper. The first noticeable thing was that I was the only black person that got locked up. Everyone's picture was posted except for the ones that were minors. They were all young kids except for my guy's father who they charged for putting money that he got from his son in a safe deposit box. Then it was the statement they made to the media which said we were involved in a drug ring selling weed to kids in high school and colleges. I didn't know any of the co-defendants nor did I know anything about selling weed to kids, adults, or anyone. The next thing I noticed was the amount of money and valuables that were confiscated from the kid. My friends and I were very surprised. He owed me money from when I tried to help him out before I had cut him off. We even joked to ourselves that we wished we knew that he had all that money. Some people were saying the white kid set me up, and others just believed everything the paper said. Even some of my closest friends believed what was written in the paper. I had heard all the comments that were being made, but I never said anything to any of them.

Knowing a person's strengths and weaknesses is how I place them in my life. Like I mentioned earlier, some remain on the floor and a few make it to the top shelf. All the others are somewhere in between. There is no need to argue or cut them off. Even the friends that run their mouths have a purpose. Whatever you need people to know, just tell them. Good or bad, consider them your media. Some people were happy that I got locked up, but whatever anyone was thinking it didn't matter to me. I knew the truth, so I focused on fighting, learning all the lessons in the process, and moving on to be a better person. I got a lawyer that charged $10,000 to take the case. Getting my car was a separate case so he said he would charge me depending upon how much work he had to do. He later informed me that they had a recorded conversation between myself and the kid about trying to buy weed. Now it was confirmed that it was that time I took him to East Orange. I told my lawyer exactly what happened, and he informed me that it was an illegal act and that the word conspiracy doesn't mean you did anything. I found out that assisting someone in any way, shape, or form in any illegal activity and even hearing someone speaking of doing a crime and not reporting it could lead to a conspiracy charge. I started thinking about all the other times I was on the phone with the kid and had told him that I didn't want to be involved in anything to do with dealing drugs. I was also thinking about all the time they spent watching the house, sending informants there to buy drugs, but it never happened.

All the cops, prosecutors, and everyone involved in this big operation worked all these hours only to run into a house where people were only partying. I wondered how they even got a warrant to raid the house when there was never anything illegal going on at that house. It was my first time experiencing how the cops use the media to cover their dirt. They put things out in the media and the community and sometimes even family believe it and turn their backs on you. No one checks their illegal activities and their abuse of power. It was years earlier that I wrote about how making a thug stop could lead to a conspiracy charge. This incident made me think of something else that I had written as well titled "To the Government".

To The Government

The government of our country
To you, I'm speaking
You have the youths running races
They never can win
With your geographical structure
And your prison system
Acting like you're surprised

Trouble Strikes Again – Always Something

With all these school shootings
When you're the farmer of war
Many seeds I see you sowing
You appoint overseers
To make sure they're growing
From afar, you watch and peep
Then you hit the streets
For ghetto youths I see you seek
Preying on the weak
Snatching up lost sheep
You're a bully, you're a beast
But in your skin, they'll be heat
On your plantations, there'll be no peace

Always making peace talks
But you don't want it that bad
Cause if your jails are not full
With your boys you get mad
Always talking against war
But you don't want it to stop
The biggest dealer or arms
You'll never close your gun shops
With your mixed messages
You have the youths confused
Telling parents they're responsible
For their kid's every move
The very same you abuse
Taking the rights from parents
To discipline kids the way they choose

Separation has been your mission
You don't want unity
With your political warfare
And your economical strategies
You're turning nation against nation
Family against family
From parents, you're robbing babies
You're raping other countries
For you they'll be no mercy

You're starving us for freedom
For justice we're hungry
Your plantations make you feel great
In your crops you have faith
Many seeds you cultivate
I'm talking jealousy and hate
That's how your business generates
To opportunities, you build a gate
To control who escalates
No longer can I wait
To see my people get a break
From the system you create
Like we're fish you set the bait
Just for us to take a taste
With all the traps you set in place
All your crops shall go to waste

I hope you have some questions for yourself after reading that. If you have any for me, I would love to answer them. Once again, I was thankful that my big brother, Natalie, and a host of family and friends were there supporting and praying for me. My two babies were all the energy I needed to keep fighting. After the incident, I was even more determined to be there for them and be the bond between them. It was already a challenge, and I knew it was going to become even more challenging.

I used to hang out in the basement or backyard with the guys playing dominoes because I love people and like to socialize with them. Sometimes I would have them doing pushups with me. It was always a good vibe. My main reason for being there so much was the sound system. The love of music was the one thing we all had in common. I was in the middle of the project I had started months ago, and my goal was to complete a demo album with at least ten songs. I knew the case was going to take a long time to litigate so I decided to finish the project. There's a saying that goes, "always make good out of a bad situation" and I had been practicing that. I was already learning some real-life lessons and whatever happened in the end, I just wanted to have this album done. I wanted to be able to play the album for anyone that wanted to hear it and for my kids to be able to grow up listening to it.

Natalie was still working in New York, and she commuted to work on the train. I was able to use her car to go where I needed to, whether it was the studio, gym, appointments with the graphics designer, and most importantly my daddy duties. I remember about three weeks after my arrest, I was working on things for the album cover. I was driving Natalie's car and stopped by the house to grab some papers that I needed. On my way to the house, I passed a detective parked on my street in an unmarked car. I didn't care because I wasn't doing anything illegal, and I wasn't going to live in fear. I got my papers, drove past him, and pulled over by the store at the corner. The store at the corner was exactly across the street from the house I was arrested at. I ran into the store to get water and two packs of peanuts for myself and my friend that was riding with me. I came back out, got in the car, and drove away.

The detective pulled up behind me and pulled me over. When he came to my window he started asking me questions like where I was coming from, why did I go into the store, what did I buy and where was I heading. I asked him why he was bothering me and told him to leave me alone. He told us to have a good day before he walked back to his car. I knew I had made a bad decision trying to connect the white kid with someone, but I was a hardworking, upstanding member of the community, and I wasn't going to let them or anyone else intimidate me.

My daughter was now four-and-a-half years old, and my son was going to be turning three years old. Things were getting easier for us now that they could tell me when they were hungry, what they liked, and when they needed to use the potty; and they could talk to me on the phone. I still had to pick them up to carry them at times but not as much. I started having more fun being a dad. They brought me a feeling that I had never felt before, and I couldn't get enough of it. I was the proudest dad. I attended all their concerts, Halloween parades, sports events, and all the events that parents were allowed to attend. I loved to see happy looks on their faces when they saw me; it was priceless. Every kid wants someone in their corner, especially their mom and dad. I promised God and myself that I would be there for them, and I wanted to be there in every way possible. I would do anything and everything to make sure my kids felt loved, safe, and wanted.

Just when I thought I was already in enough trouble, more trouble was to come. We had a party to celebrate my son's 3rd birthday. I had a rental car for the weekend. A few of my close friends, family, and a lot of kids came to celebrate with us. My two babies were now connected. My daughter was a proud big sister and caretaker of her little brother. It was more than just a birthday celebration. It was also a celebration of family. It felt good to see them treating each other as a brother and sister should. It also felt good to see the relationship my daughter and Natalie had. It was just amazing. To this day, I still enjoy looking at pictures from that day. The party went into the night so after cleaning up, I drove my daughter home. A little while later, my friends and I went to a party at the local club. It was mostly people from the neighborhood that were there. After the party ended, everyone headed back to town. I was in the middle of a line of cars. When we got to the traffic light it was green, so the cars kept driving. We were driving at a pretty good speed when the light turned orange, and the car in front of me suddenly braked. I tried to stop but ended up rear-ending the car in front of me. The driver of the car was a girl that I knew and was friends with. I told her to drive down the street to where she lived and that I was driving to that same location since my friend that I was driving home lived there as well. I told her not to worry because I would fix her car. She started shouting, "I'm calling the cops!" I begged her not to because I had been drinking. She called the cops anyway.

When the cops came, they asked if anyone was injured, and she told them yes. The girl that was riding with her was pregnant. This girl was my friend's child's mother. She kept telling the girl that she needed to go to the hospital even though the girl kept refusing to go because she was fine. The ambulance came and took her to the hospital. The cops asked me if I had anything to drink, and I told him I had had a few beers. He said he was going to detain me and take me to the police station where he would test my alcohol level with a breathalyzer. I was in shock that she called the cops. She was my daughter's mother's very close friend. She was always at her house and around my daughter. I had known her for years and we were cool with each other. I couldn't understand why she did that to me. The cops took me to the police station, gave me the test, and I was over the limit. My boy Ninja's sister came there, and I was released into her custody. It was now Sunday and later that day I called my boy who was like family to ask how his child's mother was doing. He told me she was fine, and she wasn't injured in the accident.

When I called Theresa (my daughter's mother) to tell her what happened, she informed me that they had a fallout, and she probably did what she did out of spite. Now it was making sense to me why she had done what she did. I now had a DWI and assault with a motor vehicle charge in addition to the charges from my previous arrest; all within two months. For me, I had one option and that was to fight so I talked to my lawyer and retained him for these new charges. The first thing my lawyer did was request the medical report which was negative for any type of injury. He took it to the court, and the judge dismissed that charge. Then he started fighting the DWI charge. I knew and accepted that I was guilty of that charge. I took full responsibility for that one, but we wanted to get the best deal we could. It was a mandatory license suspension so I told my lawyer that while negotiating with the prosecutor to try to minimize the time, keep pushing back the court date so I could finish working on the album I had started. With all that I was going through, I never cried or complained to anyone. I kept going to work, worked to finish my album, and took care of my kids. I still found time to party.

The child's father of the girl that had called the cops on me came and asked me to help fix the car. He was a very humble guy so out of respect, I spoke to him very politely. I asked him if he was out of his mind or if he thought I was. With the money this case was costing me, I could have bought her a better car than the one she had and still have a lot of money left. It seemed there was something wrong with her insurance policy, so she cut off her nose to spite her face. She was now without a car and had to walk. God was helping me to strive. The best part was the fact that I wasn't even mad at her. I felt bad for her because she also had two babies.

When I realized all that was happening in my life, I asked my father for a special prayer. I would ask for a prayer every so often, and he would pray for me in the house. This time I told him I wanted him to pray for me at the church altar. He had the key to the church so one morning after work, we went to the church. He anointed me with oil and then prayed for me. I'm a true believer in God's power. I've seen and experienced it enough times. I tattooed Psalm 27 on my arm to remind myself that with him I have nothing to fear. I just had to trust him and keep moving forward. I kept working hard on my album. I was determined to finish it before anything happened with my court cases. I kept going back and forth to Brooklyn to record the songs. I had met a guy in the club who some mutual friends had introduced. They knew I was doing music, and he was a singer. We exchanged numbers and stayed in touch. It turned out that this guy had a beautiful voice. I asked him if he could sing the hooks on a couple of the songs I wrote and was now recording. He was ready and willing because he loved to sing. All I would have to do is go over the lyrics with him and the way I wanted him to sing. He was American and had never worked with any type of Reggae music before. We went over the first hook a few times, and then I took him to the studio to record the song. The producer worked with him until we got it to where we were satisfied. The song came out beautifully. We worked together on three of the songs, and they all came out amazing.

Natalie is a very good singer with a beautiful voice. I asked her to sing the hook of a song I wrote called "Swimmer". It needed a female touch, and she had the magic touch. She went into the studio and knocked it out of the park. Every time I went to the studio, I met a different reggae artist. The most memorable was when I met Shabba Ranks. Shabba was one of my favorite artists growing up, and now I was talking to him. He was very down-to-earth and real cool. He said to me, "Yute put yuh stamp pan it." He was telling me "Go hard and do what you do; be original."

One day while I was recording, Junior (One Blood) Reid came into the studio. After I was done recording, I came out of the booth into the studio and was chillin' with some of my friends. He started talking to me and told me that he liked my style and personality. He said maybe one day we could do a song together, so we exchanged numbers. That was all I needed to hear. Later that day when I got back to New Jersey, I called him up and told him I had a song that I would like him to work on with me. I had already recorded the song so all he would have to do is go in the studio and record a part of the song I had already done, or he could do his own thing. He agreed so we went over the business agreement, and set up a time with the producer. Two days later, we were back in the studio recording his part. I couldn't believe it was happening. This was Grammy award-winning, international recording artist, Junior Reid that was featured on one of my songs. The name of the song was "Everywhere is Dawgs". He didn't like the dog concept as a Rastafarian man, so he switched up his parts with the word lion instead of the dog. The song came out beautifully, and now I was cool with the great Junior Reid. He even introduced me to a few people in the music industry. All my time and effort were now paying off. It felt good to see the words that I wrote now becoming songs that the world could listen to.

My daughter was only five years old at the time, and I brought her to the studio to record an intro for the album. I had recorded the ten songs and had them mixed by a guy the producer had introduced to me so now the songs were ready. I had the master in my possession. While I had been recording, I was also working on the pictures and graphics for the jacket and cd. I named the album "My World". All the songs reflected me and my thoughts. I found a company that would do everything in-house; they would even sell it on their website. I followed all the instructions they gave to me and provided everything they needed. Finally, I had an official album in my hand and not only one copy. I ordered 1,000 copies, and I was everywhere selling and promoting the album. It was a great feeling of accomplishment. Everything about the album was authentic and original. It is something I will forever be proud of. A word spoken and recorded can never die; the songs I wrote and recorded will be around forever. I gave both my kids their copies, and I will never forget the feeling I got a few years later when my daughter told me she took her copy to school for show and tell. She told me all the things the kids were saying and asking her. She was so excited, which brought joy to my heart.

I realize that it's not easy to be yourself especially when it's not popular. True love for people is the one thing that I would struggle with and still struggle with. It seems like people pressure each other with who they are supposed to love, talk to, be friends with or even say hello to. I've seen people treat their parents, kids, brother, sister, or friends like strangers all because of a new relationship or just trying to please someone that thinks differently of that person for whatever reason. Getting along with others has always come easy for me. We don't have to be friends, but I will treat you with love and respect. No one is going to tell me not to talk to you or be cool with you if we are cool. I've seen people switch up their many personas depending on where they are, who they are around or what they are trying to make you think of them. I always wondered how these people can be relaxed and be at peace with themselves. I feel like they are always in a constant state of confusion. I experienced this very same thing with having two kids that are only a year and a half apart with two different women.

To be there for my daughter, I knew I needed to have a civil relationship with her mother. I needed her to grow up seeing me treating her mother with respect. It was very hard at times, but I knew what I got myself into, and I was not going to blame her mother or anyone else for my shortcomings. I did not want to be the type of father that had to explain to my kids why I wasn't there for them. That was not going to happen. I used to visit my daughter and spend time with her at the house. It got to a point where there was always something that I was not pleased with. This sometimes led to an argument. One day while I was there, my daughter was playing on the front lawn. Her mom and I got into an argument inside, and I noticed that she heard. I had been watching her from the big glass window in the living room. She stopped playing, and she had a look on her face that broke my heart. From that moment, I decided that I was not going back into her house again unless it was necessary. I did not want my daughter growing up with any memories of her mom and me arguing.

I never regretted making that decision because our relationship got much better. I was overprotective of my daughter which caused me to find fault with a lot of things when I went there.

Even though her mother and I weren't together, I wanted my daughter to know that I respected her and the importance of family. I became very close with the family, especially Nana and Shereka. They were very instrumental in the care of my baby girl, and they became family. How could I not love and appreciate them? It was not easy being so close to my daughter's mom's family. For me, it was about my daughter and showing love and appreciation for those who were there for her. It was difficult to explain this to Natalie and comfort her. One thing I knew is that I was going to do my best on both sides. The older my daughter got, the better things got. Things were so good that Natalie would sometimes go with me to my daughter's family get-togethers. When this happened, my daughter was the happiest one in the house. She loved seeing us getting along.

People would ask me how I got along so well with my daughter's mom's boyfriends. I would tell them it was about respect. If he respected me and my daughter, there was no reason for anything but love. It was very hard to find that balance, but I thanked God for the strength and that we were one family. Fathers, I know it's not easy, but never let anyone dictate to you how you should treat your kids. Find the balance and spread love. Some friends want to tell you who to be friends with and who to talk to. Resist that type of hate and choose love. Love will bring peace.

So many people are not speaking to each other and don't even have a reason why. There are some whose reasons are so petty. I will always choose to build a bridge to bring people together as opposed to tearing them apart. When you love people and people love you back, it is the greatest feeling. Some people are envious of the love you generate and will do everything to destroy it. They will tell you all the bad things people are saying about you or tell people that you are saying this and doing that intending to tear you apart. Let love guide you. Introduce people to love, and they will love you forever.

I know it's not the norm for two people who have broken up to show love and have respect for each other, but we should all try to make this the norm. That's the way it's supposed to be. There will always be disagreements and fights, but we should draw the line and set boundaries. We should strive to not cross these lines and boundaries, and if we do, we should find a way to fix it. It might take some time to get to that place, but love will take us there. It will free our minds regardless of how the other person reacts. The fear of how the other person is going to react will sometimes hold us back from doing the right thing. I've never yet had a bad reaction from reaching out to someone that I have crossed the line with. They say that time heals everything, and I have found that to be true. If we would just humble ourselves to look into some of these altercations we have gotten into, we would realize they were over nothing, and there's still love on both sides.

Chapter 8

I See the Light

The Evolution

After the altercation between Tafari and myself, I didn't see him for a few years. Then I started seeing him around town. We had mutual friends so sometimes I would be in a group where he was or was nearby. I never would say anything to him. There were a few times that I thought to myself about how close we had been. Deep inside, I still had love for him. The few times I saw him, he never came over to me or even looked at me in any way that made me feel any hate or animosity that he had toward me. One day, I saw him with a group of friends. When I walked up, I greeted everyone except him. I kept moving around to greet others. It was a summer afternoon, and a lot of people were out for an event in the park. I had a heavy feeling in my heart from walking past him and greeting everyone else. It wasn't who I was or how I was feeling inside. Love wouldn't allow me to do this. I walked over to him and said, "Yo Tafari, let's leave all that old stuff alone; it's one love and I have nothing but love for you." We smiled at each other, and he said that he was about to say the same thing to me. It was a great feeling and was an experience of love being victorious. The weight I had was now lifted, my heart was joyful, and my mind was at peace. We shook hands, hugged, drank two Guinness Stout, and began to catch up. Our friendship was restored, and the experience made it much stronger. It was not only good for us but good for others around us. Our friends witnessed two grown men making peace and showing love and respect to each other. Our friendship is back on track and has been growing ever since.

Spreading love and making amends does not always go as smoothly as that. Always remember you are doing it for yourself, for your peace, happiness, and energy. Natalie's dad and I never had any kind of relationship. There were bad vibes between us from the start. We never had an argument or confrontation, but I had received a few warnings from him, and I would hear things he was saying. None of it bothered or scared me. I took it as if it was just a father in his feelings. I was young, fearless, and sometimes careless. I would try and say hello to him out of respect, but he would just scowl his face. It went on like that for many years. I had nothing but love for him in my heart. After all those years, Natalie and I now had a son which made him the grandfather of my son. The way I looked at things was that he was now officially family. I started putting some effort into saying hi to him whenever I saw him. Sometimes he would respond, and other times he wouldn't. I got used to it. I also understood that some of my behaviors would have made any father mad, so I had to allow him to react in his way.

The older my son got, the more I wanted to make peace with him. I wanted my son to grow up seeing us living in love and harmony. We had a few good moments in between all the back and forth. One memorable moment was at the celebration of my son's christening when we actually had a conversation. Another time was at his 50th birthday party in the Bronx, New York. I got into a picture with him which was unprecedented. I never knew what to expect with him so for that party, I had invited a couple of my boys that lived in the Bronx just in case something happened. Thankfully nothing happened, and we all had fun. It was good while it lasted because it didn't last for long. I was older, much more mature, and very confident. I started feeling like it was time to talk with him to let him know how I was feeling about him and ask him for forgiveness for some of my behaviors. We were at his son's wedding who is Natalie's younger brother. I knew her brother since he was a toddler. Natalie had introduced me to him, and from that moment he was now my little brother. We lived in the same town so I would see him often. I looked out for him and treated him like my little brother.

At his wedding, I ran into his dad in the bathroom of the hotel where the reception was being held. I sparked the conversation with him, and it exploded. We got an inch away from having a physical confrontation, and it caused a big scene. I felt lighter and at peace that I had extended an olive branch. I accepted the fact that I could only control how I acted and reacted in the situation. I walked away with love in my heart. Sometimes people are not ready when you are; always give love and try again next time. Never give up on love. Giving up on love is giving up on yourself. Loving someone does not mean you have to be friends or even cool. Just as long as you don't have any hate for that person, you are good. Some people just need to be kept at a distance for your peace and safety. Hate will destroy you from within. When I looked back at the incident, I realized I chose a very bad time for that talk to take place. We were both drinking and were not in control of our thoughts and behaviors so I learned a lesson in the process. There is always something to learn from every experience in life. Only if we are humble and true to ourselves will we see the lesson to be learned.

When I got arrested in the basement, I was very upset with the narcotics squad and the justice system that supports and backs them up even when they are being dishonest. After my lawyer got the discovery and went through all the evidence, he sat me down so we could review it all together. My charges were all from the one time I took the kid to East Orange to connect him with my guy so he could try to get some weed. They had a recording of the phone conversation when he called me before he met up with me. They had followed us to East Orange, and we did not know it. That day, I was late to meet my daughter, so I had rushed out of the parking lot and flew up the highway, so they had lost us. Everything else was supporting evidence.

They had videotaped us hanging out in the park. There were a lot of people in the park the day they videotaped us. Even my daughter and other kids were on the recording. I had nothing to do with anything they stated in the paper, but my lawyer informed me that it was a legitimate charge because I assisted a person in committing an illegal act. If someone asks you if you know anyone who sells weed and you point them in that direction, you could be charged with a crime. He told me all the things I was mad about and what I did or didn't do was irrelevant. The only thing that mattered was what they had charged me with. I did it, and they had some evidence, so it was either find something that they had done wrong or fight for the lowest penalty. He told me to leave that to him. The first thing he did was get my car back.

It took a while for the case to be called to court. I remember the first day I went to court. I saw the kid for the first time since I had cut ties with him. We looked at each other from across the courtroom, and I could see he was feeling bad for me. In our last conversation, I had told him that I was only interested in my music and being there for my kids. He had gotten to know my kids. I couldn't blame him for what had happened to me. It was my bad choice, and I felt bad for him. I'm still not sure if they started watching him after he started hanging around us.

I was going back and forth to court as my lawyer was fighting the charges. I felt like it wasn't serious enough for me to go to jail. My lawyer was fighting for probation. The kid was the only one of everyone that had been arrested that I ever had any dealings with. Therefore, he was the only one that could implicate me in a crime. One day, my lawyer called and said he had good and bad news. I asked him what was going on because even the good news was usually not good news. He said the bad news was Jay (the kid) had been in a motorcycle accident and died. The good news was that he had a stronger hand to play with. I was shocked and hurt. He became a friend, and we had been close. I didn't want to be around him anymore because I had realized what he was about, but I still had love in my heart for him. It felt really strange reading about the accident in the papers. I still have the newspaper clipping that I have kept in memory of him. I ended up getting probation and community service which I diligently completed.

My probation officer was a young woman. She told me she wished all the offenders she supervised were like me because she had no problem with me. I obeyed all the rules I was given. My lawyer even told me the prosecutor said I was a good kid that got caught up with the wrong people. After what happened to me in that situation, no one was ever going to ask me where anything illegal was. If they did, I would just act as if I didn't hear them or tell them to go ask the police. For some reason, people always chose to ask me for drugs all the time. I'm aware and conscious enough now to know that if it's illegal, the police are aware of it and all the dealings associated with it and it would just be a matter of time. It all belongs to them: the guns, drugs, the money you are making. The more serious part of it is karma. Your drugs, guns, or anything that you are doing that hurts others will come around to you in ways you could not imagine. These things will rob you of your dreams and take away your passion and belief in yourself.

I have learned some harsh lessons, but I am thankful for them. They prepared me for harsher ones to come and made me more knowledgeable which is something I can share, especially with my kids. I made it my duty to share my experiences, the knowledge I gained from it, and my struggles with all the kids in my circle and those in the community that I interact with. I have a special love for all kids even the older ones that are becoming young adults. My kids, nieces, nephews, godkids, and all my friends' kids always have my love and support. I am Uncle Dervin to all my friends' kids, and I try to attend birthdays, graduations, games, family functions, and funerals. The kids in the community know me.

My kids were now playing different sports, and it was exciting watching them. One day I was watching my son's soccer game. He was playing defense which he was very good at. A kid beat him on the outside and was rushing towards the goal. My son was running alongside him and I shouted, "lick him, Danny." This is the Jamaican word for "hit". The kid's mother was standing next to me and said, "Don't say that! That's my son." I felt so bad. I apologized to her and explained that I didn't mean he should hurt him. I meant to just stop him. I got caught up in the moment and forgot it was a kid's game. That incident stuck with me ever since that day. I even remember the expression on the woman's face.

My son and daughter lived in two different towns, but their teams would play in the same leagues since the towns were so close to each other. One day, my son was playing soccer on one field while my daughter was cheerleading for her football team on another field just yards apart. I kept going back and forth to support both of them. Natalie was doing the same thing. She always supported my daughter. After the game, we all got together as one unit which was a proud moment for me. It was rewarding to get by the hard stuff and realize it wasn't that bad. It was a very strong lesson of love for them too. We can be on two different teams with no love lost. I still have pictures from that day that I enjoy looking at. They always uplift my spirit and remind me to fight for love. It was a more challenging situation when Danny was in a game against Deedee's team. I had set a rule that our family as a team comes first. So, we would look at it as if both teams were ours, and Danny was our man in the game. They were all my kids so I would just enjoy the game and support them all. It was harder for my daughter, but we gave her room to support her team while supporting her little brother. She was very vocal about her feelings for her brother, and it was known. It was situations like those that helped to bond them together in a very strong way.

From the time they were babies, they learned to embrace and support their differences. Loving kids does as much for me as it does for them. They show appreciation for the simple, little things. Being around kids and doing things that make them happy comforts me in any storm. Some of the things I had wished for when my kids were babies had started coming to fruition. One of those wishes was for them to grow up to meet and know the kind of woman my mother was and still is. I wished this, especially for my daughter. My mom and my daughter had a relationship since birth. Her mom could drop her off to my mom at any time, and she always did. I got to watch them interact through different stages of her life. That in and of itself is a blessing. My big sister and her husband lived in Connecticut, and they would come to pick her up all the time. Most importantly we all loved enough to get to know each other.

I enjoyed watching the individual development of my kids. It was super cool to hang out with them. They knew where they wanted to go, what they wanted to do, and even what they wanted to eat. I would listen to them sometimes negotiating with each other as to what it was going to be, and when they couldn't come to an agreement they would come to me. For the most part, it was smooth sailing, but sometimes it took some compromising. A lot of the time, Shereka's daughter Quba would be with us. My daughter and she are cousins but were more like sisters. Quba was like a big sister to my son Danny. She would always make sure he was okay. She was always holding his hand when we were walking. She would help him at the park with getting on the slide, swings, and jungle gym. She was also close with my other nieces and nephews and was considered part of the family. They all grew up together. I was also very close to Quba's dad. They would allow her to go anywhere with me. With all the bad experiences I was going through, they kept me energized, focused, and motivated.

Another thing that kept me motivated was the love I had for the people in my village back in Jamaica. I wanted to be there for them in any way that would change their situation for good, both economically and socially. Things were not going as I had planned because I couldn't even visit there. One of my wishes was for the day when I would be able to take my kids to visit them. They haven't been able to visit with me, but they both have been able to visit and meet some of my family and friends and get to see the place I had been telling them about since they were babies. Until this very day, they are still a source of energy for me.

My sisters, brother, nieces, nephews, aunts, uncles, and an army of cousins were still living in Jamaica. They were close people who I loved and cared about that I hadn't seen in almost 15 years at this point. My kids and family I had here took away most of the pain, and the remaining pain I used for energy. With all that pain and hurt, I ended up in a lonely place in a world all by myself at times.

A girl who I was cool with invited my friends and me to her birthday party that she was having in the basement of her older sister's house who I knew as well. I was very cool with the whole family. It was free to get into the party, but she was selling the alcohol. Ricky, Kirk, and I decided to support her and spend some money at the bar. The party was down the street from my house, so I walked there. I was there with Ricky and Kirk drinking rum and rum punch all night so we spent a lot of money with her. There were other people there, but we were in the corner going back and forth to the bar. It was about 3:30 a.m. Sunday morning, and the party started to come to an end. I was talking to her older sister who I had been cool with for many years. She was also drinking rum punch. We walked upstairs to her room which was the first time I was ever upstairs in that house. We were both laying on the bed talking—both of us fully dressed. The next thing I knew, I heard a banging on the door. That was when I realized we had both fallen asleep. She got up and opened the door. It was almost morning by then so I left the house and walked home. Nothing happened between us—no kissing, no touching, and there was no sex. At no point had either of us removed our clothes. I went back to sleep when I got home. The rest of the day was just a normal Sunday. I went to work that night.

On Monday evening, someone called me to tell me that people were saying that I raped her. I was in shock. It was spreading all over. I was hearing all kinds of versions of what happened and that I was going to jail.

I knew I hadn't done anything, so I wasn't worried about going to jail. It was the rumors that were spreading about me and the silence of people that I was close with that bothered me. Ricky, Kirk, and I talked about it. They knew I would never do anything like that. No one else called me to ask me what happened. Everyone was hearing about it and talking but not to me. I had even heard some of their comments. I felt like I was in a world all by myself. I had never experienced anything like it before.

I went back to work that night with all this pressure in my head. The fact that I knew the truth kept me strong. My brother was the boss at my job, but he worked the day shift. He started at 7:00 a.m. but would sometimes come in early. When my brother got to work that morning, he came to see me as he would sometimes. He told me someone came to the house to tell him that I raped someone, and I was going to go to jail. He said they told him they are just waiting on the results from the doctor and that the police were involved and were the ones that took her. I told my brother exactly what happened. He turned to me and said, "I believe you." I have known you all your life, and you wouldn't do that. Then he said, "Don't worry. We'll just wait and see." This is what he would always say about everything. He said, "I'll pray for you." There's a scripture in the Bible that says, "Greater love has no one than this: to lay down one's life for his friends." That's exactly what my brother did. When my brother said, "I believe you" I was lost, and he found me. Now it was him and I in my world and what anyone was thinking didn't matter to me anymore. Now I was standing tall, head up and unbothered. Until this day, I have never told my brother what he did for me that morning. He was that one person that believed me when no one else did.

Days and weeks passed, and the police had never come to question me even though the rumors were still going around. I went by Nana's house (my daughter's grandmother), and she told me someone came to her with the claim and the person was laughing saying I was going to jail. Nana said, "Son, I know you wouldn't do anything like that," and I said to her, "Nana, I didn't do anything." She then said, "You don't have to tell me that. I know." She was now the second person who believed in me. I always had love and respect for her, but at that moment, it was cemented into my heart. Time went by, and no one was saying anything to me, and nothing happened. I kept living my life all while showing love to everyone, even the hypocrites. Until this day, I still don't know who started it, and I still don't care. Even the woman and I are cool again. I never said anything to her about it, and she never said anything about it to me. This is the first time I'm addressing the incident. It was a test of a lifetime, one that I learned so many lessons from. I would have never known how much my big brother believed in me.

A lot of people have lived their whole life not having one person believe in them. There are innocent people in jail that no one believes in, not even their families. I've experienced this feeling. Thank God for my big brother who firmly believed in me. After the dust settled, I wasn't mad at anyone. It was all love as usual. I even went to a few parties at that house again. It was all love in my heart for everyone, but I felt let down by the ones that were close to me. In my eyes, them not saying anything to me about it and not even asking me what happened but commenting on it with others was a betrayal.

It was time to evaluate myself which was kind of a blessing in disguise. For a while, Ricky was the only person I would confide in. He was a loyal little brother and the mother of his kids, who was his girlfriend at the time, was family. She was an offspring from my community in Jamaica. I would stop by their apartment and chill with them sometimes. I was still cool with my little girls' crew who were now all grown up with kids of their own. They have been around me drunk, high, straight, and I always made sure they were safe. The incident made me miss my community and the people I grew up with even more. There was a voice in my head saying, "Remember you're in a different place, and all these people are total strangers." It only took one rumor, and everyone's character was on full display. Believe me when I say I was taking screenshots and notes. I had sown seeds in the community with the result of two beautiful plants growing which I was never going to leave.

At this point, I knew it was now my community, but I needed a stronger bond with my home base of Rio Bueno, Trelawny, Jamaica West Indies. I kept a connection with them throughout the time I had been here in the U.S. After having my babies and different battles I had been fighting, the connection weakened. Sometimes all it takes is a phone conversation with a family member or friend that knows you, loves you, and believes in you to push you over a hill on a day when you are feeling weak.

My cousin and longtime friend Brent, aka Round Bread, was the type of person that loved his community the way I did. When we talked, he would always talk about the community and not himself as most others did. He would talk about the soccer team, the school, the kids, the elderly, the roads, water, and he would even talk about getting a party going for the holidays, especially Christmas. He was my guy and a figure in the community, so I chose to stay in touch with him, and he kept me connected to the people. I didn't like every day talking on the phone with different people. He was the only one I would frequently speak with. Anything I was doing in the community, I would do it through him. My sisters would take care of anything personal. I had my team on the ground. The people in the community got to know how I operated so if they had a message for me, they would tell my sisters or Round Bread.

I love my people and that love was part of my driving force. Having love for yourself and others is a blessing in every way. I was always the kind of person to break bread with people and give a helping hand when I could. It would give me priceless inner joy. Even the kids in my community in Jamaica that had never met me knew who I was. Sometimes I meet them here in the U.S. and they tell me stories about things I have done for them which gave me the most amazing feeling. The more you have to live for is the more you love and respect life. When you respect life, you value it. The more I started valuing my life, the clearer things got. Making the right decisions got easier. I started walking away from arguments that were not worth my time, freedom, or life. It's much easier to apologize, say sorry or just be nice. A part of what helped me with that was my self-confidence. Both reading and working out helped to boost my self-confidence to great heights, and I realized that I had to be consistent with both. Consistency is the key to reaching optimal levels. It was the program I completed in jail that taught me the things I was now practicing in my life. During this same program, I had committed to working out. It now makes perfect sense to me why this had been part of the program and why we were required to participate in it daily.

I started reading everything I could about the different muscle groups and their functions. I read and asked questions about the different ways to strengthen different muscles. Throughout the years, I have learned a lot about working out. One day an idea came to me to record an exercise video. I thought about it for a while before deciding to make it my next project. I planned to make it simple so anyone could use it for their daily exercise regimen. The plan was to use stuff around the house. I already had most of the team in place from making the album. I had the graphics guy, the manufacturer, the photographer, and the music for the background. The only thing I needed was a videographer. There was a guy at my job that I would talk with sometimes about music, and he would share with me his goals with his side hustle which was videography. He generally did weddings and different kinds of parties. I shared my idea with him and asked him if he could record the workout session and do the editing. Even though he had never done that type of video, he was willing to give it his best shot. I was happy to work with him because he was always giving me good advice and encouraged me with my music.

Now that I had my entire team in place, it was all about getting myself and the routine ready. I talked to the guy that ran the local boxing gym where I had been working out at that time. I shared the idea with him and asked for his permission to do the recording there. He said it was okay, but we would have to do it on a Saturday when the gym was closed so there would be no disturbances. After getting his approval, I started working on setting up a date when everyone would be available. I coordinated with everyone and came up with the date. The photographer was available that day as well to capture the shots for the DVD cover. I try to be very professional with anything that I do so I did my prep work. I got a haircut, gathered the little bit of workout gear I needed, and got Natalie and the kids as my deckhands. They were my strength on the day of the recording.

On the day of the recording, I got up that Saturday morning and ate breakfast early so it had time to digest and give me the energy I needed for the performance at hand. We met the guy that ran the gym around 8:00 a.m. and started getting everything together. The videographer came and set up his cameras, lighting, and markings for where he wanted me to position myself. The photographer was running late so we decided to start since we could do the photoshoot at any point. I thought it would be better to do the photoshoot at the end when I was pumped from working out. I did a quick full-body routine to get my blood flowing and then it was showtime. I incorporated dumbbells and water bottles into my workout program. I explained that there are items around everyone's house that can be used for a quick exercise session. There's no excuse for not working out. All you need is the will to get down and do a few pushups. My kids were there watching and listening to the message and that was all the motivation I needed. If no one ever ended up seeing the video, my main audience had and that was fulfilling.

The message was much more than exercising for them. It was determination, commitment, teamwork, being open-minded, and much more. My kids knew that I worked at night when they were sleeping. They knew that I wrote and recorded the songs for my album. My daughter had witnessed me working in the recording studio. They had seen pictures from my many photoshoots when I was experimenting with modeling. And now, they were a part of my team working on a different project. I could not wait for them to see the finished product. The photographer came and did the photoshoot. We put everything back in place and packed up the stuff we had brought there. We all left there with work to do so the final product would be of the best quality and professional standard. While waiting on the photos and the final master copy of the DVD, I had a lot of work to do. I worked on registering a name and worked with my graphics guy on the logo and the cover design. The name I came up with was "Beach Body Burn" with the subtitle "You Have to Burn It to Earn It". I got the photos and DVD, and both guys had done a great job. I went through the photos and picked out the ones I needed for the cover. I took them, along with all the information that was going to appear on the cover jacket, and the DVD to the graphic designer. He then did the final designs which I approved of. He sent them directly to the manufacturer, and I sent the master DVD to them. Now, they had all the materials for mass production.

While waiting on the manufacturer, I kept working with the graphic designer on promotional materials. We made business cards, posters, and t-shirts. It was a lot of work from the very beginning, but it was exciting for me. I enjoyed seeing all the different components come together. All I had to do now was wait on a call or an email for the date to pick up my first order of DVDs. It's a one-of-a-kind feeling when an idea comes to mind, and you put the work in for it to become a reality. After all that work, it felt good chilling for a little while before getting the products in my hands so I could get back to work promoting and selling the DVDs.

One Friday night after hanging out with my kids and my nephew who was visiting from Jamaica, I went out with a couple of guys I knew that played in the NFL. Later that night after having some drinks, I got pulled over by a cop. He said he observed me swerving and asked me to step out of the car. After asking me to perform a series of field sobriety tests, and then he arrested me for DWI. He was a pretty cool cop. I didn't give him any trouble, and he didn't give me any. He might have saved my life or someone else's. I called Natalie, and she came to the police station to pick me up. My car was towed so the following day we went to pick it up, and that's where the money spending started.

After a while, reality started to hit me as to how much of a setback this charge was going to be for me. I decided to give it my best fight and take it one day at a time. I got my lawyer to handle the case. I kept working and tried to stay positive. I knew hard times were coming, but I also knew I had no choice but to get through it. I never doubted my ability to get past any obstacle. I always told people that I was only stressed for a minute. My biggest fear was losing my driver's license and with that, losing the close bond I had built between the kids and me. Every cloud has a silver lining, and in this situation, it was the fact that my kids were older now. They knew who I was, what we do and most of all, they could communicate with me on the phone very well. The case went on for a few months. During this time, I was still driving so I had some time to prepare them and myself for what was ahead. I always kept it real with them, so we talked about it. My lawyer ended up brokering a deal with the prosecutor. My driver's license would be suspended for two years, I had to pay fines, and I would have to do community service. The suspension was the hardest part. I knew it was coming but now that it was here, it was hard to swallow.

The day came for me to go to court. Before I left, I had to turn over my driver's license. One of my favorite songs back then was "One More Road to Cross" by DMX. That was exactly how I was feeling. It was one day at a time. Some good, some not so good, and I had some really bad days. A few good things were going for me which made my life a little easier. My job was only a 10-minute walk from my house, and my dad was working the same shift as me. Working at night gave me time during the day to complete my community service. I had strong family support, especially from my brother. Both my kid's mothers were driving, and they willingly stepped up to keep us all on the same schedule we had been on. Natalie was now driving us everywhere we went. She would say she felt like she was driving Miss Daisy.

My boy Ricky had a car, and I was able to call him when I needed a ride. My son's grandmother, who I called Grandma, took joy in anything to do with her grandson. She would help with driving him when needed. From that, I developed a very special love for her which continues to grow until this day. I even met some good people along the journey. I had met people that I did community service with; there were a couple of guys I would pay to take me places, and some would just always say the right things to affirm to me that it was all going to work out. The experience also showed me the other side of some people that were not supportive. One thing is for sure; it taught me a whole lot of lessons. It was just another course on real life. I showed up every day paying full attention and trying my best not to miss any of the lessons. At some point, my connection with my kids was not the same. I started missing picking them up, driving them places, or just simply driving around with them. It was the time that we had to ourselves that was so special to me, and I was missing it so much. I felt their pain also with not having daddy to themselves like they used to.

During this time, I got the call from the manufacturer that my DVDs were ready to be picked up. It was almost a two-hour drive, but one of my boys from work took me to pick them up. When we got back, he wouldn't accept the gas money I offered him. One thing I know for sure is that God always makes a way for me. I started promoting the DVD right away. I was trying to get everyone to buy one. The Verizon Wireless Corporate Classic 5K was held in Morristown shortly after I got the DVDs. It was a good place for me to do some promoting so I went there and put posters up all around the staging area. It was held on a weekday, so I had to go to work later that night. I left before the end of the event.

I remember walking home with a feeling of achievement. I was out there alone doing my thing even though I wasn't able to drive. There

185

were a few stores in town that allowed me to put my poster up in their glass window. I have to mention the look of amazement on my kids' faces when they watched the DVD for the first time. It was a great feeling and a one-of-a-kind experience. In the middle of selling and promoting the DVD, I got a cease-and-desist letter from a law office telling me to stop using the name Beach Body. I had no idea at that time there was a parent company for workout videos with the name Beach Body. I stopped promoting it, but I kept selling it locally. I even thought about just changing the name. I decided not to because I learned so much in the process that instead of spending all the money to change the name, I would be better off making a new video. It was very disappointing, but the experience and accomplishment overrode that feeling of disappointment. After all these years, people still tell me they are using water bottles in their house to work out because of that DVD. The feeling I get when I hear this never gets old.

The most amazing thing during this time happened. Natalie and I got married. We were like best friends and lovers. It was more than a wedding for me. Our closest friends and family surrounded us with their love. The day after our wedding, Hurricane Sandy came and our honeymoon trip to Las Vegas was canceled. After hunkering down through the storm, there was no electricity, a gas shortage, and road closures. I remember driving around with Grandma trying to get gas for the generator. It was the first time since I left Jamaica that I saw people waiting in such long lines for gas. Some were trying to get gas for their cars while others had gas cans in their hands trying to get them filled. What stuck in my mind was all the fun we had during all of it. We were inside chilling. For a guy that couldn't drive, I was surely getting around and getting by. After all, I know a lot of people that never drove, and they got around just fine. It was a two-year test for me, and I was going to pass it. Keeping myself busy was a way of keeping my mind off the adverse effects of not driving and the time seemed to go by faster. I never missed work, the gym, my community service, seeing and spending time with the kids, or any of the school events. Thanks to some good friends, family, and God for the determination he blessed me with. There was no benefit to sitting around stressing about what already happened. Instead, I tried working on making the future better and brighter.

The two years went by, and I was ready to get my driver's license back. I paid all my fines and had completed my community service. I had to do a 48-hour inpatient program which I did. I had completed all that was required of me before getting my license back, including not operating a motor vehicle during the period of my suspended license. Once I got my license back, I had to install an ignition interlock device in my car for the first few months. I wasn't allowed to drive any car without that device. It was a breathalyzer that was connected to the ignition. If your blood alcohol concentration was over a certain level, the car would not start. It would beep randomly as you were driving, and when it beeped, you had to blow into the device. If your alcohol level was too high, it would warn you before it locked you out for hours. After not driving for two years, blowing into a device was nothing. It was a privilege to be driving again. Those few months went by, and I was no longer required to have the device in my car. The one different thing was my time with the kids, especially my daughter who was now 12 years old. She got used to spending time with friends and hanging with family more. It was disappointing for me, but I realized it was all part of growing up.

At this point, I was now working at my job for 14 years. Both my kids were in middle school and going through life changes. It was part of my dream to be around to hold their hands and walk them through the tough times. There were some tough times, and I was right there every step of the way. I was also making better choices and decisions. After all the lessons I learned from the school of hard knocks, I was much more informed. I started to avoid some places that I used to hang out at. I was more careful with who I associated with. With a few minor changes in my life, I was getting major results. I was more at peace with myself. I had fewer problems which brought me and my loved ones more happiness. I started feeling a different vibe from those who cared about me. They were less worried. I was a hard worker at my job but not a company guy, I was just there. It was a steady income with benefits that provided health insurance for me and my family. I was the last one arriving at work and the first one at the clock in the morning when my shift ended. I appreciated my job, but I did not like it. I was trying my best to start something of my own.

One of the days I had prayed for arrived; my daughter was graduating from middle school. I was happy for her and the fact that I got to witness her first real graduation. It was one of those days when I reflected on raising little birds. She wasn't flying yet but she was growing feathers. She would be going onto high school, and she could not wait. There were many reasons why I was so happy to witness her graduation. The main one was the fact that I did not know what would happen with my immigration case and if I was going to be around. I remember going to court one day and my lawyer informing me that if they denied my application I could be detained. I had to sit my kids down and explain my situation to them. My daughter cried. I truly believed that God would work it out as he sees best for me and my family. It was hard walking into a federal courthouse not knowing if I would ever see the outside of the country I had been living in for over 26 years at that point. My two kids were born here and most of my family was now living here. One thing I knew was that I was not going to run around playing hide and seek with the law. I went to court and the judge accepted my application so the case could move forward. He gave me a new court date which was one and a half years away. I got to come back home to my family.

The following year I got to witness my son graduate from middle school, and you can imagine how happy and grateful I was. Now both of my kids were going to be in high school and were one step closer to college. It was not easy to take one day at a time, but all these experiences were teaching me how to do that.

My close ties with my community in Jamaica had become stronger. I did not know if or when it was possibly going to be my new home again. My boy Round Bread was still living there and was very active in the community. Two of my sisters were also there along with a whole host of family. The community was like one big family. It was difficult to find someone you could trust with money for doing any business. That was something I would hear from other Jamaicans and other Caribbean nationals. It was a different story when it came to my sisters who were very trustworthy. They never asked for anything, and they would spend their own money to buy stuff to send to me. They were always sending stuff to me and that's very rare amongst other people. People are usually asking for something, but no one would think of sending you anything, especially in my situation with not being able to travel there.

Every Jamaican living abroad wished they had sisters like mine who lived in Jamaica. I was blessed to have them. They were both trustworthy, loyal, and kind. One experience I would like to share is about a situation that happened between me, my brother, and a guy in Jamaica that was like a brother. We grew up together, and he was my brother's best friend. Through the years, he and my brother stayed close. My brother was always saying good things about him. This guy was a truck driver and mainly drove tractor-trailers. My brother would sometimes mention to me that one day he would like to buy him a truck. He started to call and told my brother that if he bought him a tractor, he had a trailer that he could fix up and make a lot of money. This was a guy who we loved and trusted. My brother and I were very close all our lives, so we talked about doing something together all the time. He shared the idea with me, and we agreed to go ahead and buy him the tractor. When all was said and done, we sent over $30,000 to Jamaica.

My brother was the one who was communicating with him. He bought a tractor and worked on the damaged body of the trailer to fix it up. This took forever. After a year, he got it on the road. Our agreement was for him to work with the truck and give us what he could whenever he could to cover the cost of what we invested; then, we could start saving to get a second truck. There were no stipulations. My brother told him to drive for a few weeks and take care of himself and anything with the truck. Then he should start bringing some money to my sisters. Week after week, month after month, and there was no money. It was excuse after excuse. My brother is very patient, humble, and forgiving. My brother had been the one dealing with this guy. I asked my brother if he minded if I called him to find out what was going on. He said he did not mind. I called him to let him know that if the truck wasn't making money, then it wasn't worth it. He promised me he was going to start bringing money to my sisters. He brought some money and then went back to the excuses. By this time, I was mad at him. I ended up calling him, and I told him to park the truck and give my sisters the key and all the papers. He tried to tell me more stories, but I was done listening.

The truck sat there until the daughter of my late area leader called me. She told me that her child's father was a truck driver and was currently out of work. She asked if he could operate the truck and take care of it for us. I told her to have him call me. He called me right away. He explained to me exactly what his plans were for the truck and the money he would make. I didn't know him, but he was straightforward, and I felt like it was a good way of paying homage to my late general. I told him to get the keys and papers from my sisters. I also called Round Bread to let him know what was going on, and he agreed with the idea. When the guy checked the truck out, it needed all kinds of work. I sent him a few thousand dollars to get the truck back on the road. Our guy had bought an older truck with a fraction of the money we had given him. This new guy started driving it and did okay for a while before the excuses started. I told him the same thing I told the other guy. If the truck works, we get paid. It's simple; if it's one trip, we split the money. I said, "It's not going to be you getting paid, and we are not." At the same time, he was telling me it was slow because of this reason and that reason.

He called to tell me the truck broke down on the road. He was telling me his boss owed him money for loads he did, and that's why he wasn't able to give us any money. So I told him to get the money to fix the truck. I also told him to let me know if he didn't want to pay him so I could send someone to give him a check. He got the money and fixed the truck. It was no longer worth it for me, so I told him I was going to sell the truck. I ended up selling the truck for a very small fraction of the money we spent. I still feel betrayed by our brother but I'm over it now, and another lesson was learned.

This guy's younger brother lived here in the States and was also a tractor-trailer driver. He called me one night while I was at work. We were like brothers since we had been kids. He told me he broke down on the highway and needed a new tire. He said the tire guy was there and could fix the tire, but he needed the money for the tire. He was looking for a credit card to be given over the phone. I told him I couldn't do it, but I would try to reach my brother, and maybe he could help him. I called my brother and woke him up. He said he would call him and take care of it for him. Later that morning when my brother came to work, he told me he took care of it. It was over a $1,000 charge on his credit card. He had told my brother he would pay him the money in a few days. It has been more than six years, and not once has he called my brother. I ran into him a few years ago and asked him what happened. He tried to tell me a story that I was not believing. I told him that at this point it was not even about the money but the fact that he never reached out. He told me to tell my brother he would see him in two weeks. That two weeks still did not come yet. To make things clearer as to how cruel this guy was, my brother works hard to take care of his family and anyone he can help, and this guy was out partying every weekend. My brother probably wouldn't approve of me talking about this incident, but I was a part of both, which taught me great lessons so I feel the need to share.

They were life experiences that had an impact on me so much that they made me change for the better. I still have a love for them but for right now, it's from a distance. I'm thankful I got to know that you use money and love people and not use people and love money. I pray continuously for the strength to be loving and forgiving because things like that take a different type of strength to not stay angry or hate people who do those things to you. My brother never displayed any type of anger toward either of these guys. He never even mentioned anything about them. If it was up to my brother, this guy would still be driving the truck, or he probably would have run it in the ground by now. He would tell me it's a lesson learned while I was thinking it was a very expensive one. I thank God for him. He has been my teacher of patience, humility, forgiveness and so much more. At a point in this situation, I was blazing hot. Thankfully, my brother was not the type of person to instigate things but always found a way to defuse every situation. He is very good at it. He probably could have been a good hostage negotiator. He's a light in the darkest moments.

Both of my kids were now in high school, and they were both playing sports. My daughter was a sprinter on the track team. My son had been playing football, soccer, basketball and was also on the track team.

After his first year, he settled with playing basketball and got pretty good at it. I went to the track meets and games. I felt like I had to be there because we were one team. There were difficult periods when I had to pay more attention to one more than the other like the shepherd that leaves his flock of 99 sheep to find the one which is lost. That's exactly how I felt sometimes, especially with my daughter. There was a period when I knew she needed me closer to her than ever before. I never strayed or turned my back on either of them. My love for them never faltered. I tried my best to manage my attention accordingly. At times, I was judged for my team working ability, accused of being biased and loving one more than the other. The love I know and have for my kids was in the purest form, so I never felt pressured to do anything other than what I felt was the right thing to do. It was hard for me and others at times, but doing the right and the best thing for us was never a question for me. For that very reason, our bond grew very strong. We were like the timber that grew in the strong winds, the sailor that battled the storms, and a team that won and lost together.

Colgate-Palmolive, the company I had been working for, decided to move the plant I worked at to South Carolina. At this point, I had been working for the company for almost 18 years. All 18 years had been on the night shift. I didn't know what I was going to do next, but I knew I wanted to do something different. The company allowed us to re-apply for a job in South Carolina under a new agreement. Under no circumstances was I moving away from my kids so that was never an option for me. I watched people react in all different ways. Some acted like it was the end of the world, some were just worried, some were taking it one day at a time, and others were like me and ready to move on to something different.

I started thinking about music again. It was just that thing that I always liked and wanted to do. Peter, my Indian friend who owns a convenience store in town, was always asking me what I was doing with my music. He told me that he knew a couple of guys in the business that he could introduce me to. Now that the place I was working at was closing down, I was thinking more about my music; I took him up on his offer. He took me to Hackensack, New Jersey to meet with some guys at a recording studio. One guy was a business partner and also of Indian descent. The other guy was a producer, and he was Black. The Indian guy didn't say much. It was the producer that I was mostly talking with. We exchanged numbers so we could communicate and set up another meeting to see where we could go with my music from there. I called him, and we planned to meet. He told me to bring the recordings I already had. When we met, he listened to some of the songs I had recorded. As soon as he heard Pitbull in a Skirt, he said it was the one he thought we should work on. It was one of my favorites and everyone that had heard it loved it, so I was in total agreement.

We then moved to the business side of things. We agreed on some figures and drafted up a contract. Again, I must say God always leads me to some good people, and this time I was talking about Peter. They say, "do good and good will follow you." I found that to be so true. I communicated to Peter everything that was going on with me and the producer. Peter was playing a manager role, even though he was just a friend looking out for another. He ended up putting up some money for me even though he knew so much could happen that he might never see a dime of it back. He is one of the more real people I have met in my life. We worked on the song until we felt like we got it to where we wanted it. There was some uncertainty in my head regarding the changing of my guy who sang the hook. He replaced him with a female's voice; someone I had never met. I started thinking about Natalie's beautiful voice so if it was going to be a female's voice, it should be hers. After all, the song was originally inspired by her. He eventually won because I didn't want to make it about me and my personal feelings but more about what was best for the business. The song was good and ready to go.

He was also involved in the video recording business, so we decided to make a video for the song. We shared some ideas and met with his team. We recorded at a couple of different locations including my hometown of Morristown. I went and talked to the mayor who was my friend. He permitted me to use the same park in which I wrote the song. It was a very memorable evening. I had members of my community, family, my kids, and friends there supporting me. The cops even came to check if everything was going okay and if we needed their help. After shooting at the different locations, the footage was edited, and we had a final video. I lost the connection I had with the producer after that. He was all about the money and less interested in the promotion and development of me as an artist. The experience was priceless. It's experiences like that and so many more in this book that made me into who I am today. I was doing all this while still working and figuring out my next move before Colgate closed.

Instead of closing the entire plant at once, they gradually scaled down the production. They started moving the production lines one at a time. That way, they wouldn't have to stop production. Both plants were running at the same time at one point. It was a transition but not a smooth one. Our plant ran longer than they had planned due to difficulties in getting the production up and running in South Carolina. Every time a production line was moved, a couple of people would be let go. I left halfway through the moving process. My brother was one of the bosses, so he was there until the very end. I still have trouble sleeping at night from working the night shift for all those years. I did most of the writing for this book at night.

It's been an adventurous journey since leaving Colgate. There was a company store where all the employees and retirees were able to buy products at a discounted price. The products included toothpaste, dog food, hand soap, Irish Spring soap, cat food, Ajax, and much more. I would shop in the company store every chance I got so that I would have products that I could share with other people. Giving and helping people brings me great joy. Having these products to share with others was a blessing. That was one of the things I missed most about this job. In everything, there are lessons and one that I learned in this situation was the behavior of people. Some would call to ask me for products all the time, and then after the plant closed, they wouldn't even call to say hi or ask how I was doing. From experiences, I already knew that was how it was. It was just that some of the people who did this surprised me.

Understanding human behavior is probably one of the most challenging things on earth. It's the reason for most wars, fussing, fights, and separations. I've been learning to not take other people's behavior personally. There are a million reasons why we behave the way we do, and I think most of the time, it's nothing personal. I've had people misjudge my behaviors many times, behaviors that sometimes would hurt people I love although it was not my intention. I think it's the main reason my wife Natalie filed for divorce. I was hurt at first. She was a friend, sister, and confidant so that hurt didn't last long. I knew who she was to me and how I truly felt about her so all I had to do was give her respect, support, and be understanding of how my behaviors affected her. For me, nothing changed other than she wasn't around, and we weren't communicating like we used to. There was never a fight or any disrespect between us. I've heard so many stories about bitter and revengeful separations. The love and respect never changed. Real love never dies. After a while, it was like nothing happened between us, and we became closer than ever. We have had many arguments and breakups, but our bond has been solid from day one. I know emotions get the best of us sometimes, but I could never understand how a person can love someone one day and the next day be calling them names and wishing all kinds of bad things on them. I'm not sure what love is but that's not it.

I want to share something I wrote in the year 2001. This thought came after a conversation I had with Natalie. It was after our breakup that occurred after my daughter was born. She expressed some feelings she had. At that moment I was being selfish and was only thinking, I knew I loved her, but she was misunderstanding some of my behaviors and thinking I didn't. I love to write my thoughts on paper when I'm in a certain mindset and when I have a pen and paper around. This particular day I wrote what I called "What is Love?"

<u>What Is Love?</u>

I'm trying to find out what love is
And for now, I won't retire
Girl I'm hot for you
So love might be a fire
You're the one I'm in love with
You're my heart's desire
I tried to show you in my own way
But you still think I'm a liar

195

Don't get deep into movies
So we hardly hit the theater
Don't have a big appetite
Very rare we go to dinner
But if that's what love is
The poor man would be a loner
Or if a rich man should go broke
Would he lose his lover
I wanna know what love is
Is it a natural power

As you can see, this is something I've been thinking about for a very long time. I questioned the love I felt for people. I wondered if I was mistaking love for something else or being foolish loving someone I'm not supposed to, and the questions went on and on in my head. I've always heard the saying "love and hate can't be friends." I was now getting an understanding of what it meant. When there's love in a person, they love everyone including themself. You might ask how is that possible, just like I asked myself. One day after some deep thoughts and analysis, I realized that there was not one person, place, or thing that I hated. At this time in my life, there were only three people that I knew that I would not speak to if and when I saw them. It was anger that led to avoidance but never once a feeling of hate as these three people were like brothers. I spoke about two of them and expressed my feeling of love for them and sent a message of love to the third since he wasn't around, and I have no contact information for him. I'm currently working on getting his contact info so I can speak with him directly. The two I spoke to expressed similar feelings of love for me likewise. It is a great feeling to make peace and express love; especially when it took a lot of courage, strength, humility, and open-mindedness to the possibilities of the other person's reaction.

The word hate has been overused. This started from early childhood. When we get angry, we think we hate everyone and everything. It's very common to hear kids telling parents they hate them. That usually happens when you are already angry. It's the same for grownups. When we are angry with someone, we tend to think we now hate that person; or if a sports team beats our team, we say we hate that team, the city they are from, and anyone wearing that team's jersey. The same goes for race, religion, and anyone with different views than us. Now think about all the people and things that you are angry with for some reason or all the people and things you are indifferent with and ask yourself, "Do I hate them or am I just angry with them because of something they did or something I didn't like about them?" Most of the time, you will realize that you don't hate that person or that thing. Let's try to be more aware of how we use the word hate. I'm not in any way saying hate doesn't exist. There are misunderstandings, ignorance, intolerance and so much more in society that will continue to build and fuel hate among us. Love is patient and kind.

It only takes one person to change a generation. Bob Marley's message of love impacted many generations across the world. In his time when Jamaica came to the minds of people all over the world, they would think of slogans like "one love", "Irie mon". There is an effort by some with selfish intentions to replace the message of love with one that is of hate. Maybe unconsciously, but when someone with a voice and large audience keeps identifying themselves as Jamaican by screaming the words "suck yuh madda" or "bomboclaat," it is sowing seeds of hate and anger in society. Most of the time, we are conscious of the love in our hearts, but we act otherwise because of weakness. We think about what others are going to say or think about us. Sometimes we feel like we have to take a side in an argument between others, misunderstanding what loyalty is. Sometimes all we need to do is be the bridge and bring others together. Speak the truth that is in your heart and free yourself.

I pray for strength to love because it takes a lot of courage at times. One example of that is keeping the love I have for my people in Jamaica. The fact that I haven't seen them in more than two decades is enough to cause love to fade away. Mine never did. With all that I was dealing with here in the U.S., I still did what I could for them and often ended up getting burned. I can easily count on one hand the times I received anything from someone in Jamaica other than from my sisters; I think about it sometimes, and it's not a good feeling. I have expressed my thoughts and feelings with Round Bread. What keeps my love for them so strong is understanding. It's a very different kind of culture here in America. It's one of giving gifts, working, paying bills, and opportunities. Nothing is free. We are exposed to so much more than they are. I think the biggest difference is the access we have to information. People who have migrated tend to judge the ones they left behind and expect so much more of them when in reality, we were just like them before we left. I still laugh at the list of things I asked my sister for one Christmas. The more I get to understand my people and their way of life, the stronger the love gets. There's a saying that says, "the heart is willing, but the flesh is weak." That's basically how it is with my people. I've learned to take more responsibility for my actions and decisions.

When we sent the guy the money to buy the truck, that was where we went wrong. We can't expect to run a successful business with a person that doesn't have money management skills or money to invest in the business. That should have been the first sign that he was not the person to be handling the money. Too many times, we expect the people we have known for years who have no experience in any kind of business to all of a sudden have the know-how. If you give a rat cheese to carry or a person a bucket of water with holes in it to carry and expect it to reach the destination, then all the blame is on you. A better understanding will always keep the peace and love. They sometimes expect more from you than you can offer, or you could easily slip into a mindset that makes you feel if you can make it, they can make it too. So, it takes understanding on both sides for the love to flourish.

During this time, my daughter got her driver's permit. I was excited to be around to witness this very special milestone. As a very experienced driver, I was happy for the opportunity to be one of her instructors. On the day she got her permit, an instructor from the driving school took her to the Department of Motor Vehicle (DMV). I met her there. Now that she had her permit, I told her she was going to be the one driving anytime we were in the car together. She was excited and ready to drive. I directed her to the highway, and she drove to Boonton, New Jersey where we had Jamaican food for lunch. Then she drove back to Morristown. She was confident and very relaxed. For the first time, I was in the passenger seat with my daughter driving. I remember one Saturday she drove her brother and me to the same restaurant in Boonton. On our way back, there was a rainstorm. It was pouring so I thought about telling her to pull over and let me drive, but she was doing so well I didn't stop her. At no point did she seem uncomfortable or nervous. After that day, I was convinced that she was going to be a very good driver. Months later, on her 17th birthday, she went back to the DMV with an instructor to take her road test. She passed and she got her driver's license, and I was there waiting for her. We went for a late breakfast at IHOP and then she went on to celebrate her birthday and this special milestone. It was a dream come true for me.

I had an eye-opening experience when one of our very own Reggae superstars, Charly Black, rose to international fame. Years before his international hit song "Gyal You a Party Animal," he had a minor dancehall hit called "Buddy Buddy". He came on tour to the U.S. and one of the shows was in New Jersey. My boys and I were partying hard at that time. We were everywhere and everyone in the party circle knew us. We went to the show and after his performance, the party ended. I walked around trying to find Charly, and I couldn't find him. A guy who I knew pointed me to a door and said Charly was inside that room. I knocked on the door a few times before someone opened it. I asked for Charly, and he told me I couldn't see him and closed the door. With the alcohol in me and the disrespect, I was super mad, so I started banging on the door feeling like I wanted to kick it down. They opened the door and there was an argument between me and the guy. I had my whole team with me, so I was good. This guy knew us, and we knew him which was the reason for his disrespect. What he didn't know was my connection to Charly. Charly told him to let me in the room.

They were the promoters, and Charly was a young artist from Jamaica. He was in my zone, and it was only right to make sure he was good and not being taken advantage of. We talked for a little bit, and he told me everything was good. Now, these guys were mad as hell. The artist that they were trying to show off about was family. The following night, we went to another party and one of my boys came and told me that Charly was in the club. I immediately walked over to where he was. Upon approaching him, one of those same guys tried to stop me. Charly could see him blocking me from passing, and he immediately told him to let me through. I've always been proud of my hometown of Rio Bueno and love the people. If it's trouble, death, wedding, or any kind of celebration here in the U.S., they know they can call me and I'm there. I think of it as we are all one grand team broken up into smaller teams, so we are supposed to support each other. It felt good to see someone from my town in such a position that was still humble and loyal. It was a morale booster for me and my boys. Charly kept working hard and was releasing song after song. He was making his name in the dance hall. It was years later that he found the hit song every artist dreamed of, "Gyal You a Party Animal." This song became an international hit and one of the biggest dancehall songs at the time. It will hold its place in dancehall history. Charly Black was now touring the world while the song "Gyal You a Party Animal" was playing on every radio station, club, wedding, birthday party, dancehall, barbecue, and playlist. It was playing everywhere, and his name became a household name all over the world.

After telling people about the place where I grew up, I felt like I finally had a breakthrough. I couldn't have felt prouder. Other than his success, the next best part about his story was the fact that he was traveling around the world declaring himself as the Country Boy, Trelawny Son. He was from Rio Bueno as well. That in and of itself was legendary. I heard that a few people from the community were saying unpleasant things about him. I knew how people were from my experiences, so I contacted Round Bread to find out what was going on. He informed me that Charly Black was a good guy, and he would never forget about them. He even went as far as to say anywhere in the world Charly was, he would contact him or most times he would just send him a video clip. He informed me that some expected him to do all these things. Some of it was jealousy and some of it was just plain ignorance. I understood everything he was saying because unfortunately, that's how it was in my community. After talking to Round Bread, I was even happier for Charly and all of us.

All I wanted and was waiting on now was for him to come to perform in my zone which is the tri-state area (New York, New Jersey,

Connecticut). My wait was over when I saw all the promotions for a show in Brooklyn that he was headlining. I felt like it was the perfect place for me to link up with him because it was an outside evening show. It was a family day celebrating Jamaica's independence. Gramps was living in Brooklyn, so I called him up and told him to meet me there. I drove to Brooklyn by myself and met Gramps at the entrance to the venue which was a football field. The entrance fee was $40 per person. We paid and went in. There were a lot of people including children. There were also vendors. We walked toward the stage and on our way, Gramps saw a guy he knew from Jamaica. He stopped to talk to him. He, too, was there to see Charly. What got my attention was when he told Gramps that he had gone to a club in Manhattan to see Charly. While he was outside, Charly walked by, and he was shouting his name, but Charly and his team kept walking. When I heard that, I joined the conversation and told him that was the wrong place and time to be shouting his name expecting him to stop and come over to him. I informed him that Charly was now a superstar working with a team. It's nothing personal. We proceeded closer to the stage where Gramps saw another guy he knew. This guy was part of the promotion team. Gramps told him we were there to see Charly. He said Charly wasn't there yet, but we could come backstage and wait for him there. He opened the barricades to let us in. We hung out backstage until Charly came. We kept chilling watching him and his team situating things with the promoters and stage managers. He saw us and walked over to us. I had a good conversation with him and right away, I knew nothing had changed between us. He was still the Charly Black I knew—humble, kind, loyal, and authentic as ever. He gave me his number and introduced me to his road manager. He let him know that I was family.

The road manager showed me where the drinks were, and it was time for a toast. We hung out until it was time for Charly to perform. They brought him the mic backstage where he was starting his performance from. He walked on the stage while singing and we walked up behind him. He smashed it. His performance was electric. He even gave me a shout-out. After the show, there was a big crowd around him. People were trying to get a picture with him. He waited until everyone got a picture and that's when I said to myself, he has my support 1,000%.

The first thing I did when I got in the car was called Round Bread. I said to him, "Charly is good yo." The man is more real than real. He was happy to hear what I was saying because he was trying for a while to connect me with him. I told him he should strengthen the foundation on the ground in the community. It must be full support for our brother. From that day, the team which is called Team Unstoppable has been growing and strengthening. Charly Black would let me know every time he would be in my area and when possible, we linked up. I'm even featured in two of his music videos. He is an icon, an inspiration, and a living legend of our community and throughout Jamaica.

It was now my son's turn to get his driver's permit. Just like my daughter, he went to the DMV with an instructor from the driving school. I met him there. After he got his permit, it was time for him to hit the road. Once again, I was excited for him and to be there to share such a special moment. I directed him to the highway and just like I had done with my daughter, we went to the Jamaican restaurant in Boonton to eat. It wasn't about the food so much; it was more about the drive up the highway. I wanted them to know that the highway was just another kind of road to get used to, enjoy, and not to be feared. My son had his cap turned backward and was comfortable in the driver's seat. He was driving like he had done it for a while. One of the differences between my daughter and him was his love for speeding. Our conversation was mostly about speeding. I felt a little guilty talking to him about speeding when he had been driving with me all his life. I explained to him all the dangers that come with speeding. He did well, and I was proud of both of them for now being on the road.

I bought a parcel of land in my old community in Jamaica, which was located on the main road along the beach. Someone was occupying the land, and it was now my responsibility to get them off. I had to retain a lawyer to work through the court to remove them. It was a long, drawn-out process. My intention was always to bring and keep the people of the community together. This parcel of land was now causing all kinds of issues. My sisters were the ones representing me there and because I didn't want them to have a problem with anyone, I asked Round Bread to take over the everyday dealings. I made it clear to my sisters, Round Bread, and my family and friends that I did not want any arguments over the land. I would prefer to let the money go because too often Jamaicans kill each other over parcels of land. I wasn't worried about it, so I didn't want them to worry either. There were days that I got angry that I had to go through all that with people I loved and cared about. I would remind myself that it was all a misunderstanding and ignorance. Round Bread is still there to this day representing me and taking care of things. There are some lingering issues concerning the land, but we are taking it one day at a time while living and taking care of more important things like family.

It was my daughter's final year of high school, so it was time for her to begin to prepare for college. It was another milestone that I had prayed I would be able to witness. I was very happy to be a part of her team, along with her mother, guidance counselor, and college coach. The whole process brought me back to my reference of raising birds. My daughter was now getting closer and closer to flying. While she was preparing to leave for college, my son who was a year behind her was starting to visit colleges. He was in the very early stages of preparation, and I was happy that I was around to share this great time with both of them. After all that I had been through and was still going through, it was nothing short of a true blessing.

On Danny's 17th birthday, he went to take his driving test with his instructor from the driving school. I met him at the motor vehicle agency where he took the test. He passed so we went inside where he got his driver's license. That was probably his best birthday present. He had a car before getting his license so now he was driving around on his own.

The day of high school graduation came for my daughter, and I must tell you it was a very emotional day for me. I was happy that I made it, she made it, and my mind was thinking about all that we had been through together throughout the years. We went through some rough patches, but we got through them because we had a strong team. A part of the team got to witness it and celebrated with her. Her mom, brother, and both her grandmothers were there.

Duke and Julie's son, Kevin, also graduated with my daughter. After graduation, their family went to Jamaica for a few days. They left their house key with me and asked me to check on things while they were away. When they got back, Julie gave me a thank you note which I still have. I kept it because it felt special to me. Some people don't even say thank you. It felt different, and it touched a part of me that made me feel appreciated. I love to write my feelings on paper and once I'm holding the pen, my heart, mind, and soul engage to express my true thoughts and feelings. That's exactly how I felt about her note. It wasn't just lip service. It was genuine. Her note read:

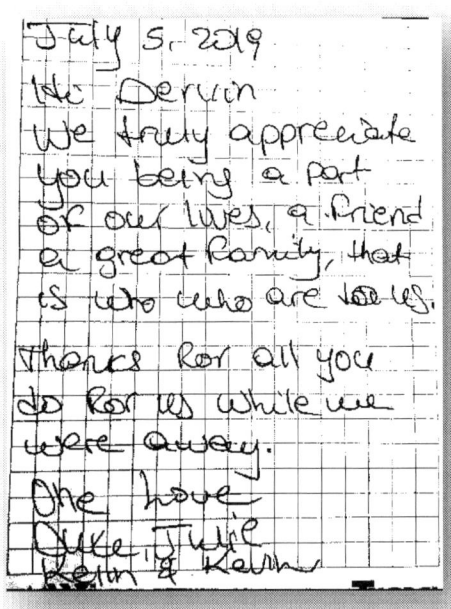

I've never expressed to her or Duke how this note made me feel mostly because there was so much going on at that time.

Chapter 9

The Great Battle

David Against Goliath

In 2017, I had gone to a doctor's appointment for my annual checkup. I expressed my concern to the doctor about a hard lump I could feel under the skin slightly to the right above my belly button. He felt it with his hand. He then asked me if I had any pain associated with it and I told him I didn't. He told me it was nothing to worry about, and that it was just my muscle. At that time, I had six-pack abs and was close to making it eight. It sounded a little weird, but I didn't give it any thought. I was in good shape, no pain, and I didn't have any second thoughts, so I left his office as usual.

The following year in September of 2018, I went back for my annual checkup. This time I was more concerned about the lump because it was now bigger and protruding out. He again told me it was nothing to worry about, and he was still thinking it was my ab muscle. This time I wasn't willing to accept that as the answer. He said for my comfort, he would send me to see a surgeon. He gave me the surgeon's business card to call and set up an appointment. I set up the appointment and went to see the surgeon. After examining the lump, he told me it was a desmoid tumor. He said if it was not bothering me, it was best to leave it alone because if it was removed, the chances were, it would come back and come back aggressively. He suggested I leave it alone and later on we could do a biopsy. I agreed. He also told me to read up about desmoid tumors which I did, and my research confirmed what he had said. This lump had now become visible through my t-shirts and was growing. It was now the Spring of 2019, and I started to feel uncomfortable with the size of the lump. I started feeling a slight sensation in it sometimes. By the end of June, I called his office and set up an appointment to see him.

Just after the 4th of July holiday, I went to see him. I wasn't going to live the rest of my life with this lump that was growing. I told him I wanted the lump removed. He kept asking me if I was sure and if I had read about it. I told him I did, and I would worry about it if or when it came back. He agreed to remove it, so he told the nurse to schedule an ultrasound and a biopsy. This was standard procedure for the removal of a tumor. I had the biopsy on July 9th. Two days later, on July 11^{th,} I flew to North Carolina with my daughter for her freshman orientation at the college she committed to going to. The orientation was scheduled to start the next morning, which was Friday, July 12th.

When we got to North Carolina, I rented a car at the airport, and we drove to the hotel. I had booked a hotel close to the college. We got some lunch before we checked into the hotel. When we got to the hotel room, both of us fell asleep. When I woke up that evening, I was hungry so I searched for a Jamaican restaurant online and found one that was close by. It was going to be closing soon so I woke my daughter up and told her we should go get some food before it got too late. She said she didn't want anything to eat. I told her to still come with me, but she didn't want to. I didn't like the idea of her staying there alone. We came together, and I felt that we should stay together. I tried to talk her into coming with me, but she decided she was not coming. I had to eat so I left her there and went to the Jamaican restaurant. When I got there, I tried calling her a few times to ask her what I could bring back for her, but I got no answer. I bought a few different types of food from the restaurant. There was a convenience store next door, so I stopped in there and picked up some snacks, water, and juice.

When I got back to the hotel room, she was lying on the bed with her phone in her hand. I asked her if she saw me calling her, and she said she didn't because she had just woken up. I asked her how she could have fallen back to sleep and woken back up in such a short amount of time. I asked her if that was the case, why didn't she return my call when she woke up and saw I was calling. I didn't know what was going on with her, but she had an attitude all day. I tried to tell her that next time she should answer the phone because something could have happened to me, and I could have been calling to let her know. She started yelling back at me. She said some hurtful things which made me upset. I put the food that I was eating back into the plastic bag, picked up a bottle of water, and went downstairs. I was so upset and wished I could catch a flight home. I sat on some steps at a side door of the hotel that faced the street. All kinds of thoughts were running through my mind. I called my brother to tell him what happened and how I was feeling. He talked to me for a while. I also called Natalie and told her how I was feeling. I even messaged Round Bread in Jamaica. I didn't go into detail with him, but he told me about his girl and that it was just how they get sometimes. I was sitting on the steps for a while until it was dark.

About 8:00 p.m., I got a call from a strange number with a New Jersey area code. When I answered, it was the surgeon. He started telling me that the results of my biopsy were back and there were some cancerous cells. Once he mentioned the word cancer, I could not hear anything else he was saying. He was rambling on about cancer. I stopped him and said to him, "What are you saying? I have cancer?" He said, "Yes." I couldn't tell you how I felt at that moment because I went numb. All I remember about the rest of the conversation was that he was trying to get me to come to his office the next day. I told him I was in North Carolina with my daughter, and I wouldn't be back until late Friday evening. He told me to call the nurse in the morning because we needed to schedule some appointments right away. As soon as I got off the phone with him, I called my brother. I couldn't come out with the news, so my brother thought I was calling back about what happened earlier with my daughter. He started to tell me not to pay any mind to it, that it was just how kids are sometimes, and they say things they don't mean. I said to him, "No, it's not that." The doctor just called me and told me that I have cancer.

I honestly don't remember what his immediate reply was or the details of our conversation. The one thing I do remember was God is able, just trust him and that he always asked God not to let any of his siblings die prematurely. My brother was doing most of the talking until we hung up. I'm not sure if he prayed over the phone, but I remember him telling me he was going to go talk to God after we got off the phone. After I got off the phone with him, I remember wanting to call Natalie, but I was hesitant because I didn't want to give her bad news right before bedtime. I wasn't sure how she would react. I thought about waiting until the morning or later the next evening when I would be back in New Jersey. I needed to talk to her to let her know what was going on. She knew about this lump from the beginning, and she had been more concerned about it than I had been. Through all that I had been through in the past, she always was an optimistic voice in my ear. She was not the kind of person that worried very much or at least she didn't show it. No matter what it was, I would always feel better after talking to her. All this might sound like it went on for hours, but it was only minutes before I couldn't resist any longer, so I called her. Just like the conversation with my brother, I don't remember the details. I think we talked mostly about the doctors and the fact that for one-and-a-half years they had told me not to worry about it. I called her a couple of times that night.

I went back to the room to get my workout gloves and the peanuts I had bought at the convenience store. Working out always helped me to release stress. I went back downstairs to the gym to work out while going back and forth on the phone. After I was done working out, I went back to sitting on the steps outside. All this time, I think I was numb from the shock. I just wanted to get back home. It started to get late, so I decided to go take a shower and go to bed. My daughter and I had to get up early to be at the college. When I got upstairs, I realized I had forgotten to bring the band-aids they gave me to dress the spot on my abdomen where they had done the biopsy. From where I had been sitting on the steps, I could see a gas station up the street with what looked like a store. I went back downstairs and walked there in search of band-aids. I was able to get band-aids there.

It was a little way from the hotel, so I had time to think and tears started running down my cheeks. Here I was in North Carolina walking on a lonely road by myself, just found out I have cancer, and my daughter who I took there for college orientation was being rude to me minutes before I got the news. I knew I wasn't going to tell her while we were there, and I had no plans of telling her before she left for college. I didn't want to put any kind of pressure on her. I went back to the room, took a shower, and went to sleep.

I got up very early the next morning, got ready, and packed my stuff. I woke her up and told her I would be downstairs in the lobby when she was ready. The hotel had a complimentary breakfast in the lobby area. I practically forced myself to eat something. My daughter came downstairs, we checked out, and got on our way to the college. She still had an attitude, so she sat in the back seat of the rental car. All I was thinking was if only she knew. We got to the college, and I was pretty much following her lead. For the most part, she acted like I wasn't even there. The first place we gathered was in the auditorium. I had to step outside to take a call from the doctor's office. It was the nurse who gave me some numbers to call to set up appointments. She wanted me to call as soon as I was able to. We went from "don't worry about it" to total panic very quickly. I was dealing with my daughter, on one hand, and the doctors on the other.

While my daughter was waiting in line to have her picture taken for her school ID, one of the cameras broke so I knew it would be a while. I left her and went outside to set up my appointments. I was going back and forth between calls to check on her. She went from one booth to the next until she said to me, "I'm done." Everything was done ahead of schedule, so we had a lot of time before our flight. With her attitude and what I was going through, I just wanted to get to the airport, return the car and wait until it was time for our flight. I got on the highway and headed to the airport. She asked me where I was going, and I told her to the airport. She asked why we were going to the airport so early, and I didn't even reply. All I thought was, "Where are we supposed to be going with you in the back seat not talking to me?" Now she was really mad at me. She said she needed something to eat so we got food and then went to the airport.

I returned the car, and we checked in for our flight. Our flight wasn't for another four hours. I sat on a bench by the security check, and she went and sat a distance away from me. Now I finally had time to think, and I broke down crying to myself in the airport. My brother checked in with me, and I spoke to Natalie. My daughter's uncle Chinkie had called me while I was sitting at the airport. I shared with him how she was behaving, but I didn't mention anything about cancer. After waiting for what felt like a whole day, it was time for us to go through the security check and head to the boarding gate. As if what I was going through was not enough, after going through the security screening, I got pulled over to the side, and my hands were swabbed for explosives. After waiting all that time, our flights were now delayed. I went to the bar, got a drink, and made some new friends. We finally boarded late that evening and landed in Newark around 9:00 p.m. My brother came to pick us up, and my daughter still had an attitude.

The following week, I had all kinds of doctor appointments. The same doctor that told me it was a desmoid tumor was now the one rushing me to have surgery to remove the lump. He scheduled a date for me to have the surgery the following week. He was the one that was going to remove the tumor, and then the plastic surgeon would reconstruct my abdominal wall. The surgery was supposed to be on Thursday, so I was to have pre-surgery consultation with both of them on that Tuesday before. I saw the plastic surgeon in the morning, and he explained to me the procedure he planned to do. Later that afternoon, I went to see the surgeon. It was my first time seeing him since the diagnosis. He started twisting his story and said he had told me to get the biopsy done months ago which was not true. I got so mad. I won't even say what was going through my mind. I sat there and stared at him. He kept telling me to say something, but I didn't open my mouth. The nurse was standing there like she usually did but this time was very quiet. She knew exactly what had been said at the previous visits. If he had wanted me to do a biopsy, she would have been the one to set it up. She knew the truth. While we were in the room, someone came to the door and told him pathology was on the phone. He was gone for about 20 minutes. Natalie was with me waiting for the doctor to return.

When he came back into the room, he said, "Change of plans." He had received the final pathology report, and it was a lot more serious than he thought. This doctor was not an oncology surgeon, yet he was making decisions about my cancerous tumor. After he got the pathology report, he consulted with an oncology surgeon who told him because it was a very aggressive type of cancer, it would require chemotherapy before surgery.

The type of cancer I was diagnosed with is called Rhabdo-myosarcoma. He canceled the scheduled surgery and set up another appointment to install a port under the skin of my upper chest that would attach to a vein in my neck. This device would be used to administer the chemotherapy drug and to take blood samples. On July 24th, I had surgery to install the port. It was a minor surgery, and I was only at the hospital for about four hours so my brother took me. I was given Tylenol before I left the hospital and a prescription for a pain killer. We stopped to have the prescription filled, but I didn't take any since I wasn't in any pain. I came home and went to sleep. When I woke up a few hours later, I was in excruciating pain. It just so happened that my brother had stopped by and asked me how I was feeling. I was in pain and feeling sorry for myself. Before I could answer, I burst out in tears. Reality began to set in. The fight was real. I took the pain medication and about an hour or two later, I began to feel better. The surgeon had told me that I couldn't work out for a week but after four days, I started doing push-ups, and I felt perfectly fine.

Now there was a change in the surgery plan, so I was getting ready to start chemotherapy. I was in a different state of mind. At first, I had no intention of telling my parents that the tumor was cancerous. I figured I could have the surgery as planned earlier to remove it, and they wouldn't need to know. I didn't want them to stress over me as I knew that would in turn stress me out. Now that I was about to undergo chemotherapy, I knew I had to tell my parents. Other than losing my hair, I didn't know what effects the chemo drugs would have on me. I knew they would be worried about the way I looked and what was going on with me if I didn't tell them. I told my brother that it was best for him to tell them and to please tell them not to worry about me. I would be fine. I started telling people that were close to me. The word cancer sounds like a death sentence to most people. Throughout my experience, I have received all types of reactions. I will share some of them with you as they happened.

The first memorable one was when I told Duke and Julie. Julie asked what the treatment plan was, and I told them. Duke then said, "Yeah they can buy you some time." I was saying to myself, "Who says something like that to a person that is sick, especially with cancer?" I was much more optimistic than he was, so I laughed about it. Everything was moving at a super high speed. I didn't have any confidence in these doctors from the very start, and now it was getting worse. They were all over the place with what course should be taken. It was a rare form of cancer, and they were not familiar with it. They were consulting with a doctor at Mount Sinai Hospital in New York City. The doctor even sent me to see him so he could explain to me the recommended treatment he gave to the doctor. They sent me for a PET scan on August 2nd. This particular scan checked for cancer from my head to my toes. It had now been almost two years since I had discovered the lump so imagine how I felt waiting for the results of the scan. The results came back showing it was isolated in the tumor and hadn't spread. It was my first real sign of hope. I felt it was a miracle that it hadn't spread being that it was two years later, and I was being told I had a rare, aggressive cancer. That was enough to convince me that God was already working on my behalf.

Nine months earlier on November 2, 2018, there was a celebration for my parents at the church. The church had moved into a new building a few months earlier. My sister in Connecticut called me a few weeks before the event and asked me to sing a part of a song that a group would be singing. She said it would sound good if I did the part she was talking about. How could I say no to singing in the church and more so at an event for my parents? She told me she would send me the song to listen to. She said, "You'll love it." The name of the song was "I Worship You" and the part that she wanted me to sing said, "Way Maker, Miracle Worker, Promise Keeper, Light In The Darkness, That Is Who You Are". On the day of the event, a group of us sang the song, and I rocked my part. The whole church joined us in singing. We kept singing and repeating the song. While singing those words, I had a cancerous tumor, and I didn't even know it. God knew and was already on the job.

My faith was strengthened, and my fears were calmed. I was scheduled to have chemotherapy on August 5th. A few days before, I was talking to a church leader that worked out at my gym. I told him about my cancer diagnosis and all that was happening. He told me about a place in New York that he usually worked at called Memorial Sloan Kettering Cancer Center. He said they were the best in the world, and I should obtain a second opinion from them. I told my brother about this, and he said he also heard that they were the best concerning anything to do with cancer. He strongly suggested that we cancel the start of my chemotherapy and get a second opinion. I was a day or two from what was supposed to be the start of chemotherapy. I told my brother I didn't care, and I would go with whatever. That was how I felt at that moment. He said he was going inside to make a few phone calls to see what he could find out. Later, he called me to give me a number and the name of someone to contact at Sloan Kettering Hospital in New York. He said he spoke to them, and they needed more information to connect me with the right doctors. I called and spoke to them, and they scheduled an appointment for me to go and meet with a doctor.

I canceled the start of my chemotherapy and had them send my scans, test results, and records to the doctor in New York. I figured after having this tumor for two years, how could two more weeks make anything worse. It would be worth it to speak with more knowledgeable doctors. If you have been paying attention to my story, by now you should realize that God always provided someone to help me.

Among all these doctors that I had no confidence in, there was one that I did. It was the oncologist who was the same doctor that stopped the surgery and suggested I undergo chemotherapy before having surgery. He had explained everything to Natalie and me in a way that we were both able to understand, and we had both agreed that he knew what he was talking about. When I called him to let him know that I was going to get a second opinion at Sloan Kettering, he told me that was where he had trained and worked before working in New Jersey. He also told me to keep him informed. After hearing that from him I felt very confident that I had made the right decision.

My brother was very calm about the whole situation. Natalie was worried about the delay in the start of my treatment. She had received advice from friends in the medical field that I should start treatment right away. My daughter still did not know what was going on, and I planned to not tell her for a while. She was getting ready to start her first year in college, so I wanted her to at least get settled in her new home and start her new routine. It didn't go as I planned. I decided it was time to let her mother know. I called her mother, and the first thing I asked was if Deedee was around her. She said no so I told her what was going on with me, and I tried to answer her questions. Her reaction to the news was making me emotional so I had to get off the phone. My daughter had been in her room and heard what her mother was saying to me. So now she knew I had cancer. She asked me about it, and I tried my best to comfort her. I told her I was going to be fine; I just had to get through the chemotherapy part, and then it would be smooth sailing. She was pretty good other than being mad that I didn't plan to tell her before she left for college. My son was the type that was never too concerned about anything, so I was less worried about him finding out. Natalie said she would take care of breaking the news to him.

I went to meet the doctor at Sloan Kettering in New York City. It was a team, including the surgeon, that would be performing the surgery to remove the tumor. They already had a plan from reviewing my records, scans, and test results. It was a rare type of cancer that mostly affected children, and they knew about this type of cancer. I told the Doctor about the oncologist in New Jersey, and he immediately knew who I was talking about. He said he had trained with him and his team. Their plan was different from the one in New Jersey. The plan nowwas for four rounds of chemo, each round consisting of three consecutive days, each being eight hours of treatment. At the end of the fourth round, they would do a scan, and depending on the results they would decide to do the surgery or if another round of chemo would be needed. Then after the surgery, they would decide if radiation would be needed. I had no second thoughts about their plan. I knew I was in the right place and the right hands. I called the oncologist in New Jersey on my way home to share the plan with him. When I told him the surgeon's name, he said he is the best in the world. I felt like God was putting together a team to fight with me. After all, I have Psalm 27 tattooed on my shoulder. I put it there to remind myself that he is the strength of my life. All that was happening at this point was living proof of that.

I agreed to start chemotherapy on September 5th. I was informed that they had a treatment center in Basking Ridge, New Jersey and that would be where I would do some of my treatments. This place was only a 15-minute drive from my house. I was still working out in the gym. I was told to avoid doing ab exercises and to avoid any pressure against the port in my chest. I started sharing what I was experiencing with more people in the gym. Other than my closest family and friends, they were my biggest support. Another memorable reaction I received was when I told a young lady that I was cool with at the gym. She immediately hugged me, and she held me for a while. Next thing I knew, I started crying in her arms. Since that day, I have had a different view on hugs and what a simple hug can do for a person; I give them with heartfelt feelings. The young lady that owned the gym started hugging me every time I walked into the gym. If she wasn't there when I first walked in, she would come over to me when she saw me working out to hug me. Every one of those hugs meant a lot to me. Some days, I wished she would just keep holding me. It was an emotional roller coaster. Sometimes it would only take a song on the radio to bring tears to my eyes. Other times I would feel like superman. Out of respect, I told my brother that he could tell the people at church, but I didn't want them to come to me with any talk of sympathy. I grew up around them, and they were always praying for me. I knew that they were very sympathetic by nature. I needed to stay strong, calm, hopeful, and in a stress-free mental state. I understood how scary the word cancer was to most people. I had to do what was best for me to put forth my best fight.

It was almost time for me to start chemotherapy, so I went back to New York for my first official doctor visit. The plan was to take my vitals, meet with the oncologist and his team, and then meet with the surgeon and his team. After that visit, I would go to Basking Ridge for a pre-treatment scan so they could record the actual size of the tumor before the start of chemo. On September 5th I would start my first round of chemo in Basking Ridge. I took the 7:00 a.m. train to New York for my appointment and had to walk about 20 minutes to reach the hospital. I checked in with the front desk on the floor they told me to report to. After checking in, they told me to sit in the waiting room, and I waited for my name to be called. After sitting there for a while, I heard someone call my name from the other side of the waiting room, and the waiting room was big. I got up and rushed over to where my name was being called from. It was a black girl, and she said to follow her. While walking behind her, all I was thinking is, "This girl is walking like a Jamaican." She led me into a small room where there were two others, all taking vitals.

When I sat down for her to draw blood, we started talking. She asked me if I was from Jamaica, and I told her I was. She then asked me where in Jamaica and I told her, Rio Bueno. She said that she saw my tattoo with the name Rio Bueno on my forearm which was the reason she asked. She went on to tell me she has family there, including her uncle. When I asked her who her uncle was, our conversation got more serious because she started talking about my cousin Cubby who I mentioned earlier in the book. She said Cubby's mom was her aunt which meant her father and Cubby's mom were brother and sister. God always leads me to someone, but this time it was family in a place where I least expected it. She introduced me to the other girl that was working with her, and she gave me her phone number. She told me to keep in touch with her and let her know how my treatment was going. Her name was Cherine, and she was super cool. All I could say was it had to be God. As soon as I got back to the waiting room I called Cubby to tell him what had just happened. He, too, was excited to hear the news. He explained in more detail her closeness to us. I went on to my next meeting which was with the oncologist. I mostly talked to his assistant who was a very nice, well-mannered woman named Rosemarie. She told me the do's and don'ts, what to expect when I go for treatment, and answered the questions I had. My third and last appointment was with the surgeon and his team. He inspected the area around the tumor, went over what they were hoping for with the chemotherapy, and answered the questions I had. All I had to do now was get my final scan before I started treatment. I went to Basking Ridge to have the CT scan and was now ready to start my treatment.

The morning of September 5th came. It was just short of two months since I had been diagnosed with cancer. It was time to start my chemo treatments and I was ready. I had heard how sick it made some people, and I had seen how sick it made people look. Some even think it was the chemo drug, not cancer that killed most people. Up until this moment, I had never been sick, and I was feeling perfectly fine. My mind was made up to ride through this valley with no fear because I felt the presence of God with me. The craziest part of all this was the people that were trying to give me advice despite never having asked me what type of cancer I had. For them, it was the word cancer and what they had heard about it. I was never the type to take advice from anyone. I always tried my best to make an informed decision, particularly when my life was at stake.

On that morning, my brother drove me to Basking Ridge because we didn't know what to expect, and they said everyone reacts differently to the drug. When we got there, they put me in a cubicle where I sat in a reclining chair. The cubicle was in a large room with many other cubicles. They hooked up the IV to the port in my chest. First I was hydrated with fluids for two hours. Then, the chemo started to be administered which was another four hours. For the final two hours, they hydrated me with fluids again. The whole process was painless and very boring. There was a TV screen attached to the chair with limited channels, or you could do whatever you wanted on your phone. I could go to the bathroom or walk the hallways if I felt like it. The bag containing the drug hung from a movable stand so I could freely move around. They recommended drinking a lot of water to flush the drugs out of my system, so I drank water throughout the day.

Once again, when I got to the treatment center there was a Jamaican girl that I knew very well working there. She was Marie's cousin, so she too was family. My brother was sitting there until I convinced him to leave and come back later to pick me up. It was more comfortable being there alone. I could go to sleep when I felt like it, be on the phone, or go for a walk to stretch my legs. It was a long day, but it came to an end and went smoother than I had anticipated. My brother came back to pick me up. Now we knew that I would be able to drive myself. I felt perfectly normal after my first day and was looking forward to repeating it the next day.

The following day was a Friday. I drove myself for treatment, and it was just a repeat of the prior day. The only difference was I was much more comfortable. I now knew some of the nurses, the routine for the day and, I was more familiar with the place. I knew where the bathrooms, water fountain, and refrigerator were. I brought my snacks and lunch. At the end of my treatment for that day, there was something at Duke and Julie's house for her uncle that died. He was being buried the next day. I was feeling fine, so I went by Duke's house. Food, music, and drinks were there. They had told me to drink a lot of water to flush all the toxins out of my body. I was there until very late that night and was drinking water the whole time. I was nauseous later that night when I was in bed and was going back and forth to the bathroom. I later did some research and found out that it could have been the over-drinking of the water that had caused me to be nauseous.

Saturday morning when I woke up, I felt fine. I got ready and went to the funeral. I only went because we were close. He was from my community in Jamaica. It was very hard for me mentally because he had died from cancer, and here I was in the early stage of my fight with the very thing that had killed him. I saw Marie's sister, Andrea, at the church. It was the first time seeing her since I had gotten the news of my cancer. I wasn't sure if she had heard, but I felt like I should tell her myself. We had been close for a very long time, and she was like a sister. I called her to the side to tell her. She asked a few questions, and I saw the tears coming so I walked away. Anytime someone started crying or expressed great sadness, it would break me down.

It was the following Monday before I completed my first round of chemotherapy. The only thing that was different from my previous days of treatment was that at the end of the day, they placed a device on the back of my arm on my tricep. This device would automatically inject me with medicine within 24 hours of it being activated. The chemo drug lowers the white blood cell levels so the medicine in this device helped to boost it back up. At the end of each round, they placed this device on my arm. It made a beeping sound before it injected me, and then I would feel a pinch. It also had a green flashing light that would turn off once the process was complete. At that time, I was to remove the device, place it in a special container they gave me, and bring it back to the office on my next visit.

Now that I had completed my first round of chemo, I was bracing for its effect on my body. The first day afterward, my head felt heavy, and my energy was low. My doctors advised me not to go to the gym because of the possibility of me getting sick from any germs there. The chemo drug compromised my immune system so I would have trouble fighting any kind of germ. The gym was helping me to stay sane so on the third day after my last treatment, I went back to the gym. The first day back was hard as my head was still heavy, but I worked through it. After that first workout, I felt pretty normal again. Almost two weeks after my first round of chemo, my hair started falling out. I realized I could pull my hair out simply by running my hands through my hair without feeling anything. I pulled all I could out, and there were lightly scattered batches of hair remaining. I cleaned up the rest with clippers. Eventually, there was no hair on any part of my body. I didn't even have eyelashes. I was looking different. My fingernails and toenails started getting dark, and I was told that they could fall out.

The plan was for me to do a CT scan a few days before every round. I was to go to New York for the first day of treatment. They would check my vitals, my white blood cell level, and I would meet with the doctor before starting the treatment. I would then do the next two days of treatment at the Basking Ridge location. Going to New York for treatment was very overwhelming. I had to be there at 8:00 a.m. so I was up by 5:00 a.m. to catch the 5:50 a.m. train. I would prepare my lunch the night before which was always a tuna fish sandwich. I hardly ever eat tuna fish anymore because of the bad memories associated with it. I would drive my car to the convenience store by the train station. My friend Peter that owned it allowed me to park there for the day. The train arrived at Penn Station right around 7:00 a.m. Then I had to walk 20 minutes to the hospital. The 20-minute walk helped me relax my mind before the long day ahead. It was the loneliest train ride you can imagine. My mind would be all over the place, and I would start to feel sorry for myself. It all depended on how early I got to see the doctor after my vitals were checked that determined what time I got to go home. My treatments were about eight hours long so the earlier I got to see the doctor the earlier I got to go home. After the eight hours of treatment, I would walk 20 minutes back to the train station. Some nights, I wouldn't get home until 9:00 or 10:00 p.m. I would leave in the dark and return in the dark. I would eat when I got home, prepare for the next day, and get ready for bed.

One day while I was in New York receiving my treatment, I called a friend and asked him to pick up something for me to eat and drop it off at my house. He was asking me a lot of questions and telling me what he was doing and all he had to do. He told me to call and order it. I said to him, "I'm at the hospital in New York getting treatment." By the time I finished saying that, I was broken-hearted. I told him to forget it and hung up the phone. That was one of the lowest moments in my fight. When I got home later that night, the food was there, but I didn't feel like eating it at that point. Right after my second round of chemo, I noticed that I was getting irritated easily. I would get a slight headache anytime I thought too hard. Even watching TV was aggravating. I started to avoid talking to people on the phone. My brain was not processing things normally anymore. At times, I would feel like I was losing my mind. Working out was the only thing that would ease the pressure in my head and for that reason, I was going hard at the gym.

Just a simple conversation could change my whole mood. One day my big sister in Connecticut called me. She asked how I was feeling, and the conversation went from one thing to the next. She went on to tell me how she remembered when I was a baby, and I was sick with sores all over my legs. She said that when my mother had to take me to the doctor, she was the one always carrying the bag. Now all I was wondering was what made her think of that. All my life, she had never once brought that up. That had me thinking she probably thought I might die. It sounded like the type of story a person would share after someone's death. After I got off the phone with her, I kept thinking about it until I started to cry. A day or two after that happened, Nana sent me a song, and it was the same song I mentioned earlier, "I Worship You". I listened to the song until tears started running down my cheeks. Now I started to feel like it might be more serious than I had originally felt and thought.

In the early stage while I was still seeing the doctors in New Jersey, it was Natalie that was mostly talking with the doctors. I asked her to please tell me the truth. I wanted to know what she was thinking and if I was going to make it or not. She told me that she thought I was going to be fine, and she assured me that if she was thinking otherwise, she would let me know. Hearing that from her was all the energy I needed. I doubled down on working out and avoided talking to people on the phone. The people in the gym were always motivating, encouraging, and very supportive. Some would send me encouraging words daily and they meant a lot to me.

One day, I was on my way to the gym, and Chinkie called me. I stood by the gym door waiting to finish the conversation before I went inside. I will never forget when he said, "Let me know when you're ready. I have a good studio waiting for you." It went in one ear and out the other, but my mind recorded it. Here I was in the middle of a battle with cancer, and this man was talking about a recording studio. Music was the last thing on my mind, but it was the message of hope that I got. Hope was all that I was living on and every bit of it counted.

After my third round of chemo, the drugs started taking a toll on me. Both of my legs were covered with a rash, and the pressure in my head got worse. The doctor said the rash was an allergic reaction, so they prescribed a cream for me to put on it which worked very well. One of the strangest effects that the chemo drugs had on me was they took away my dancing spirit. I started realizing this sometime after my second treatment. I had been loving music and dancing to it since I was a baby. For the first time in my life, I would hear my favorite songs and not even have a nod of my head. I no longer felt the beat in my heart, soul, or mind. I would hear music and follow the words but with no emotion. I didn't even know that was possible. This was most noticeable in the gym. I always vibe to the music in the gym. I would even sing and dance while working out. Sometimes, you would think I was at a party and not the gym. I would go for chemo every three weeks, and it would be that way for the first two weeks afterward. In the third week, my dancing spirit would come back. It went on like that until I finished chemotherapy.

The only reaction I would have to some songs was tears. Some songs would make me feel lonely, sad, and pitiful. Since then, I look at people differently when I see them dancing, especially the older ones. Dancing is spiritual. It's an expression of inner joy and happiness. Even babies start dancing before they can walk or talk. I've seen pregnant mothers play music close to their bellies. It makes sense to me now. Now I wonder what is going on in the hearts and minds of people that I never see dancing. Please understand when I say dance is an expression of the spirit. There's nothing like the whole church standing on their feet dancing or a baby standing in front of the TV dancing. Personally, for me, I'll dance anywhere, anytime. Remember I mentioned that I used to walk around with a boombox. One of the intimate ways to express your love for someone is through dancing. Embrace and enjoy your dancing spirit. It is a blessing.

The chemo was supposed to shrink the tumor before I had surgery to remove it. After the three rounds, it didn't look any smaller to me. It was another thing in my head that I was dealing with. One of my uncles in Jamaica that had been battling cancer died a week before I had to start my fourth round. It was one of those days that I will always remember. I wasn't surprised by the news. My sister had told me a few days before that he wasn't eating and that he was going to see the doctor that Tuesday. I told her to stop forcing him because he couldn't eat and that's how it is on the last days of life. I told them that he might not make it to go to the doctor on Tuesday. Sunday evening, I was on the highway driving when I got a call from my brother who was on the highway returning from a funeral in Canada. He told me that my uncle passed away. I told him that I didn't want to be the one to deliver the news to my mom. I felt like he would be the better one to do it because of his calmness, patience, and his way of articulating things.

We agreed that he would deliver the news when he got back. I kept thinking about it as I was driving and kept thinking it was going to be close to my mom's bedtime by the time my brother got back. I thought it would be better to tell her before so by her bedtime she would have calmed down. I called my brother back and told him I would tell her. I called my dad to the side first and told him. We then went into the living room where my mom was sitting. I told her as calmly and as gently as I could. She started crying, and I hugged her. I felt for her not only because her brother died from cancer but because I was here battling it as well. My dad was standing there. He had his battle going on with Parkinson's Disease. It was a lot for her all at once. I was standing over her trying to comfort her while holding back my tears. After a while, she calmed down and was able to make some phone calls. By bedtime, she was in a good place which was good because it hurt me to see her in pain.

A few days later, it was November 5th and it was time to start my fourth and hopefully final round of chemotherapy. Just like usual, I went to New York for my first day of treatment and to meet with the doctors. The nurse told me that they were going to schedule me for another round. It was the last thing I wanted to hear. I was tired and my brain was not handling the drugs very well. I told her if I had to, I would but I really didn't want to. She could tell that I had had enough. She promised me it wasn't written in stone. They were scheduling it just in case they needed to. She said it was easier to cancel it than to get it scheduled last minute. I asked God to let his will be done. If I got this far, I could make it to the end. I completed my fourth round of chemo and thankfully I didn't throw up once nor did I get sick. It was my brain that was affected. I found out what I was experiencing was called chemo brain. My fifth-round if needed was scheduled for November 26, 27, and 28th. I was scheduled to go to New York on the 26th when I would find out if I had to complete the fifth round. If another round was needed I would be there all day, and if not, then I would get to be home for an early Thanksgiving.

My mom and my brother were getting ready to travel to Jamaica for my uncle's funeral. It was another pain that I had to deal with. So many relatives and friends passed away over the years, and I was not able to attend the funeral because of my ongoing situation with INS. A couple of years earlier, I lost an uncle and aunt hours apart. I couldn't attend any of their funerals, and it pained my heart. To add to everything my mom and family were already going through, my nephew was now hospitalized in Jamaica. They left for the funeral in Jamaica while I was here in the states recovering from four rounds of very aggressive chemotherapy. At that point in my treatment, my appearance had changed. I had no hair. I had no eyebrows or eyelashes which made my eyes look weird. My skin was a different texture and pale in color. Thankfully, I was willing to put up my best fight with my team. I wanted to be around for my kids and my family so chemo was a small price to pay. My mom, brother, sister, and my nephew that was sick came back from Jamaica together.

I went to do my CT scan in Basking Ridge a few days before my appointment in New York. On the morning of my appointment in New York, I took the train like usual. On the train, I was hoping and praying that I didn't need the fifth round. After doing my vitals and bloodwork, it was time to hear the verdict. My nurse informed me that after checking the scans, they decided it was time to do the surgery. It was the best news I had received since I started this fight. It was such a relief. I was so happy you would have thought they told me that my cancer had disappeared. I met with the surgeon and his team, and I was scheduled for surgery. The surgery date was December 12th which was only two weeks away. I was the happiest man walking through New York City later that day. I even threw away my tuna fish sandwich. I was tired of all of it. I had not been looking forward to possibly having to go to Middletown, New Jersey for a fifth round of chemo the day before Thanksgiving. I had a milestone to give thanks for that Thanksgiving.

Now I was looking forward to the surgery to finally have the tumor removed from my abdominal wall. The surgeon told me that he would not know if the tumor was attached to my bowels until he started the surgery. He said if it was, he would have to cut out a section of my bowels. I told myself that if that was the case, there was nothing I could do about it but let him do his work. I wasn't having any problems with my bowels which was a good sign. My surgeon's confidence and easy-going spirit made me very relaxed.

My aunt in Canada who had been checking on me throughout my treatments was always telling me that God was going to work a miracle for me. I was thinking he had worked it already or he was working on it. It was when I told her I had finished chemotherapy and the surgery was scheduled that I understood what she had been thinking. She kept asking me if I was sure the tumor was still there and if the doctors knew what they were talking about. I admired her faith, but it was kind of strange to me. She sounded like she thought if the tumor was still there, then she didn't get the miracle she had prayed for. It made me think of the story in the Bible when Jesus turned water into wine. That is the only way a lot of people perceive miracles. If that had been the only way I saw it, I would be disappointed, discouraged, and maybe angry. That would have all led to a feeling of hopelessness. I felt miracles were happening from the time he led me back to the doctors to tell them I wanted the lump removed to then find out this very aggressive cancer did not spread anywhere else in my body despite it had now been almost two years since I noticed the lump. Imagine how long it was there before I noticed it. It had to be God that led me to the team of doctors in New York who I later found out was one of the best in the world. I felt I had experienced so many miracles up to this point while my aunt was there hoping for the one she expected.

Expectation sometimes blinds us from seeing miracles right in front of our eyes. This blindness leads to disappointments and complaints when we are supposed to be singing songs of praise. God has people around us turning water into wine every day, but we are waiting to see him doing it. It's his way and not ours. Instead of waiting to see my tumor disappear which I knew was possible through God's mighty powers, I was praying for God to work through my surgeon to remove the tumor from my body. I asked God to take control of the surgeon's mind and body and do the surgery for me. I knew he was already on it, and I had no doubt he would finish it.

I knew that I was not going to be able to work out for a few months after the surgery. So, I spent the next two weeks going hard in the gym. I worked out up until the day before my surgery. A few people gave me their numbers and asked me to keep them informed. Days before my surgery, my sister and good friend Ann and her husband, Glen came to New Jersey to visit my brother. She called me a few times, but I was sleeping. When I woke up, I saw the missed calls and called her back. She said she wanted to see me before she left so I should come to see her. I got dressed and went to my brother's house to see them. Ann was one of the people that was in the battle with me. She would send me a message every morning. When I got to my brother's, we talked for a little while, took some pictures, and then they left. Seeing them cheered me up. Since I was a little kid, I always got excited to see her. After they left, my brother handed me a $100 bill and told me they left it for me. At first, I said, "No I can't take it." My brother said, "No mon, Take it." I took the money from him with a heavy heart. Their act of kindness and compassion touched me in a way I can't explain. With what I was going through at the time, money meant nothing to me. All I wanted was to survive this battle. I'm hardly ever on the receiving end so that in itself felt special. The support I felt from the people I loved and cared for when I needed it was a once-in-a-lifetime feeling. I thought to myself that God led them to New Jersey for that reason and not to only visit my brother.

Five months after getting the news that I had cancer, it was finally the day of my surgery to remove it. It was December 12th, and I was ready for an early Christmas present. They told me I would be in the hospital for about five days. This was going to be my first time spending the night in a hospital. I had packed my bag the night before. It almost felt like I was going on vacation. I had been in a dark spot, and I knew on the other side of the surgery was the brightness. I had been looking forward to this day, so I was a little excited. I had received some instructions before the surgery, like the need to fast and some hygiene do's and don'ts. My surgery was scheduled for early that Thursday evening. I got ready late morning, and then it was time to leave. My brother and Natalie were accompanying me to the hospital. We got together for a customary prayer. After the prayer, we got ready to leave, and my dad started to cry. It was one of those moments that will stick with me forever. I had only heard my dad crying a couple times in my life, and this was the second time for me. It touched my heart.

We planned to take the train to avoid any kind of traffic and because we were not sure about the parking situation there. We drove to the train station, parked the car, and got on the train. I was as comfortable and relaxed as I was going to be. I had two of my favorite people with me, and I knew they were going to make sure that I was good. We arrived in New York and checked in at the hospital. I was taken into a room where they prepared me for surgery. Now I was just waiting. A lady came and told us that the surgeon was running late with the surgery before mine. I laid there for a while longer waiting until the surgeon came to speak with us. He said it was getting late, and he was still finishing up with surgery; then the operating room needed to be cleaned and prepared for my surgery. He then asked if I would be okay rescheduling my surgery for first thing the following morning.

The next day was Friday the 13th. He even mentioned that he was tired and would prefer to go home to get some rest and come back fresh in the morning. All that he said sounded to me like it was not a good idea to do it that day. There was no way I was going to have him operate on me after hearing all that he had said. We agreed it was a good idea to wait until the next morning. The first thing I told him was that I was really hungry. He told me that he would have someone bring me to a room so I wouldn't have to redo the admission process in the morning. He instructed them to get me something to eat right away so I would be ready for surgery in the morning. I also expressed my concern about waiting for surgery the next day. He promised it would be first thing in the morning, and I was brought upstairs to a room.

Natalie decided to stay in New York so she could be there first thing in the morning with me. My brother took the train back home by himself. The plan was for Natalie to keep him informed the next morning. I was disappointed with the delay, but I felt like it was God's plan. The hospital was clean, and relaxing, and the staff was awesome. Natalie stayed with me in the room until it was time for her to get some rest. She got a hotel room close to the hospital so she could get to the hospital at a short moment's notice. I felt a little lonely, but I was tired and anxious, so it wasn't that bad. I made a few calls before going to sleep.

A little after 7:00 a.m., I woke up to loud talking and all kinds of movements in the room. It was two young ladies. One of them was the day shift nurse and the other was her aide. It was the start of her shift, and she came in to see a request for me to be downstairs for surgery right away. She asked if I already showered, and I told her I hadn't. She started rushing me around while complaining that the night shift nurse should have woken me up earlier so I would be ready for surgery. It didn't take me long to realize she was Jamaican. They practically pushed me in the shower. They stood by the door waiting on me to get out. They were helping me to do everything. It was like a mother trying to get her kids out the door before the school bus arrived. I had to ask her to allow me to call Natalie, so she knew I was about to go into surgery.

We had been told the surgery would be first thing in the morning, but we weren't thinking it would be that early. It was a good thing the hotel Natalie stayed at was close by. The nurse had the patient transporter waiting to bring me down. Even though they were rushing me, I felt loved. They just wanted me to be there on time for my surgery. They were rooting for me. Once again, I'm saying God always has someone there for me. This time it was my Jamaican nurse named Rose. She held my hand and said, "You're gonna be fine. I'll see you when you get back." I was taken downstairs where they went over some of the same things that were done the evening before.

Now I was ready and waiting for the call to go to the operating room. It wasn't too long before Natalie showed up which brought me some comfort. Someone came out to talk with her about the procedure and took some information so they could communicate with her. It was finally my time, so they came and wheeled me into the operating room. There was a team standing by the operating table and others were moving around. They wheeled me over to the operating table and assisted me with moving over onto the operating table. They were talking to me while getting me ready. The last thing I remember was one of the girls telling me that she was from Boonton, New Jersey.

When I woke up, I was in a different place with a bandage on my abdomen and a drainage tube running from the area with a plastic bulb on the end. I don't remember much between the recovery room and being back in my room. Later when I was back in my room, Natalie told me that the surgeon informed her that the surgery went very well, and he said I would be fine. The tumor was not attached to my bowels which was good news. I was still medicated, so I was very relaxed. Natalie decided to stay with me in the room. She called my brother to let him know that it went well, and I was okay. I knew it would be more comforting if my family got to hear my voice, so I called them when I was feeling better. It was comforting for me as well, especially after talking to my dad to let him know I was good. Natalie was there with me, so we talked every hour or two throughout the night. The chair she was sleeping in was very uncomfortable for her and the nurse kept coming in to do some things all night. She even took me for a walk around the floor in the middle of the night. I never thought that taking a few steps could be so painful. I felt bad for Natalie because she could not get any sleep.

The next morning at 7:00 a.m., a whole team came to see me. They asked me how I was feeling, and I let them know I was feeling fine. They took off the bandage that was covering the incision. It was about five to six inches long, swollen, red, and scary looking. They left the bandage off and informed me that I would be on a liquid diet until I had some kind of bowel movement. It was now a waiting game, and the wait was for me to pass gas which would mean my bowel was moving. Once I had a bowel movement, I would get to eat real food and if everything was okay after eating, I would get to go home. Walking is supposed to be the best thing for achieving a bowel movement; however, walking after a surgery like mine was very painful. It was one fight after the next to get where I wanted to go, and one by one I was getting there. The will to survive and God's strength kept me going.

Natalie and my brother agreed that she would stay with me until Sunday. On Sunday, my brother would come to visit, and she would get a ride back with him. Saturday was my first full day with Rose, and we got to talk about family, Jamaica, and our personal lives. It felt like she was family. The one question I had to answer all day and night was whether I had passed gas, and it hadn't happened yet.

Sunday was my worst day in the hospital. When my brother was there visiting, he went for a walk with me around the floor. I think ten times around was a mile. It was painful but I pushed myself because the quicker I got my bowels moving, the quicker I could go home. Later that evening after they left, my belly started hurting. I called for the nurse and Rose came. I told her how I was feeling, and she told me she was going to give me something special. She brought me a tablet. After taking it, I was still in pain and my belly was cramping up. Rose was standing by my bedside talking to me, trying to comfort me. I remember her saying "You just had surgery two days ago. You're going to feel some pain." The pain was so bad I started crying and grabbed onto her hand. She talked to me for a while until the pain subsided.

The rest of the evening I was in very deep thoughts. I thought about death, my funeral, my kids, my family, and all the people I'm close to. The thought of death brought me to the loneliest feeling I ever felt all my life. It was the kind of loneliness that had nothing to do with the lack of company. A hundred people could have been around, and it wouldn't have mattered. I was on a journey that I had to travel by myself. It was that day and at that very moment that I felt like no one knew me. All that I had been through during my life was just replaying in my mind. I saw people talking at my funeral, telling my kids about me, and it felt like it was a whole lot of hypocrisy. I decided that day that if I got the chance, I was going to write a book to tell the world who I am, dedicating it, especially to my kids.

Very early Monday morning, my stomach made a low growling sound and by late Monday morning, I passed gas. Monday evening, they gave me semi-hard food for dinner. I got fish, mashed potatoes, and greens. After eating it I felt fine, and I had a very good night. My bowels were fully functioning again. I was using the bathroom like regular times. The team came to see me early Tuesday morning, and after talking with me, they told me I was going to be discharged later that morning. I was very surprised that they were sending me home that quickly. I thought they would keep me for observation for at least another day. I called my brother and Natalie to let them know. It was about a 90-minute drive. It was also raining that day so by the time they got there, I would be ready or close to it.

For the remainder of the morning, I was getting visits from doctors, nurses, and pharmacists. They gave me a care package to take home with me. By the time my brother and Natalie got there, I was already downstairs getting my discharge papers. After five days in the hospital, I was heading home cancer-free. I was now on the road to recovery. I still had no hair, my nails were still black, the bottom of my feet was dark, my fingers were wrinkled, a part of my abdominal muscle was gone, and I had a 5-inch cut almost up the center of my belly. That was all a very small price I had to pay to survive. They were badges of honor to me. I walked out of that hospital with a different mindset. The two soldiers that had been in the trenches with me came back to pick me up and drove me home.

It felt so good to be back home. I can't even express the feeling other than it felt like I was coming in from the cold. I was still on the battlefield but out of very dangerous territory. I was wounded but alive. I was happy to see my family, and they were happy to see me. My biggest fear at that point was getting up out of bed. A part of my abdominal wall was gone; the area was sore and swollen. The first thing I did when I got home was take a shower. That was when I realized how difficult it was to stand up for some time. When I got out of the shower, I had to sit down for a while before getting dressed. There was a hole at the base of the cut that I had to keep bandages on, and I had to empty the bulb of the drain. They also gave me a form on which I had to record the amount of leakage I emptied each time. I also had a spirometer to help strengthen my lungs. They gave me one in the hospital after my surgery. I could not believe how painful it was to blow in it.

My first night home in my bed felt so good, and I had no issues. Getting out of bed was painful but before I left the hospital, they reviewed with me the way I should roll out of bed. After doing it a few times, I got the hang of it, and I was in fighting mode. I was going to do anything I had to do to get back on my feet. My next time showering was better than my first time had been. I also got the hang of dressing my cut and emptying the bulb.

Around my third day home, I went to the gym. It was cold outside, so I went there to walk on the treadmill. Everyone was happy to see me. The owner even took a picture of me and posted it on their Instagram page. She wrote in the caption that I had just had surgery for cancer a few days ago and was already back in the gym. I was restricted from lifting more than five pounds so I couldn't work out even though I so badly wanted to. A few days after I got home from the hospital, my sister Allison and her husband migrated to Morristown from Jamaica. She was a nurse in Jamaica so I would sometimes ask her to change the bandage for me. My two sisters that had been living in my community in Jamaica were now living in the USA. The week after I got home, it was Christmas. I went back to New York on Christmas Eve to see the doctors and have my drain removed. It was a big relief to have the drain removed. Moving around with the drain had become uncomfortable especially when I was in the shower or laying down. Other than going to the gym, Christmas was my first time going out around people. My big sister Maxine and her husband came from Connecticut. For the first time in more than a decade, my whole family got together at my brother's house. This time, we had a whole new generation in the house including my two kids. After leaving my brother's house, I went by Duke and Julie's house for a little while before heading back home. The following week on New Year's Eve, I went back to the doctor to have my stitches removed. I had internal stitches as well that were used to hold the mesh in place. After cutting a part of my abdominal wall out, they reconstructed it with mesh.

It would be my first New Year's Eve staying home, and I couldn't have been happier. I was happy to be alive and not in the hospital. I thought about all the people I left in the hospital and especially about the man in the room next to me who had already been there for a month. He told me that after he had a bowel movement, they gave him his first meal and he thought he ate too much. He said when he was getting ready to be discharged, something went wrong. His wife was already on her way from Philadelphia to pick him up. He was the one who warned me not to eat too much, so I only ate half of my first meal even though I was hungry. He had been there when I arrived, and I left him there. There were so many sad stories around me. I felt very blessed.

When I started feeling down, all I had to do was look around or just think of other people's situations. Everyone on that hospital floor was recovering from surgery and we all had to go for a walk. I remember there was an older lady that could barely walk. They would push a wheelchair behind her, and every few steps, she would sit down in the wheelchair for a while. After my experience trying to walk, I truly realized what a blessing it was to be able to walk. I started walking every day after I got home. In no time, I was jogging on the treadmill. When the weather got better, I started walking outside. The hole at the base of my cut which was next to my belly button was draining longer than expected so my nurse asked me to cut back on the walking and not to jog at all. It took a while, but it finally started to dry up. By the 2nd week of January, my hair had started growing back. I had lost one of my toenails. The rest of my nails were dark, but I started seeing the new growth that was the normal color.

My son was playing basketball, and it was his senior year in high school. I was happy to be back at the games. Some of the parents had heard about my diagnosis and were happy to see me. It was very uncomfortable to sit down for a long period so I would go for a walk or just stand up sometimes during the games. There was a senior night for all the senior players, and I was happy to be able to be there to support him. I sometimes wondered what was going on in my kids' heads knowing that their dad was battling cancer. Walking out onto the basketball court with his mom was very emotional for me. I had been through so much and was able to be there on his special day.

Chapter 10

Life Goes On

Still Steppin'

By the middle of February 2020, I had started lifting some light weights. My nurse didn't want me to, but I was feeling good. I didn't do any exercise that would put pressure on my abdomen. I went for my first CT scan since the surgery, and I was officially cancer-free. I would still have to go for cancer screenings every four months. The nurse had told me it would be every three months but my surgeon said every four months so that was what was agreed upon. I had also been previously told that I might need radiation after the surgery. My surgeon said that I did not have to have any radiation, and he thought the area was too delicate for that. I was happy to hear all of this as I was mentally tired.

Uncle Tee, my boy Killa's father who I mentioned earlier was battling cancer had passed away. His death hit me hard, not only because we were close but because he died of cancer. I had to fight to think positively. While he had been sick, I saw him at church, and we took a picture together. Long after I found out I also had cancer, I was looking back at some pictures on my phone, and I came across the picture I took with him. In the picture, my tumor was visible under my t-shirt. I did not know at that time it was cancerous. We both had cancer at the time of that picture, only I did not know. In this life, you just never know, and I mean never. Talking about never, the following week after Uncle Tee's funeral something happened that no one could have ever seen coming. The discovery of the new COVID-19 virus occurred. There was a lot of talk about COVID-19, and the talk kept getting louder at a very fast pace.

By the following week, which was now the middle of March of 2020, places started closing and it was recommended to wear a mask when going outside. It was also recommended to keep at least a 6-foot distance from anyone when possible and to wash and sanitize your hands as often as you can. People were getting sick, and a lot of people started dying. There was a great panic because no one knew anything about this virus. It was an unknown killer. No one was safe from this dangerous virus. It was all over the world and was spreading like wildfire. There was a mask shortage, and if you were able to find one, they were more expensive than usual.

I have mentioned the word miracle a few times already, and I'm about to tell you about another one I experienced. Before I started chemotherapy on September 5, 2019, the nurse had told me to get a face mask. The chemo drugs were going to suppress my immune system which would make me very vulnerable to getting sick. It was the reason they didn't want me to go to the gym. Everything the health officials were recommending people do because of the COVID-19 virus, I had already been doing for months. I had been wearing a mask on the train rides to New York. People would avoid sitting next to me on the train. Even walking to and from the hospital, I was wearing a mask which seemed to make people avoid walking close to me. This avoidance by people became a part of my sadness. At the hospital, wearing a mask was the norm. They had masks at the front desk. I would always take some extras when I left. I tried to wear my mask most times in the gym, but it was uncomfortable so sometimes I would remove it. Once I finished my last round of chemo on November 7th, I would only wear my mask if I had to take the train to New York.

I was out and about, going to the gym, funerals, get-togethers, and I had even been to the local bar to see my old friends a week before everything shut down. One of the bouncers that I would talk to who had expressed his hurt and support for me during my battle with cancer died from the virus a few weeks later. I remember going to New York for a doctor's visit after my surgery. At that point, my cut was no longer draining, and they had told me to leave the bandage off when it stopped draining. At the doctor's visit, the nurse covered the hole at the base of my cut with a bandage. She was concerned it could get infected from being on the train. All this time, the COVID-19 virus was all around me and had been for months before we knew it even existed. It goes back to what I had said earlier; you just never know. My doctors were worried about the everyday germs around us not knowing that there was a lethal virus spreading all around us. All I can say is it must be the mercy of God, a miracle within a miracle.

When everyone was complaining about how bad the year 2020 was, I was actually on the rebound and celebrating life. I felt like there were things we could do to protect ourselves from the COVID-19 virus, but protecting ourselves from cancer was a different story. When I would hear people complaining about the need to wear a mask, it would give me a bad feeling. I had been around many people wearing masks: patients, doctors, nurses, healthcare workers, family, friends, kids, elders, and even drivers. This was one group of people protecting the vulnerable just like I was. Not once did I hear anyone of them complaining about wearing a mask. I had so many masks at home from before the COVID-19 outbreak that I shared them with my family during the mask shortage.

When it was time to do my first four-month screening, New York was shut down due to the COVID-19 virus. The city was on lockdown and a lot of people were dying. I was supposed to have my scan done in Basking Ridge, New Jersey, and then go to New York to meet with my doctors a few days later. They canceled my in-person visit and decided to schedule my doctor appointments through their telehealth system. My first appointment that day was via a video call. They told me my scans came back clean. There was no cancer detected and everything was looking good in the area. They asked how I was feeling and if I had any problems or questions. The nurse asked me to lift my shirt so she could see the area from the surgery. The nurse from the surgeon's team later video called me as well. She went over the same things we had discussed on the first call. Hearing that I was cancer-free was all the news I wanted to hear. It was like nothing else mattered. Looking back at all the events surrounding my cancer diagnosis, it's clear that it was a miracle that I am still alive. The timing of my surgery, getting the drain and stitches removed, and then getting my first scan all before the COVID-19 outbreak is evidence of that.

People were getting their treatments and procedures pushed back, and with the outbreak in New York, the hospital would be the last place I would want to be. With all the people sick, dying, out of work, or just living in fear of the virus, I was just thankful to be alive and cancer-free. The gyms were closed so I started working out at home. I was doing push-ups and some workouts with dumbbells. Sometimes I would work out in the park up the street from my house. I would mostly do push-ups at the park. My brother had some gym equipment in his basement, so I started going there to work out as well. I had been restricted from working out for more than two months, so I was eager to get back to where I had left off before my surgery. Working out was fun and very therapeutic for me. It made me challenge myself instead of feeling self-pity.

The COVID-19 virus changed our way of life, but it was my son that I felt bad for. He was coming to the end of his senior year in high school when schools closed, and students could no longer physically go to class. He had to finish his last weeks of high school completing his classes via online learning from home. He didn't get to have a prom or spend his last few days saying goodbye to his teachers and friends. He had a COVID-19 restricted graduation that was far from normal. It was a small ceremony outside just to hand out the diplomas. The entire senior class was separated into different groups that attended the ceremony at different times. It was a bitter-sweet moment for me. I felt badly for him and all his friends, but I was happy to be alive to witness him reach this milestone. He didn't let it bother him. He still went with some of his friends to the Jersey shore. Even though most places were closed, they didn't let that stop them from having a good summer before they headed to college.

I spent that summer doing yard work, cutting a few trees down, and trimming some branches. I even built a few brick walls. It was about 3½ months since my surgery when I started this project. I worked almost every day for around four months. That in and of itself was a miracle. One day I was on a ladder about 15 feet from the ground. I had a chainsaw in my hand and was cutting a branch from the tree. The branch snapped back and hit me which caused me, the chainsaw, and the ladder to fall to the ground. I hit the ground first. The ladder fell over me with one end landing on a fence. The branch fell on the ladder over me, and the chainsaw went flying in another direction. My brother-in-law who had been holding the ladder when I was on it panicked and ran. He came back, picked up the chainsaw, and started cranking it up. I yelled "What are you doing? Help me!" I had hit my knee and wasn't sure what was going on with it. He said that he was going to cut the branch off the ladder so he could remove the ladder from over me. That wasn't necessary as there was enough room for me to get up from under the ladder. He came over and helped me up. I had a few bruises on my body, but I was okay.

So many things could have gone wrong, especially with the chainsaw. All I could say was angels were watching over me. We laughed about it for a few days; the part when my brother-in-law ran was particularly funny. I told him it would be messed up to survive my battle with cancer only to fall from a ladder which could have resulted in a bad injury or death. I considered that a miracle. Miracles are happening all around us daily, but we tend to pay more attention to whatever initially happened. The wound from my surgery was still healing, yet it didn't hurt at all. Imagine what could have happened to my reconstructed abdominal wall. Other than the bruise on my knee, I was okay after the initial shock. At this time, the COVID-19 virus was sweeping through the tri-state area. The hospital was the last place you would want to be. Once more, God was on my side.

My son was now about to go off to college. He chose to attend a college in West Virginia. He had visited his friend who went there, and he was sold. I was happy for him and that I was around to witness such a great event. My daughter was going into her second year in college. I had a lot to be happy and thankful for. These had been the things that were energizing, encouraging, and strengthening my will to survive and live. The time came for him to leave for West Virginia. We had a very special moment the day before he left. It was customary for my family to pray and invite God into all our family affairs. COVID-19 was running wild, and my dad was considered high-risk because of his age. My son, on the other hand, was moving around like nothing was happening. It wouldn't have felt right for my son to go off to college without a prayer circle. If there's one thing I believe in, it is prayer. It's the only way to talk to God and he's always listening. We gathered outside in the driveway so we could keep some distance apart from each other. My parents, sister, Natalie, and I stood around him. My dad said a few words while anointing his head with oil. At that moment, I was really touched. I just survived a battle with cancer and my dad who was almost 80 years old was still around to perform this honor for his grandson; my mom, his mom, and my sister were there to witness it. It reminded me of his christening 17 years prior when my dad anointed his forehead with oil. I had prayed that we all would live to have moments like these.

The following day, his mom and I drove him to West Virginia. It was my first time there, and I definitely had the wrong impression of the location and the surrounding area. It was more diversified than I had thought it was. We even found an authentic Jamaican restaurant. It was an honor to be there on move-in day. I was glad I was able to give my son and his mom my support. It was not easy for his mom to leave her boy hundreds of miles away from home even though she was happy for him. I wasn't sure what was going on in my son's head, but he seemed happy, relaxed, and ready for his new life. My daughter, on the other hand, was pretty much running her show. She got the hang of things very quickly. She was now a Resident Assistant at her college, and she had a side hustle doing eyelash extensions. She was driving herself back and forth from North Carolina to New Jersey and vice versa. They both now had feathers and were flapping their wings around basically practicing flying.

Summer had come to an end, and I got some bad news. My aunt who I lived with when I first came to America was sick. She had been having some stomach problems for a while which had now gotten worse. After some extensive examinations, the doctors discovered she had cancer. Further examinations had revealed that cancer had already spread throughout her body. There wasn't much that the doctors could do for her. She was on hospice care. She was treated with a couple of rounds of chemotherapy that they thought would ease her pain. It was tough for me to hear any kind of news like this, especially when it was someone this close. Like I said before, you never know. My aunt had sometimes called me or sent me some form of encouraging message when I had been fighting cancer. And all the while, cancer was spreading throughout her body slowly killing her, and she didn't know. Her situation made me feel so blessed to be alive and cancer-free. She was going back and forth to the doctor complaining about her stomach pain, and they had not yet detected cancer. I could have ended up in that same situation. One doctor had told me that it was a good thing I was in such great shape; otherwise, it would have taken much longer for my tumor to be visible, if ever visible. The tumor could have been there until I got sick which would probably have been too late for me.

It was a struggle for me to visit my aunt because it sent my mind into overdrive. Every four months, I have to face the fact that I could receive bad news from my scans. I tried my best to surround myself with positive vibes. Every time I turned on the TV or opened my phone to read something I was always running across something about cancer and usually not good news. My aunt was a very strong woman and was in good spirits considering the circumstances. With COVID-19 quickly spreading, it made things more difficult for her and the family. She needed to be very careful. Everyone around her needed to be very careful as well. It makes a very lonely journey even more lonely. I was feeling her pain. While my aunt was in the hospital, my cousin Karen and her husband came from Texas to visit her. They stayed for a few weeks and did some work at the house to make sure she would be as comfortable as possible when she got home. It was a surreal feeling being in the house I had lived in when I first arrived in

America. I had lived there with my cousins, uncle, and aunt. This time it was just me and my cousins there. My uncle had passed away, and my aunt was now fighting for her life. I was grateful to be with them to support them and do what I could to help our wounded soldier.

It came time for us to pick up my son from West Virginia for his fall break. Because of COVID-19, the college planned to have the students remain at home until late January. The students completed their fall semester classes online. Once again, I was grateful to be around and a part of his life.

December 13th came around and it was one year of being cancer-free. I couldn't thank God, my family, and my good friends enough. It's a blessing to be alive for a day and I got a whole year cancer-free. I was now going to the gym, lifting weights, and doing more sit-ups than most guys in the gym can do. Every time I walked out of the gym, I said a quick prayer to thank God for healing me.

In January, my son decided to stay home and complete the rest of his school year online. He planned to work and save up some money. Businesses started to re-open but with some restrictions. I was back in the gym working out hard. Two COVID-19 vaccines became available. At first, there was a limited number of doses, so they made those available to a select group of people. Gradually, more doses became available, and more groups of people were eligible to receive the vaccine. Eventually, everyone was eligible for the vaccine, and the distribution of the vaccine improved. There was a lot of legitimate concern about the vaccine and then there was a lot of misinformation being spread. I talked to my doctor and read as much as I could about the vaccine. I observed what was going on with the people that I knew who had received the vaccine. As soon as the vaccine was available to me, I got it. After gathering all the information I could, I felt like COVID-19 was a bigger threat to me than any of the possible side effects. It was a decision that every individual had to make. I made my decision and thankfully I have been doing great.

At this point, I still had the port on the right side of my chest. It was a constant reminder of the battle I fought. The doctors wanted to have a couple of clean scans before they would remove the port. The reality is that cancer can return at any time. They told me after the one-year scan, if I was still cancer-free, the port would be removed. My one-year scan was cancer-free, but they then decided to wait for the next four-month scan. I was disappointed because it was in my face every day reminding me of cancer, and it started sounding like they were expecting cancer to come back. The whole thing was messing with my mind. I was having to go to Basking Ridge every one to two months to have the port flushed. I was cancer-free, but it was still an active battle.

Two weeks before my next scan, I had a pain in my back that was lingering. It wasn't muscle, spine, or any kind of pain I had felt before. It felt internal. I started thinking it might be my kidney and of course, was wondering if cancer had come back. I wanted peace of mind and waiting two weeks until my scan would be a lot to bear. I called my doctor to let him know what I was experiencing and asked him to move up my scan appointment, and they did. I went for my scan, and it came back cancer-free and showed the mesh that was used to reconstruct my abdominal wall was intact. I was relieved. The pain I was feeling gradually faded. When I received the video call to get the results of my scan, I asked about having the port removed. The nurse told me she would set it up. The next day someone called me, and the removal of my port was scheduled for a few days later. I had no idea things would be moving that quickly. They called back to reschedule the surgery a few more days later than the original date. It was still only two weeks after my scan, and I couldn't wait for it to be removed. This was going to be the closing of a chapter. I went to the Sloan Kettering facility in Middletown, New Jersey for the surgery to remove the port. Natalie came with me so she could drive me back home. It was a short procedure and afterward, I was feeling good. Within a few weeks, the area was all healed. Now I have another battle scar that I am proud of.

It was now a few months from the time I started writing this book. Some things were harder for me to write about than others. It was like reliving the experiences. I had stopped writing for a few days which turned into a week and that week quickly turned into a month. Throughout my battle, Shereka would check on me. One day her daughter, Quba, came to visit me. It was amazing how mature and well-mannered she was. She sat with me in my bedroom for about an hour talking to me. It cheered me up. Because of the COVID-19 virus and my situation, I hadn't seen Shereka for a long time. She had dropped off a Christmas gift for me, but I didn't get to see her. One day, Shereka called me and said, "Bro we have to go for a drink. Mother's Day, Father's Day, and both of our birthdays passed, and we haven't gotten together." I told her to let me know when. Julie's mother had passed away so that Friday night I was at Duke's house talking with him while having a drink. Shereka called and asked me where I was. I told her I was by Duke's, and she said she'd be there in a minute. She came with a friend, and the four of us had a drink together. She went inside to show her sympathy to Julie and the family. Shereka, her friend, and I then left the house and went to the bar. We talked about some stuff that was going on with her and had a few drinks before retiring for the night.

The next day, which was Saturday, I saw her again in town. We had a drink at a friend's house before she went out with another friend. Two weeks later, it was Sunday, July 11th which was exactly two years from when I got the phone call from the doctor telling me I had cancer. I had gone out earlier in the day with my son. Later that day at home, I was watching TV and thinking about my journey. I was happy to be alive and cancer-free, but my mind was running wild. I was having a bad day. A little after 6:00 p.m., I got a text from Shereka. She sent me a link to a song on YouTube. She then texted me and this was the conversation we had:

Song: Tony Rebel – If Jah Is Standing By My Side

Shereka: I love you so much…If no one appreciates you, I do. You're my idol, and you're my number one guy. I look up to you in every way. You're as strong as they come.

Me: I appreciate you as well sis and I think I can say I love you more. Thanks for the song, that energy!!
Shereka: I was willing to share that song because it reminds me of you

Me: I love you!
Shereka: Love you too like Fa real

After listening to the song and reading those words, I felt energized, hopeful and was now in good spirits. I got up and took a shower. While I was in the shower, I thought about what had just happened. I was wondering why Shereka had texted me in the first place. I was thinking it must be God's doing. As soon as I got out of the shower, I immediately texted her. This was the conversation:

Me: I went in the shower after my last text, and I was thinking about you. I could write a book about my love for you but let me just speak on today. I know most people say things just to be nice but please know that my expression of love for you is as genuine as it gets. Today, 7-11 is a very special day to me, it's the day I found out I had cancer. First thing I did this morning when I woke up said my prayer to thank God that I'm still alive and doing great and I've been here thinking about life. When you texted me that song and those words, you have no idea where I was at that moment and how you made me feel. I was in the shower thinking why you are so connected to me, it must be God cause there's no explanation for this. I could not make this up. You are very special to me, thanks!

Shereka: Oh my God I had no idea I just felt that you needed to know that you're loved, respected, appreciated and you're a soldier. You're everything a man should be.

Me: It's a divine connection.

After that conversation, I was in a different space mentally. I got dressed and called my brother to tell him it was two years since I got the news. I told him that I wanted him to know how much I appreciated him and all he has done for me. After I got off the phone I picked up my notebook and my pen, and I started writing. It had been two months since I last wrote anything. Thanks to Shereka, I started writing again. I spent the entire next week writing. It was the most I had written in a week's timeframe.

It was now the following weekend. Saturday night, I was in the house writing. It was raining outside, and I was tired, so I decided to stay home that night. I left my room for a little while and had left my phone on my bed. When I got back in my room, I looked at my phone and I saw that I had missed a call at 12:47 a.m. from Nana. Immediately, I started to wonder why she called so late. I then received a text at 12:48 a.m. that said call me when you can. I called her immediately. She answered the phone, and said Shereka was in cardiac arrest, and then she started crying. Shereka's brother Chinkie got on the phone. I asked him what was going on and he said, "She's on the other side." I said, "What do you mean?" He replied with the same answer, "She's on the other side." He said it a third time, and I asked him if he meant she was dead. He said, "That's what they're saying." I said to him, "What?" He said, "Yes, I'm standing right here looking at her now." I told him I would call him back. I walked around for a minute trying to digest the news. I got dressed, jumped in the car, and started driving. I called him back to ask where they were. He said they were at the Beth Israel Hospital in Newark. I told him I was on my way. When I got to the emergency room, I called him, and he came out to get me.

When we got inside, he pointed and said, "Go around there and you'll see her." When I went around and pulled the screen, I saw Nana leaning over her crying and Quba standing there in a daze. Shereka was laying there on her back looking like she was sleeping. After a while, they both left the room. I stood there staring at her in disbelief until Quba came back into the room and said, "Uncle Dervin, they said they're about to move her downstairs." I started thinking about our last conversation just a week ago. When I got back home, I sat down and kept re-reading our text messages. I couldn't even go to sleep. I planned to attend church that Sunday for a baby's christening. Even though I didn't get any sleep, I got up and went anyway. After church, I came home and went to sleep. When I got back up, Shereka was still on my mind. I caught myself talking to her. I got my pen and paper and started writing what I now call "The Last Talk".

<u>The Last Talk</u>

Sis, I'm always there
Anytime you called my name
I heard you passed away
And immediately I came
I saw Nana over you
Crying out in pain
Quba there looking lost
I wondered what's going on in her brain
Three generations in the room
With a broken bridge
I'm thinking about so much
Especially your kids
What can I do for you
I wondered to myself
Then reality hits me
That's it, ain't nothing else
Got really close to you
Face to face, what did I expect
Wishing that I could feel
A little air from a breath
I felt nothing, nothing
Sis, you're really gone
I stood there staring at you
What's really going on
Now our last conversation
Came back to my mind
Was it a cry for help
Should I have read between the lines
Probably wanted to say goodbye
And tell me you love me one last time
It had to be God
Working through his mighty powers
Last time we talked
We gave each other flowers
You were a light on a dark day
A rainbow during the showers
Saying there'll be brighter days

Just bear these couple hours
It was a blessing
When you sent me that song
I'm gonna use it for strength
To keep going on
With all your family and friends
Sis, you were all alone
Dying in your car
Miles away from home
Not one last call for help
You didn't pick up the phone
Always put up a fight
This one on your own
Every time I think of you
I just break down and cry
You'll be in my heart forever
Sis, this is my last goodbye
I'll see you when I get there
Forever your number one guy.

Rest in Peace Reka
Salute

I read this at her funeral, and everyone loved it. A young man walked up to me after the funeral service to tell me how much he loved what I wrote. He said his dad was battling prostate cancer, and he thought about writing something about it. I made a commitment to myself after Shereka's funeral that I was going to write non-stop until my book was complete. The words she left me with made me want to do great things and do great things for her daughters.

My daughter was starting her third year of college and decided to do her courses online for the first semester of the school year so she could be around to support her mom and cousins. My son sold his car and bought a newer one. He drove himself back to West Virginia for the start of his second year in college. My two little birds were flapping their wings preparing to fly and I was right there with them. God is great. After all that I had been through and being alive, healthy, and around them was a miracle. I have spoken of miracles throughout this book. The journey I traveled with my cancer battle was a miracle from the start and this book is evidence of that. If one day you should hear that I passed away, don't ever ask yourself how I could have said that God worked a miracle for me. No one will live forever. It has been more than two years since I found out I had cancer and over one and a half years since being cancer-free. That's a miracle. Every day that I am alive is evidence of the miracle. When I am gone, let this book be a reminder that God is still working miracles, answering prayers, showing mercy, and never forget, He's still in control.

One summer evening after returning home from the gym, I sat on the front steps of the house. I went to check the mailbox, and I continued to sit there for a while to relax. My neighbor, Sister Velma, came by the fence to water her sunflower plants. Sister Velma had been my Sunday school teacher in Jamaica. As always, she said hi and we talked for a little bit. We talked about how beautiful the sunflower plant was. She told me that her grandmother that died had first planted a sunflower in that same spot. She said that she used to plant her sunflowers in the backyard, but they weren't growing that well, so she decided to try her late grandmother's spot. After she went inside, I was still sitting on the steps. I had seen her sunflower plant just about every day. There was something different about it that day. I was looking at it and thinking how I had never seen one that tall with such a large flower. I got up and walked over to her driveway to take a closer look. I was so amazed, I video called my friend and said look how tall and beautiful this sunflower plant is. Before walking away, I took some pictures of it and the two smaller ones that were growing right next to it. This plant was located between the edge of the asphalt and our fence and about five feet from the sidewalk. It was about nine feet tall standing straight up and because of the weight of the sunflower, it was bent at the top, so the sunflower was facing the ground. It looked like a streetlight. Anyone that walked by or drove by could see it. I was still writing this book, so I went inside to eat and shower before writing until very late that night.

While I was sleeping, the sunflower came back to my mind, everything about the plant was explained to me. The plant was me and how I should be. I should strive, grow, be successful, solid, and strong. I must shine down on people and that way I will see clearly where I am heading. To me, that's helping the helpless, the poor, the needy, and everyone less fortunate. People in society don't usually want to help people that have nothing to give in return. I had seen sunflowers of all different sizes that pointed in all different directions but never had I seen one this tall with such a large flower that faced the ground. Most of us that have been blessed with a little bit of light choose to shine it up or sideways. It's the reason we often fall. It's dark at our feet. The light we receive to brighten our path, we use to shine on the ones above us to try to impress them. If they are shining down on you to allow you to see the way and you are shining upon them, it will cause a glare that could blind you. At your feet, it's dark so you are going to stumble and fall. It should be everyone's dream to put their best effort forward, to grow, change and be successful. Never turn your back; never forget the ones on the ground. Your feet are on that ground. Shining down is a way to help yourself while helping others.

Sister Velma had used a piece of string to tie the sunflower to the fence. Without that string, the sunflower would have fallen over before it was able to get to that size. We all must be anchored to survive the strong winds, the storms, the tribulations, and the attacks. Surround yourself with family, friends, different groups, and mentors. The anchor of them all is God. There were so many messages presented to me with this sunflower. Two smaller plants were growing beside this giant sunflower. Always lift up the people around you, share your knowledge, teach someone, and it will benefit you more than them. Loving and helping people is the biggest motivator and a very satisfying feeling. To me, the bigger sunflower represented myself and the two smaller plants were Deedee and Danny beside me.

I was already in the writing mood and was so close to the end of my story. I knew I had to write about the messages I had received from this sunflower. About two weeks later, I was in deep thoughts about this sunflower, and I wrote a poem. The bees kept coming to the sunflower until the flower was gone. The squirrels got in on the action and had been climbing to harvest the seeds. The large naked bulb of the flower is still there and is just hanging with no glow. The leaves are withering from the lower temperature outside. It told me it wouldn't be around for long. One thing I know is I got its message, and now I'll share it with you.

My Sunflower

Your shape caught my attention
Your beauty drew me closer
Something special about you
You were different from all others
Standing tall, looking down
Like a giant tower
I kept staring at you
Happy that I walked over
Thinking how special I was
To have you as a neighbor
I just could not walk away
Without taking your picture
So I can show you to the world
And have it to admire
If they ask me your name
I'll just say you're my sunflower

You came back to me in a dream
This time you were talking to me
Thanked me for my admiration
For thinking, you're a cutie
You said you had a message
You were much more than beauty
And you wouldn't be around for long
So I should listen keenly
You are a light, you said
Don't waste your energy
Stand tall, shine down
Shining up is unnecessary
That's trying to impress the higher-ups
Be a light for the poor and needy
Brighten lives, light up your way
Be a sunlight for humanity

There's Always A Light

I got your message
Glad I answered your call
You gave your beauty to the bees
But you're still standing tall
You gave your seeds for harvest
Your leaves withered in the fall
You've brightened many lives
I'm gonna miss you when you're gone
Your light will be shining
In many hearts forever
Everyone that reads this poem
I hope you will inspire
Thank you for your message
My very special neighbor
If I don't see you next spring
I hope I'll see you in the summer

Shortly before the book was printed, my daughter got an assignment for one of her classes. She had to write a speech of tribute paying homage to someone who has impacted her life positively. She was instructed to write about three laudable qualities about that person. She told me I was the person she chose to write about. When she sent me the speech she wrote, it touched my heart. My daughter had not seen a word I wrote in the book, nor did I discuss it with her. The speech felt like it was from the book, so I called up the editor and told her about it. I asked her if it was too late to put it in the book. Fortunately, she said it was not, so we added this beautiful speech.

"Imagine being blessed with an individual who constantly challenges you to become a better person! I believe everyone needs a person like that in their life. For me, that person is my father. A Jamaican man, who came here on a visa when he was only 17 years old by himself and continues to fight for his own legacy. Many call him Dervin, but I call him dad. My father, Dervin Walker, has been present in my life since I was born, from being a little baby growing up in his hands to being the young adult I am today. He has made a huge impact on me for many reasons, three of which are how strong he is, the loyalty he has, and the respect he has gained from others and the community.

"The first quality I would like to discuss is how strong my dad is. On July 11th of year 2019, my dad was diagnosed with cancer. I had no idea he was diagnosed with cancer until I overheard a phone conversation between him and my mom accidentally. At the time both my brother and I were getting ready to pack up and move for college, but my dad kept his head high and never poured his emotions onto us. He continued to push us and encouraged us to chase our dreams and not worry about him. I remember throughout his whole journey fighting cancer he never once claimed himself as a "sick person". He only spoke encouraging words into the universe when it came to his cancer journey. My dad continued to live his life in the light, and not let cancer scare him or change him within. He continued to work out daily and participate in the daily activities that he partook in before he had cancer. And now I can proudly say my dad is CANCER FREE!

"The second quality I would like to discuss is my dad's loyalty. I personally have never seen anyone in my life with such allegiance as him. Since I was born and able to understand how life works I have always seen my dad with the same group of people. Do not get me wrong though, my dad is always open to meeting new people and making new connections. But he has never turned his back on anyone. Even when the other person was wrong he always tries to look past that and focus on the bigger picture. My dad has shown me what loyalty is by never leaving me since I was born. He could have made excuses like many fathers out there or left me for another family, but he didn't. He did as any real man should. He sacrificed a lot just to make sure he was and is actively present in my life. He always reminds me that he will die before he gives up on me. Even when I don't deserve his devotion because I get stuck in my ways, he is always right there when I need him at any time.

"The last quality I would like to discuss is the high respect my dad has gained in our community where we reside. My dad has always been an advocate for the children. He makes sure that one they have goals, and two they do everything they can to achieve their goals. It does not matter if you're his family or not. He will even go as far as encouraging a stranger and helping them if need be. My dad is active in the community. He attends all events for children, fundraisers, anything that is positive he shows up for and supports no matter what. He is so well known that anywhere he goes no matter the location at least a few people know him. Since I was little my dad has always taught me to do everything with love and to remain steadfast in any situation.

"As we are ending, I hope I was able to show through my speech how magnificent of a father Dervin Walker is. He has some of the best qualities that any individual would want to have; being loyal, staying strong, showing love, and giving back to others around him. I try every day to be the female version of him. Many would call him a superman, but I am lucky to call him dad."

MY FINAL THOUGHTS:

I decided to write this book because I felt like no one knew who I was and all that I have been through. It was very hard to revisit some of the things I have experienced and to be honest about them. My wish is that everyone that reads this book will find some kind of benefit that will help them in their own life. Some of the messages I hope you get from my story are:

You never know what a person is experiencing so be kind, show love and be forgiving.

There's something positive in all of our experiences. Find it and then use it for energy to move on.

Life is a journey, keep moving. The more you dwell on the initial incident, the harder it is to move on.

Never give up; there's no benefit in giving up. Whatever it is will pass with some work and time. In the meantime, keep busy.

Life is an adventure; enjoy its challenges.

The blame is on you for whatever happens to you. That's a hard one although it's simply the truth. Until you understand and master this, you are going to spend a lot of time in the same spot. It's like playing a video game and continuing to get stuck in the same spot. Blaming others will only hinder you from learning your lesson.

Stay close to family, friends, and the community. I have been through a lot, but I have a strong and loving family beside me always. I have a church family, gym family, street family, and a community that I stay close to. With all these people around me, I never have to fight alone. If you followed my story closely, you would see that throughout my life, my big brother was never far from me.

Treat people well, with respect, and be understanding. Taking care of humanity is as important as taking care of oneself. We are one unit, one people, and we cannot survive without each other. Until mankind understands this truth, we are destined for doom.

Life is a gift. Enjoy, love, and cherish it. There will be obstacles on the journey. Some we can avoid and others we cannot. It's good and bad; the wheat and the tares so let's find our way. Whatever your religion is just know that God is greater than any obstacle you will ever face. Believe in him, his power, his strength, and his might. In the darkest of times when you can't see your way out of a situation or feel alone because it's so dark that you can't see around you, your faith in him will be your only light. Only then will you see a way out. He is the light.

Every Day is Beautiful

I used to associate a beautiful day
With the weather
Sun shining bright
Eighty-five degrees temperature
Light wind blowing
Swaying the curtains at the window
Stress-free
No pain, no worry, no pressure
All that changed
In my battle with cancer
I didn't care if it was raining
Or Hurricane Katrina

255

There's Always A Light

Ice on the ground
Or a blizzard in October
All I want is a day
And it will be one to remember

Comes what may
All I want is a day
Give me breath I pray
And I will find my way
Every day is beautiful
If you're by my side
Every day is beautiful
Every day is beautiful
Every day is beautiful
I'm thankful for life

What makes my day good
Is that I'm here to touch and feel
Get to see the fakes
And experience the real
If tears are good for the soul
Why is it so bad to break the seal
And let the waters flow
So our hearts can heal
Have a problem, solve it
Then be on your way
How come losing a job
Makes it a bad day
Couldn't get what you wanted
So now what you say
Today sucks?
Better be thankful when you pray

As a kid
I used to hate the rainy days
I'm inside
I couldn't go out to play
No friends
Cause my mom would say no way

Dark clouds
And this is what we all would say
Rain, rain, go away
Come again another day
Rain, rain, go away
Little Johnny wants to play
Now I miss the raindrops
On the metal sheets
Even though sometimes
Holes in the roof would leak
It was so soothing
Sometimes I would fall asleep
On rainy days
The food would taste so sweet
Playing in the rain
You could not beat
Even though
We had to do it on a sneak
Paper boats
Racing down the streets
Every day is beautiful
With every breath that I breathe

There's A Light

There's always a light. When it's dark and you don't see it, it is within you. That light within you is your faith. At times we have to walk by faith and not by sight. Life is a journey and as long as we are moving, we will come upon dark periods. Without faith, we'll be stuck in the dark or stumble around and lose our way. The ones who stumble their way into the light often stop moving because of the fear of darkness. Never give up, never stop trying. There is a way and **there's always a light** to show you that way.

The journey continues...

Acknowledgments

To everyone who shined their light on me or helped me to find the light within me, I am forever grateful for all the love, support, and encouragement. My children, Derishe' and Daniel, are the two brightest lights of my life. They gave me the courage to pick up the pen and start documenting my life story—thank you for the pure love and happiness you have brought to my life. To my mother and father, Hyacinth and Vincent, thank you for the encouragement and love, especially that of my mother who always believed in me and taught me great morals, values, and most of all how to take full responsibility for my actions. To my sisters and brothers, they have shown me their love, encouragement, and inspiration with the remarkable way they navigate their journey. My brother Rohan gets a Special thanks for being a light over me all my life. To Natalie, she has been there for me in more ways than I can write about and for being my light in some of my darkest moments. Floyd Green (Round Bread) has been the bridge between me and my community in Rio Bueno, Trelawny, Jamaica, and has shown his love and support throughout my journey. To the late Shereka Williams (Sher), she has shown a constant expression of love for me, and her kind words have strengthened, inspired, and given me the courage to get back to writing this book after two months.

Many people assisted, inspired, and had some kind of impact on me throughout my journey that led to the writing of this book. Thank you to everyone that ever called my name in their prayers, sent me words of encouragement, or shared words with me. There have been so many people that helped me in some way or another on my journey—I am grateful for all your love, encouragement, support, and for the light, you shined my way. Kim Pfarrer provided wonderful assistance with her typing and editing skills. Doreen Ernandez, my "Eagle Eye" editor, did a great job providing editing and publishing assistance bringing this book to its final version. Veronica Chandler, the graphics and web designer, did an outstanding job designing the book cover. Last but not least, to the brightest light of all and the writer of my life story, God; for getting me through all my battles, for everyone he used to assist me, especially in my battle with cancer. God gave me the wisdom, knowledge, understanding, and courage to document and share my journey with the world. In the darkest moments when all other lights are out, within you there's always a light.

About The Author

Dervin Walker has always believed in community and doing what he can to make a difference. He enjoys sharing his experiences with others to help them make better decisions, especially the youth.

He enjoys writing, music, socializing and is very dedicated to working out in the gym. He is a strong believer in family, friendship and is very involved in the lives of his children. They are everything to him.

His main message is that people should respect each other's differences and allow everyone to choose what is best for them. Spread love, do good, and take responsibility for your actions.

His battle with cancer inspired him to write this book in hopes of giving hope to the disheartened and to let everyone know that there's always a light even in the darkest moments.

Dervin grew up in Rio Bueno, Jamaica. After finishing high school, he migrated to the United States. He currently lives in New Jersey with his family.

In Memory of Scorcha

A few weeks before this book was published, Scorcha suddenly passed away in Jamaica. May his soul Rest In Peace.

Salute

Made in the USA
Middletown, DE
27 September 2022